Praise for *Extraordinary Transformation*

"An outstanding business book to help you live, learn, and lead through any challenge."

—Dr. John C. Maxwell, New York Times *best-selling author*

"Anyone seeking to transform an organization will find this book filled with life lessons and practical advice from an engaging leader brimming with optimism, determination, energy, and an unshakable faith that the seemingly impossible can be achieved."

—Dr. Vincent Price, *president, Duke University*

"Nido Qubein is an extraordinary university president. He cares deeply about the holistic growth of his students. You'll love this book. It's captivating."

—Steve Wozniak, *co-founder, Apple Computer, Inc.;*
HPU's Innovator in Residence

"This work is an inspiring blueprint for achieving business and personal growth. Nido is a heartfelt leader who measures success in the impact we have on others. The book uses real examples of transformation in entrepreneurship, business, and academia."

—Russell Weiner, *CEO, Domino's Pizza; HPU parent*

"Nido Qubein shines a light on the challenges facing higher education and gives principles and a vision to guide innovative leaders in our world today as they face an ever-changing environment."

—Dr. Kevin M. Guskiewicz, *chancellor, Michigan State University;*
former chancellor, University of North Carolina

"President Qubein has proven it *is* possible to transform higher education in a responsible way—and anyone curious how they did it will find this book to be innovative, substantive, and resourceful."

—Marc Randolph, *co-founder, Netflix;*
HPU's Entrepreneur in Residence

"Whether you are a university leader or a business entrepreneur, you'll find this book full of valuable lessons about work and life. It's a must-read."

—**Todd Wanek,** *CEO, Ashley Furniture Industries; HPU parent*

"At a time when other universities have faltered and even closed, High Point University has thrived. This book gives us a blueprint on how that happened. A must-read for anyone interested in how to lead."

—**Cynthia Marshall,** *CEO, Dallas Mavericks;*
HPU's Sports Executive in Residence, HPU parent

"Nido Qubein delivers quite the master class on how to use solid business principles to save and grow an organization. He provides valuable lessons on how to succeed in business while leading a life of meaning and purpose."

—**William Kennard,** *former U.S. ambassador to the European Union;*
chairman of the board, AT&T; trustee at Yale University; HPU parent

"Everything Nido champions ends up being impactful and substantive. He left a highly successful business career to lead his undergraduate alma mater—and the rest is history. Wow! This book will inform you, inspire you, and activate you to new heights of extraordinary achievement."

—**Bonnie McElveen-Hunter,** *former U.S. ambassador;*
chair, American Red Cross Board

"This book proves that an entrepreneurial mindset is powerful in shaping a stronger approach to learning and leadership. President Qubein shares valuable lessons for grounding our pursuits in genuine purpose, all while demonstrating his unique ability to inspire curiosity, courage, and compassion in our future leaders."

—**Daniel Lubetzky,** *founder and executive chairman, KIND Snacks*

An Entrepreneurial Blueprint for Leaders Who Seek
Transformational Growth in Any Organization

EXTRAORDINARY
TRANSFORMATION

**Proven Lessons on How a Small College
Became the Premier Life Skills University and
Inspired the Next Generation of Leaders**

NIDO QUBEIN

**HIGH POINT
UNIVERSITY**
THE PREMIER LIFE SKILLS UNIVERSITY

Published by High Point University Press
High Point, North Carolina
www.highpoint.edu

Copyright © 2024 High Point University

All rights reserved.

Thank you for purchasing an authorized edition of this book and for complying with copyright law. No part of this book may be reproduced, stored in a retrieval system, or transmitted by any means, electronic, mechanical, photocopying, recording, or otherwise, without written permission from the copyright holder.

Scripture quotations are from the ESV®Bible (The Holy Bible, English Standard Version®), copyright © 2001 by Crossway Bibles, a publishing ministry of Good News Publishers. Used by permission. All rights reserved.

Distributed by Greenleaf Book Group.

For ordering information or special discounts for bulk purchases, please contact Greenleaf Book Group at PO Box 91869, Austin, TX 78709, 512.891.6100.

Design and composition by Greenleaf Book Group
Cover design by High Point University

Publisher's Cataloging-in-Publication data is available.

Print ISBN: 979-8-9866663-0-3

eBook ISBN: 979-8-9866663-1-0

To offset the number of trees consumed in the printing of our books, Greenleaf donates a portion of the proceeds from each printing to the Arbor Day Foundation. Greenleaf Book Group has replaced over 50,000 trees since 2007.

Printed in the United States of America on acid-free paper

24 25 26 27 28 29 30 31   10 9 8 7 6 5 4 3 2 1

First Edition

Dedicated to my grandchildren: Austin, Charlotte, Grayson, Robert, Wesley, William, Oliver, Victoria, and Miles. May each of them invest one-third of their life in earning, one-third in learning, and one-third in serving—as I have.

CONTENTS

An Extraordinary Blueprint

By Dr. John C. Maxwell

Every time I step onto the campus of High Point University, I can't help but be amazed.

I look around me, and I'm surrounded by physical beauty and extraordinary educational opportunities. I see the gardens, the academic buildings, the inspiring statues, and the quotes chiseled into granite squares along the promenade. Then, I talk to the students. I hear about their dreams and aspirations of what they want to do and who they want to be. Right away, I realize they want to do more, be more, and strive for better. When I hear their conversations and see what surrounds me, I say to myself without fail four words:

"Thank you, Dr. Qubein."

For decades, Nido and I have spoken to audiences about the importance of leadership and the best lessons to follow in business and in life. Ever since we first met, I've admired how he reaches people in such a deeply emotional and purposeful way. I've watched him use his infectious spirit to energize his own life and the lives of others. He's done it as a father, husband, entrepreneur, philanthropist, business owner, CEO consultant, and a highly sought-after speaker who has earned many awards and inspired so many people worldwide with his words.

But I do believe one of his biggest accomplishments is in North Carolina, in the city of High Point. It's the city where he and his wife, Mariana, have raised their family and lived, worshiped, and worked for more than half a century.

That accomplishment is High Point University. His alma mater. So many university and business leaders have been asking Nido to tell us how he did it all. We finally persuaded him, since this is his twentieth year as president and this is HPU's centennial year, too. This book is not intended solely for academic leaders. Everyone can learn from this book. It is more of a biographical story that focuses on leadership and innovation in general. In another book, Nido and his team are outlining and describing the incredible substantive achievements of the university's academic performance, including student outcomes and faculty research.

In 1970, Nido graduated from what was then High Point College. In 2005, he became the president of High Point University. Through our friendship, I've seen how assuming the presidency of HPU was such a highly personal mission for him, a monumental work of impact in his distinguished career.

I love what he's done with this new book. He shows us how he took solid business concepts and his own leadership lessons, applied them to the world of higher education, and helped resurrect a struggling university. But what really captivates me is how what he did at HPU can be an extraordinary blueprint for anyone reimagining distinctive solutions and dealing with future challenges.

Business leaders and higher education administrators.

Budding scholars and aspiring entrepreneurs.

Just anyone looking for a higher way, a better way to live, learn, and lead.

Throughout *Extraordinary Transformation*, Nido becomes the teacher; his book, his masterclass. He gives practical tips through the stories he tells and the reflections he gives and shows us all how to lead people, build trust in a community, and remain resilient in the face of seemingly insurmountable obstacles.

His judgment, awareness, and his faith have helped him every step of the way and helped HPU to thrive.

Under his leadership, HPU has quadrupled the size of the faculty, the campus, and the student body. He has helped raise and provide nearly $3 billion for the university, and he has shepherded the creation of eleven new academic schools—so far. According to *U.S. News & World Report*, HPU has become the south's No. 1 regional college for more than a decade and the most innovative for the past eight years. Today, 99 percent of HPU's graduating class find employment or start graduate school within six months of receiving their diploma.[1]

That is fourteen points higher than the national average. That is something to celebrate. And Nido's *Extraordinary Transformation* is something to celebrate, too.

Nido shares with readers his own fears. In 2008, he had many sleepless nights when he faced the Great Recession and worried about future construction on campus. But a member of the board of trustees, the chair of the finance committee, told him not to worry.

"Nido, you're building a great school. Look at what you've done."

Yes, look what Nido has done. He has created what I call a "'Who Luck' University."

"Who Luck" basically means meeting the right people who turn your life around. At High Point University, students do meet the right people, and their lives do turn around. Parents who send their children to High Point University find that out right away. Their children start the most transformative time of their lives at a God, family, country school, a place

---

1   Data collected by High Point University in accordance with the National Association of Colleges and Employers (NACE) standards shows 99 percent of all graduates in the class of 2022 were employed or furthering their education within 180 days of graduation, which is 14 points higher than the national average reported by NACE.

of higher learning and higher living where they connect with mentors who help them grow.

In *Extraordinary Transformation*, Nido shares their stories and writes about their triumphs and their heartaches. There is one particularly poignant story about a young woman named Ali, a junior who wanted so badly to graduate.

After dealing with a number of health complications, she was battling to stay alive in an ICU in Connecticut when Nido and other university officials heard about her story. They then created, printed, packaged, and shipped her honorary diploma by overnight express to her hospital. The next day, Nido received a photograph from Ali's mom. Ali was sitting up in her hospital bed, grinning big and holding up her diploma like a trophy.

Ali died a few hours later. A few days later, Nido received a letter from one of Ali's cousins who had been there with her at the hospital. The cousin wrote:

> When I spoke to Ali's mom Saturday afternoon, she told me what you did. It's hard to put into words what an amazing act of kindness you showed to a girl with mere hours to live. Her mom sent me a picture of Ali in her hospital bed with her diploma and a graduation cap. She had a smile on her face and passed knowing she was a proud alumna of High Point University.
>
> I really want to thank you and to let you know that your act of kindness was recognized and very much appreciated. I hope someday I can perform such a meaningful act for someone in need.

Nido still has that letter. And that letter says volumes about the type of leader Nido Qubein is.

Such stories are found throughout *Extraordinary Transformation*, and Nido writes about them all in such an empathetic way. To me, his book is an ode to practical optimism and a ringing homily on the enduring values and virtues of American business. It shows us all what transformational leadership can do. Everything in life rises and falls with leadership, and Nido has helped High Point University rise prominently and significantly.

When I read *Extraordinary Transformation*, I was amazed, but not surprised. I know Nido. I know his faith, and I know he sees the families of High Point University as his own family. He wants their children to have a solid foundation so they can overcome any obstacle or withstand any crisis they might face in life.

High Point University helps students think big, dream big, and believe big. In turn, students believe in themselves. They embrace what they see and feel, and they choose to be extraordinary.

I do love HPU's signature call to action: Choose to be Extraordinary! I love it because what High Point University is doing is truly extraordinary in the competitive world of higher education. These students live and learn at a premier life skills university, and they receive a stellar education that helps them hone two key life skills every great leader needs: competence and great values.

Great leaders possess an inner core of values that guides them to do the right things for the right reasons. They become an asset to everyone around them, and they realize that if you're bigger on the inside, you're bigger on the outside. You no longer ask, "How long will it take?" You ask, "How far can I go?" High Point University is teaching their students to ask, "How far can I go?" By doing so, High Point University is producing some of the greatest leaders for the future of this country.

Yes, *Extraordinary Transformation* is a story about a business leader returning to his alma mater, and with God's help and the influence of others, he transforms a university and creates purposeful outcomes for tens of thousands of students. But it's also a story about the American Dream. It shows how the foundational principles that built this country nearly 250 years ago are still relevant today.

So, enjoy *Extraordinary Transformation*. May it enlarge your own vision for innovation. May it move you to effect change in your own corner of the world. May it become a purpose-centered gift you can rely on for years to come.

Thank you, President Nido Qubein.

Dr. John C. Maxwell is a No. 1 New York Times *best-selling author, coach, and speaker. He is the founder of the John Maxwell Company, the John Maxwell Team, and EQUIP, an organization that has trained more than 5 million leaders in 180 countries. He also serves as the Executive Coach in Residence at High Point University.*

Before the Butterfly, a Caterpillar

In January 2005, I went on a campus tour with my two college-age daughters. The place, alas, was not terribly impressive. At one point, gazing at the rust flaking off an old shower head and thinking about the ancient furnishings and drab feel of the dorm room I'd just seen, I glanced back over at my daughters. They didn't need to say a word; I could see it in their eyes.

No way would we go to school here.

If I wouldn't send my own daughters to live in this environment, how could I expect anyone else to do so? My heart sank as I imagined young students, not even out of their teens, trying to learn, to be inspired, to expand their potential in the midst of such uninspiring surroundings. There was no other way to put it: This building was a wreck—one of several on a campus that looked worn out and exhausted.

But we weren't touring the place because they were thinking about enrolling. We were touring the place because I had already enrolled. It was the first month of a brand-new president's first term, and that new president was me.

This had come as a surprise to me as much as it did to everyone else. After all, I am not an academic by training or past career path. I'm a businessperson.

I came to this country on a one-way ticket, a teenage immigrant seeking an education. When I arrived on these shores, I had a limited English vocabulary and no more than $50 in my pocket. I fell in love with America.

Finding the American Dream

I fell in love with the culture, with the big-hearted sense of friendliness and hospitality I found everywhere I looked. I was enthralled by the exceptional freedom of speech and extraordinary focus on enterprise, by the spirit of benevolence and generosity.

I fell in love with the American Dream. Not that my new home promised simply the pursuit of financial success, but that it promised to support and encourage the pursuit of a meaningful life and a virtually unlimited sense of possibility—and it delivered on that promise.

I came seeking an education and got it. First, in my formal schooling; second, from the people and the culture; and third, through my own experiences in business. In my adopted home, I discovered what I have come to believe is the greatest education in the world: creating business ventures from nothing but the seeds of clear ideas and strong principles, planted in the good soil of American possibility.

I see the character and values of America coming into question a good deal these days. This is nothing new. It happened during the Vietnam years, when I first arrived here, and I saw it again during the economic crisis of 2008–09. But these are passing circumstances, regular difficulties and challenges that test the soul of a nation.

I believe in the American Dream today more than ever before, and I define it not by wealth but rather the achievement of one's goals. I've seen these principles in operation for more than four decades, in every industry from baking to banking, publishing to real estate, retail to education, and I believe they are stronger than ever. And since 2005, I've found evidence of these convictions arising in the most unexpected quarters: the college campus.

The academy might be the last place you'd expect to look for business-like innovation. The halls of higher learning are often viewed as the very embodiment of tradition, places of cautious thinking with an innate resistance to change. Many of America's famous entrepreneurs, from Bill Gates to Steve Jobs to Mark Zuckerberg, were college dropouts and even wear that pedigree as sort of an entrepreneurial badge of honor. It was Mark Twain, the most distinctive of American voices, who said, "I have never let school interfere with my education."

I thought about Twain's quote as my daughters and I continued our campus tour and reflected on the scope of the challenge in front of me. High Point University had a storied past as a very good school. Back in the 1960s, I'd been a student here myself. But its glory days were in the past. As I stood there in 2005, the university was struggling. Freshman enrollment had fallen nearly 20 percent just that year and was still dropping. With some $120 million in deferred maintenance costs, the institution was living on borrowed time. In *U.S. News & World Report*'s annual survey of private colleges in our region, our little school on Montlieu Avenue ranked No. 17. And I must confess, staring in the face of all that deferred maintenance scared me half to death.

Still, as I glanced once more around the cramped restroom and out through the doorway at the dorm room, I found myself smiling.

What needed to happen here would require taking some risks, and I have always been a risk-taker—a calculated risk-taker. If you avoid risk, you avoid opportunity, which means you also avoid the possibility of excellence. As I learned from American baseball, you can't steal second with your foot on first. Not that I endorse being foolhardy, not at all. I do not believe in diving headlong off steep cliffs into unexplored waters. I believe in first finding out how deep that water is, doing one's best to make sure there are no hidden obstacles in there, no sharp rocky outcroppings or lurking sharks.

And then jumping off.

The presidency of High Point University was a position for which I was, in one sense, entirely unprepared; yet in another sense, I had been preparing for this position my whole life. No, I was not an academic by background or profession; I had not risen through the ranks of the academy. Yet, in my career as a businessperson, entrepreneur, and educator, I had learned a set of core principles that I believe anyone, whether CEO, business owner, or leader of any type of organization, could apply to create success, significance, and value in any field. Now it was time to put those principles to the test on the campus of my undergraduate alma mater, an alma mater that enjoys a rich history and an impactful legacy.

Call it Day One of a decade-long lab I called Transformation 101.

And did it ever transform!

First and foremost our attention was on academics—providing an extraordinary education for every student who enrolls at HPU. While this book is not entirely focused on all the enhancements in our academic programs, do not let these pages mislead you. HPU is a superb institution with truly learned, dedicated, and outstanding faculty focused on student outcomes.

Among our achievements, our faculty did something distinctive when they adopted and embraced growth mindset strategies as a campus-wide effort. The positive impact of growth mindset strategies on student learning is best exemplified by work published by faculty in the natural sciences. When faculty shared weekly growth mindset messages with the students enrolled in introductory biology and chemistry courses—messages that emphasized that growth and improvement are possible with hard work and good strategies—students' overall academic performance improved significantly.

We were among the pioneers in this area. In academia, we are trained to address the cognitive aspects of learning, not the social-emotional skills required to learn well. Few faculty are even comfortable addressing social-emotional skills in the classroom. And yet at HPU, we have recognized how crucial these skills are for students to learn well and to feel confident in applying what they have learned in a professional setting. We recognized that students can't learn deeply if they are struggling with their own mindset. So we embraced this topic wholeheartedly, and we have the published data on academic performance to show how our students benefited tremendously.

We also wanted all students to benefit from a life skills education. So we designed an educational core that fosters in students curiosity and a love of learning but teaches them important life skills. These life skills include critical thinking, persuasive communication, teamwork, coachability, emotional intelligence, resilience, appreciating differences, and more. We lead the university to serve the learning interests of our students, and we insist on making our values the center of our focused efforts.

I am so proud of the achievements of our faculty: NIH grants, Phi Beta Kappa memberships, authorship of significant books and papers, and important research. I rejoice in the accomplishments of our students, especially when I see so many selected for Fulbright scholarships or Goldwater Scholars and more. Someday I'll write a book dedicated to the outstanding learning outcomes at HPU and explain in more detail the steps and strategies we took to create an extraordinary university.

Our Faithful Transformation

Since 2005, we have grown the campus size from 91 to 550 acres and grown enrollment from 1,450 to more than 6,000. We have invested almost $3 billion in renovation and new construction, mostly in establishing eleven new academic schools but also in expanding our graduate programs and offering our first doctoral degrees. Some of the nation's greatest thinkers and innovators regularly come to High Point to teach our students.

Today, HPU students flourish both academically and socially, collectively investing nearly 500,000 hours a year in local community service during their time on campus. They land top-notch internships with employers from Ernst & Young to Microsoft, the New Orleans Saints, and the Boston Ballet, and graduate to careers around the world at Fortune 500 companies, international service programs, public school systems, and top-tier law, medical, and graduate school programs. As for life after HPU, 99 percent of all our seniors land a job or enter graduate school within six months of graduating. That's fourteen points *above* the national average.

The overall focus of our transformation was on impacting student outcomes. We made great strides in enhancing the rigor of what we do academically through STEM, research, and experiential learning.

We put emphasis on the influential aspects of learning and became a premier life skills university. How students feel about their learning matters. Professional identity matters. Confidence matters. Faithful courage matters.

And, by the way, there would be no more rusty showerheads!

Of course, along the way, we faced hurdle after hurdle, many of them seemingly impossible to surmount. We attracted nationwide attention, and we endured the worst public health crisis in a century, and twelve years before that, we went through the worst economic downturn in generations without cuts or furloughs. Meanwhile, we continued to build, invest, and grow through those two dark times. Our ranking in the category "Best Colleges in the South" in the *U.S. News & World Report* survey would go from No. 17 to No. 1 with a score of 100. We've now been No. 1 for 11 years in a row. Some called it a metamorphosis, a "controlled explosion," or "the Miracle on Montlieu Avenue."

I call it *the art of the possible*.

This is the story of what happened to create that dramatic turnaround. More importantly, *how* it happened and *why* it happened; and most importantly, what you can learn from it and apply to create transformation and success in your own organization and, hopefully, in your own life.

We may not have met, you and I, and I may not know the circumstances of your work—whether you are a manager striving to lead your department to greater results, or a business owner, or a leader within a community organization, a nonprofit, or a university. Yet, regardless of the specifics of what you do, if you are in any sort of position to build or influence an organization of people, you have faced—or will face—many of the same kinds of challenges I've faced in my career. In all those situations, I have seen some principles emerge that, if followed with care and diligence, would likely assure the success of any endeavor.

I believe you can do the same.

The record of what our faculty and staff here achieved at High Point University from 2005 to 2024 is not just the story of what happened on the campus of a private university in the middle of North Carolina. It is also the story of what anyone can accomplish—anywhere, under any circumstance. May this book be helpful to you in some way. My intent is to share with you our story without suggesting that somehow we did it all perfectly or that somehow we believe "we arrived." Our future is bright. We will continue the work with the right balance between academic excellence and life's demands. Some readers will embrace this book with an open mind. Some will choose to critique it. I hope readers enjoy this book and find it meaningful and stimulating. Thank you for reading.

Nido Qubein
High Point, North Carolina

CHAPTER 1

Yes, You Can

It was the last Friday in September 2021, and I was sitting onstage under a beautiful blue sky, looking out onto nearly two thousand guests seated in chairs and standing shoulder to shoulder in front of us.

Finally, after years of planning, the day I'd longed to see had come.

Our band, the Marching Panthers, stood in formation off to the side with our cheerleaders, and I could feel the excitement all around me. It seemed to swell with each note the band played. I saw so many faces I recognized, so many people who had meant much to me in my life. Beside me was my wife, Mariana. On my other side was Bob Brown, the chairman of our HPU Board of Trustees. I know Bob well. For decades, he has worked behind the scenes with some of the most influential leaders and biggest corporations to help heal the racial divisions of our world. Bob has made the world a better place, and he has helped High Point University and his hometown of High Point become a better place. I am proud to call him my friend.

In the front row, I saw my family. They are so important to Mariana and me. My son Ramsey; my son Michael with his wife, Morgan; my daughter Cristina and her husband, Cole; and my daughter Deena and her husband, Brad.

Everyone had come to celebrate High Point University and the unveiling of a new complex. Under one roof was 350,000 square feet of space, a pavilion that integrates academics and athletics *and* provides a strikingly beautiful venue for entertainment, sports, community events, and educational conferences.

But the building is bigger than that.

It shows how much we care about our students, our parents, our alumni, our community, and the entire region.

It shows parents first how we provide the best learning environment, the best resources, and the best experiential learning opportunities so their children can aspire to be who they want to become.

It shows the city of High Point how we have created a place where they can be inspired, entertained, and proud of their university.

It also shows our students how we give them significant and impactful hands-on experiences to help them succeed in an increasingly competitive global marketplace so they can become more relevant in a meaningful way.

All those thoughts raced through my mind that Friday afternoon. Our family gave the lead gift for the project, and because of our support and service, the board of trustees voted to name the building after Mariana and me. As I waited for the festivities to begin, I thought about how far we had come as a university. This building—an arena, conference center, and hotel—represented an excellent example of how HPU embodies what I tell our staff and faculty often: "Yes, we can!"

Our talented team at HPU had made this happen.

As the afternoon sun bathed Vert Stadium and the Witcher Athletic Center with an ethereal glow, our Marching Panthers broke into The Temptations' classic, "Get Ready." It felt so appropriate, so right. It was the grand opening of the arena and conference center. The day before, we had celebrated the grand opening of the Kahn Hotel.

As the energy rose around me with the magic of our band, I felt the importance of this defining moment in our university's history. I wanted to shout from the mountaintops, "I am the most blessed guy on the face of the earth because of you. You are the ones building High Point University!"

We as a university had taken a calculated risk with our expansive vision since 2005. I knew we couldn't remain at 1,450 traditional students as we were back then. We wouldn't survive. We had to enroll more students. We placed our faith in God, and our collective vision fueled our drive. As I tell our students, you take the risk out of life, you take the opportunity out of life, and we all wanted to make a difference in the lives of our students. We have.

There's a wise Chinese proverb that says, "The journey of a thousand miles begins with one step."

I took that first step. But so did many others. We did it together. And that, my friend, is how it all began: One team. One vision. One purposeful future.

How to Become a Transformational Leader

Our team knows that the highest order of leadership is to tell the truth. Yet, that is just the beginning. You consciously and intentionally have to bring your business, social, spiritual, and family lives together; each plays a part in who you are as a leader. When you do, your life is like a beautiful song. Its harmony influences others, it can move people, and anyone looking at you will know what kind of person you really are.

People value authenticity ahead of charisma. Charisma gets you in the door, but it takes substance to deliver results. We all must remember it's not about us. It's about everyone around us. They are our team; you are their coach. You have to listen to what they say and engage your mind to absorb and understand their concerns. We need to listen twice as much as we talk, and others will hear twice as much of what we say. By listening, you will gain information and knowledge. Write it down to remember it. Then, execute. The end result? Wisdom begins to blossom.

When you do, you'll understand the importance of SLOW: Speaking, Listening, Observing, and Writing. It'll help you become a person of substance, a person others can trust. Through your actions and your words, you can challenge the people around you to do their best, and like a well-trained team before a big game, they'll want to play their best—and win.

Vince Lombardi, the legendary football coach of the Green Bay Packers, knew how to get the best out of his players. Today, he is considered one of the greatest football coaches of the twentieth century—if not the greatest. But he taught his players about more than just the game of football. He taught them about life. I'll always remember his comment on winning and that after the cheers have died and the stadium is empty, what matters is the dedication to excellence, victory, and doing the best we can to make the world a better place.

Lombardi's actions and his words unveil much about the impact and influence leaders can have. A good leader can tell us so many things about how to live, how to reach our full potential, how to serve others, and how to leave the world a better place.

A good leader then becomes a transformational leader. Remember, managers change behaviors, but leaders change minds.

A transformational leader can create competence in the people they lead. It's one of the vital lessons every leader must learn. Create competence to create confidence. Authority is earned, not granted. A good leader is an enabler of learning who knows that people don't respond to what you say, they respond to what they understand you to say. And to how you make them feel.

No matter the decade, those lessons never become outdated.

So, at High Point University we heed these lessons and live by them. And, as time progressed, our team took many more steps to ensure that our students grew in wisdom and served with stewardship.

CHAPTER 2

Aim for Extraordinary, Act with Urgency

A s my first official act as president of High Point University, I invited a few friends over for lunch. I told them we needed $10 million.

Let me start again. I'm getting ahead of myself.

It was Tuesday, January 4, 2005, and I was just one day into my new career. I stood at a small lectern and faced a group of the city's most influential people gathered around eight or nine tables in the art gallery of the university's Hayworth Fine Arts Center. The mayor of High Point was there as well as the city manager, members of the city council, civic leaders, and executives from High Point's prominent businesses. Maybe sixty people in all. For some, it was the first time they had ever set foot on our campus. We had invited them to this luncheon meeting because I wanted to share with them what I saw happening at our university. And I didn't mention the $10 million until after the second course.

The way I saw it, there were three big issues facing us at High Point University: fundraising, our relationship with community, and our revitalization and reputation throughout the region and around the country.

After thanking them for coming, I came right to the point.

"I invited you all here to tell you a little bit about our plans for the future. I want to share a vision with you. I call it a shining university on a hill."

Everyone there knew the reference to John Winthrop's famous "city upon a hill," that enduring vision the future governor of Massachusetts painted of a place that would serve as a model of the highest values to the rest of the world. The fact that these words had been later evoked by both President Kennedy and President Reagan (who added the "shining" part) gave the phrase a well-freighted pedigree. To say nothing of the fact that the image originated with the Gospel of Matthew.

"This room is filled with people who make things happen in High Point, and I want you to know that we are about to make things happen on this campus. Our university is about to come out of the shadows and attract the attention of people across the nation.

"We want you and everyone in our city to be proud of this university, our students, our faculty, and our academic programs. We want you to know that we are dedicated to creating excellence in every aspect, and that we are destined to be one of the finest universities in America.

"However, I also have to be honest with you and say that, as things stand at this moment, we have some miles to go before we reach that goal."

This was the understatement of the year.

"Our auditorium is falling apart. Our dorms are not in good shape."

I looked over at the dean of the business school—a business school that did not, at this point, even have its own building.

"The Phillips School of Business is a fine school, but it has no home," I said. "We need to build it one. We also need graduate school buildings. A new student fitness center. A new athletic building. Funding for new academic programs and faculty development. And our dorms—oh, how we need to renovate our dorms!"

In fact, the situation was a good deal worse than what I described. We not only needed to renovate our existing dorms, but we also needed to build some new ones. More than that, we needed to attract more students—more *paying* students—to go into those dorms. For years, the university had been extremely generous with scholarships. In other words, we were giving away our education for close to free and creating significant deficits and deferred maintenance in the process. Which practically meant that the university hadn't had the funds it needed for essential maintenance and improvements on its buildings, many of which were built during or right after World War II. Our noble intent to assist students and provide financial aid had left us out of balance and in a fiscal mess. We must assist those who need scholarships based on need and merit, but we must do it logically and prudently.

But that was just the beginning.

As for our landscaping? Scarce or nonexistent.

And the decor in the cafeteria and elsewhere? Lackluster, institutional, and uninspiring.

Furniture in the dorms and lounges? Old or broken down.

Dorm bathrooms? In disrepair. With rusting pipes.

On paper, our budget was balanced—but only by neglecting major repairs and improvements. And enrollment was dropping like a rock.

"Our biggest practical challenge," I continued, "is admissions. Bringing in just 100 more paying students next year would add $2.6 million to our annual budget, which would make a significant difference. But in order to bring in more students, we need to become a place of distinction."

There were nearly a dozen accredited four-year colleges and nine very good community colleges in the Piedmont Triad, an area in central North Carolina with 1.7 million residents defined by the cities of Greensboro, High Point, and Winston-Salem. So, you can understand why competition for dollars, students, and every other academic resource was intense. High Point University was not a name that stood at the top of very many wish lists of high school graduates, locally or nationwide. Frankly, it was typically seen as a "safety school," and we needed to transform it into a first-choice educational institution.

"Right now, HPU is not that visible nationwide. We have to brand it. We have to advertise it. We have to transform High Point University into a widely known and respected name, not only in the Piedmont region but throughout the southeast and across the nation.

"And when I say *we*, I am not invoking the *editorial* we."

I paused and looked around the room.

"No, I mean *we*," and I gestured with both hands in a sweeping motion that said *all of us gathered here in this room.*

"The reason I've invited you all here today is not to come see *our* university.

"This is *your* university."

A "Shining University on a Hill"

At the time, not much of a relationship existed between High Point the university and High Point the city. HPU was a fairly remote island in the midst of its surroundings—as universities so often are—and school and community felt little relevance to each other.

High Point itself was known not for education but for furniture. The city of High Point had been a nexus for the international market ever since the nineteenth century, and by the 1960s, it was the world's leading manufacturer of wood furniture. Its semiannual event known as the High Point Market made it the hub of the home furnishings universe.

Meanwhile, High Point University was practically an afterthought. Our residential student body numbered less than 950. Individual apartment complexes in town housed more people than that. As I said, quite a few of the people I had spoken with had never even visited the university before. Why would they? To the city leaders, the school was hardly a top-of-mind concern.

This was about to change. Or so I hoped.

"One of our principal reasons for calling this meeting," I said, "is that we want to build stronger bridges between our school and our city—and we want to start doing that immediately. Right now, starting today. For too long, there has been a sense that HPU exists off in its own corner. That sense of separation is something we need to overcome. We need your support. And this is not a one-way street. We believe you need our support, too."

I pointed out that, while this was not widely known or publicized, HPU already generated some $140 million per year in economic impact to the community.

"As we grow to become that shining university on a hill, that flow of benefit to the surrounding community will increase greatly, both in ways we can readily measure and in new ways that none of us has even begun to envision yet. It is a relationship rich in potential, one whose surface we have barely scratched."

I stepped back and pointed to the banner unfurled on the wall behind me. It said "High Point University" in big white letters against a purple background—except that to the word "Point," we had added an *apostrophe-s* in brilliant gold, so that it now said:

High

Point's

University

"We are High *Point's* university—and together, we will accomplish great things!"

The group then burst into a round of sturdy applause, and it was evident that they were not merely being polite. They were starting to see the same vision I was seeing, and they were catching on to my excitement about it.

Which was perfect timing because this was where we came to the money part.

"Yes," I added, "there is a great deal of work to be done, and we must have the facilities, the resources, and the capacity to do it. So, in order to begin achieving all this right away, we're going to raise $10 million in the next sixty days."

Now *that* got a serious reaction.

Ten million dollars—in sixty days? Up to that point, HPU might typically raise $1 million or $2 million a *year*. The university's entire annual cash budget was barely over $30 million. They were too polite to say so, but I had no doubt that there were at least a few people in the room that day thinking, "Nido, do you think you may have bit off more than you can chew here?"

I knew it was a risk to declare such a big goal with so short a timeline. And if we failed to meet our deadline, it would not spell a very auspicious start to my presidency. It might even cast skepticism over everything I wanted to accomplish here.

But I announced the fundraising goal for a reason. I wanted to convey a sense of urgency.

In one sense, nothing was really *that* urgent. It wasn't as if the school was on the verge of collapse. But that's often the way crisis works. It sneaks up on you.

You've probably seen this yourself. The biggest threats to our existence typically don't show up with trumpet fanfares or cymbals crashing. In a movie, you might see an explosion within the first two minutes or a plane crash or a murder before the opening credits roll. But life is not a movie. There's no Hollywood director spelling it all out for you, no soundtrack with low, ominous cellos and trombones telegraphing what's about to happen. You have to peer into the interior of events and circumstances and find out for yourself what's *really* going on there.

What was really going on at High Point University was that it had become lost in ***an ocean of sameness***.

It wasn't that our university did not have its strengths. It did. There were great people here, including stellar faculty. Yes, we provided a liberal arts education—but many colleges did that. I knew we couldn't compete based on our strengths because they were common. How were we different? How could we stand out? In what ways could we become exceptional? We needed to become extraordinary.

Extraordinary.

The Power of One Word

If there is one solitary word that most encapsulates the vision and mission that would drive us for the next decade, it is the word "extraordinary." And while I use that word a lot, I mean it each and every time I do.

You have to know that English is not my first language. When I arrived in America at the age of seventeen, my first task as a newcomer to this land was to become fully proficient in its language. I knew that if I wanted to have a successful career in America, I needed to be able to speak the local tongue in a fluid, fluent, and flowing manner. As I fell in love with America, I also fell in love with its language. Which means that even today, when I use words, I'm acutely aware of what they mean.

For example, the word "extraordinary." By definition, it means something *other* than ordinary. Something above and beyond, something different and distinct.

Distinction was what we lacked at High Point University. But it was *exactly* what we needed. If there was one driving principle behind all the changes I had in mind, it was that we had to become extraordinary. But how? Just so many questions.

How could we help our students become genuinely exceptional?

How could we make our academic programs and educational resources incomparable?

How would we make everything else, from the campus grounds to the campus cafeteria, awe-inspiring?

How would we do all that? We were about to find out.

Everything we would do in the months and years ahead would be focused on that ultimate aim.

Normally, change happens slowly in academic institutions, and to be fair, there are good reasons for this. There is strength in continuity, and within the trappings of tradition there often lies a great storehouse of wisdom, of lessons learned well over many generations. I wasn't intending to move quickly purely for the sake of shaking things up. But gradual change doesn't attract attention. People don't tend to recognize incremental change. If we added one new academic major every few years, or built on an existing building every few years, or grew our enrollment by a percentage point or two each year, that would not be a *bad* thing—but there would be no story to tell.

This is not to say that incremental change has no value at all. There are places where incremental development is precisely what is called for, where moving fast may even be counterproductive. These are situations where making small improvements consistently over time can add up to have a powerful cumulative effect. Exercise is like that. So is the accumulation and assimilation of new knowledge or the learning of a new discipline.

But in the context of transformation, incremental improvement simply will not deliver the amplitude of benefit you need. The story of the tortoise and the hare is a nice fable, but there are times when "slow and steady wins the race" is dead wrong. This was one of those times. And this was the central reason I unveiled that $10 million goal to our small gathering in the university art gallery. We needed to be noticed, and when you want people to notice, you have to make your moves big.

We were about to make some big moves.

The First Step

After the formal part of the event finished, we all stood around talking. You could feel the excitement in the room. We could have stayed there talking for hours. But after thirty minutes or so, people began to leave.

I walked the 100 yards or so back to Roberts Hall, the main administrative building and home to the office of the president. I ascended the steps, went into my office, and stood for a moment, thinking. Then, I retraced my steps back out to the main entrance, stepped outside the front door, and closed it behind me.

It was cold, a freezing January day, and I could see my breath. I stood on the front portico, gazed over to my right at the Hayworth Fine Arts Center, and thought about what we'd just talked about at our lunch meeting.

Destined to be one of the finest universities in America . . .

Those bold words rang in my ears. And now, we needed to turn them into reality.

A few days earlier, before formally taking office, I had met with Dr. Dennis Carroll. At the time, he was our dean of academic affairs. A few years later, Dennis would be promoted and become the first provost of High Point University. He became my right hand in all matters academic until he retired in 2020. Our work together began that day in 2005 when we talked about the future of our academic program.

"Dennis," I said, "what will it take to build one of the best academic institutions in America? What tools do our faculty need to inspire and prepare our students for the most significant careers and occupations in the twenty-first century?"

I told him that whatever it took, whatever resources we needed, whatever changes and innovations he and the deans and faculty thought would be necessary to transform our university, I was committed to seeing them happen. He and the faculty had carte blanche for a complete overhaul of our curriculum—if that's what was needed.

"It's good," I told myself. "But it's not enough."

We couldn't just talk about excellence or simply teach it. We had to *embody* excellence.

I looked out across the rotunda in front of Roberts Hall toward Montlieu Avenue and the front entrance of the campus. This was where visitors—including the parents of prospective students—gained their first impressions of our university.

The place felt lifeless.

I looked off to my right at the series of sidewalks that connected this entrance area to the rest of the campus. I could picture students trudging along the sidewalks from building to building as they moved from one class to the next. No energy. No inspiration. We needed an infusion of energy here. We needed a new mindset. We needed to create an environment that motivated students to learn more, be more, serve more!

"Why is it that universities sometimes feel like places created for young people—by old people?" I asked.

I thought about Niagara Falls, the Grand Coulee Dam, about my kids when they were little, laughing and running through sprinklers on a hot summer day. *Water.* That's it. Call it fractal patterns or negative ions—I see it as *energy.* What if there were a huge fountain right in the middle of the rotunda, with great gushing jets of water sparkling like diamonds in the sunlight?

I looked over to my right again. Now those same students were picking up their pace, walking with purposeful steps, because the environment was calling them to do so.

I made a mental note: *Fountain. Maybe more than one.* It's a start of a journey dedicated to excellence in education in an environment stimulating for learning, inside the classroom and everywhere else.

I continued watching those students in my mind's eye, heading off to their next class. Walking in single file. I frowned.

"No," I murmured, "not good."

The sidewalks were too narrow. In order not to bump into people coming the other way when the place was busy, students needed to walk one behind the other. And I didn't want our students walking single file, lost in their own thoughts. I wanted them walking side by side, talking to each other, getting to know one another and possibly building relationships that could last a lifetime. So, these sidewalks needed to be twelve feet wide.

Another mental note: *Change the sidewalks.*

I proceeded down the brick steps and out onto the lawn, then turned and looked back at Roberts Hall and off to my left at the campus stretching out beyond it. There was a building there, Harrison Hall, kind of an ugly old thing, poorly constructed and in bad shape. Inside it was a single basketball court, with just enough room to walk around it. The Hot Box, students called it. The campus already looked small, and that building blocked the view and made it look even smaller. Hmm. If we took down the Hot Box, that could open up the whole space.

That building has got to go.

I looked back over to my right, toward the library. The trees were so overgrown I could barely see it from here. Now there was a bit of irony:

Here we were, an institution of higher learning, and the library was completely obscured!

I looked back over to the left again, past Harrison Hall. All the trees there were so full that they obstructed the view of the campus. We needed to limb up those trees so that people would be able to see all the way up and down the walkway. A simple thing, but it would completely change the view of the campus.

For that matter, it would also make the campus a safer, more inviting and welcoming place at night.

There was so much that needed to change. A myriad of little things—and a host of big ones, too.

I headed back into my office. It was time to roll up our sleeves and get to work.

Investing in HPU's Future

I've always been a hard worker. It's just my nature, the way I'm built.

I tend to rise early and start my day with energy. The truth is, I have never in all my years worked as hard, as long, or as full out as I did those first months at High Point University. All that January, I came to work at 4:00 in the morning, a good three hours before sunrise. The maintenance people would come in early, see me already there, and whisper, "What in the world is *he* doing here?"

Most days, I didn't leave my desk, and I didn't close up the office until 8:00 or 8:30 at night. Some days, I actually felt chest pains—and it wasn't angina. My doctor assured me there was nothing wrong with my heart. I was just working myself as hard as I possibly could. I felt responsible for this $10 million goal we'd set.

Part of that work was simply getting up to speed. I had run businesses before, from start-ups to good-sized companies, and I had coached CEOs of gigantic corporations. Universities are different. An academic institution has its own organizational structures, its own values, norms, systems, even its own vocabulary. It is a unique ecosystem unto itself, and it was one that I needed to learn inside and out—and fast.

While it was not vast in size, the university ecosystem was fairly complex in its human aspects. There were more than 100 faculty members, including deans and other key academic positions, and more than 300 people on the staff, from vice presidents to the people who cooked in the cafeteria and maintained the grounds. Then there were the students and the parents, the alumni and the donors. I had to get to know all the personalities, the interplay of systems. There were a thousand things involved in the running of a campus that I had to understand.

At the same time, there was a mountain of change I was envisioning, and every change brought with it its own complications. Trimming trees, widening sidewalks, installing fountains—none of these projects would be as simple as they sounded, but they paled in comparison to such projects as moving a road, or erecting a building for the business school, or negotiating the purchase of additional land where we could *put* that business school, along with new dorms for the additional students we'd have coming in as we grew our enrollment numbers. A thousand tasks and enormous complexities lay ahead.

Still, there was one task that came at the front of the line. It was time, as I'd told my audience of sixty friends and influencers, to go find some money.

Fast.

The Art of Raising Money

Ten million in sixty days: That broke down to well over $150,000 a day. Nearly $200,000 a day if we didn't count Sundays.

Typically, when you raise money, a lot of preparation is involved. For an organized capital campaign, you bring in consultants. They do a feasibility study, talk to a list of the people you know, organize committees, and create print collateral with beautiful artistic renderings showing where all the money will be invested and what it will look like. On consultant fees and other costs, you could spend as much as 10 percent of the money you hope to raise.

I didn't have time for all that. I needed to go find that money myself and do it now. Forget the brochure. If we didn't have an artistic rendering, I would paint the picture myself, one conversation at a time.

I did have some advantages. For one thing, in my years as a citizen of High Point, I'd been quite active in the nonprofit world, and I'd chaired almost every major civic team and charitable board in the city, from the local United Way to our chamber of commerce, and I knew more or less everyone else who had been active in that world too. In the days before contacts on iPhones, I had what we used to call a loaded Rolodex.

Plus, in my quest to raise $10 million in sixty days, I also had a secret weapon: I had kicked in the first major gift. Fortunately, I'd been blessed in business over the years, and this was something my wife and I were able to do, and we did it because we believed in this vision and mission. I also knew that when I sat down to lunch with a friend and said, "You know, I just put in the first gift myself," it would make it a good deal harder for them to say no to me.

People don't give you their money because you need it. They invest their money in something of value. They want to see "returns on their investment."

Raising money for a university is somewhat different from finding investors for a business. Investors are looking for a clear financial return on their money. That's the whole point. Money you donate to a university, on the other hand, is never going to pay you a dividend, at least not the financial kind. So why would you donate? Because it *does* pay you a dividend—just not the cash-in-your-hand kind. It is an investment in the future, in the quality of the students who will emerge from the institution years from now and contribute to society. And while this is a noble investment, it is also an intangible, invisible one—and people like to invest in things they can touch, hold in their hand, or in something they can *see*.

We needed to show them. We needed to put them in my car and take them on a tour of something that didn't yet exist.

Over the next few days, my assistant Judy Ray and I set the pace that we would follow for the rest of that month. Judy made calls, set up appointments, arranged lunch meetings, organized tours of the campus, and typed up pledge agreements. Together, we operated as a fundraising machine.

We invited people I knew to come meet me at my office in Roberts Hall. When they arrived, we got in my car, and I drove them around campus, stopping at intervals to describe what I envisioned. This couldn't be about the plain facts. We had to paint the picture, let them actually feel it, make it come alive. "Facts tell, emotions sell," goes the old sales adage, but there was little about the campus the way it *was* that was going to generate any positive emotion. We needed to show them the way it was—and the way it *could* become.

One by one, I began gathering the pledges from nearly three dozen individuals and couples. I'd spend up to three hours or more with each one—bringing them to the campus, taking them around in my car, using my words to paint pictures of what we planned and where we were going.

It became a joke around the city of High Point. "If Nido invites you to take a drive in his car, or to join him for lunch—don't go!"

But they did. And we're grateful.

Not Just a Chocolate Bar

A month later, on the first Thursday in February, we held a second meeting. Again, we gathered at the Hayworth Fine Arts Center. This time, though, the cozy art gallery wouldn't do. This time, we assembled in the main theater because the meeting was not for 60 but for 600: faculty, staff, donors, student leaders, trustees, community leaders, and representatives of the media. The proceedings were being simultaneously broadcast on the web to all those who could not physically attend, including alumni, students, parents, and others.

Projected onto the wall behind me, against a High Point purple background, were the words "High Point's University" and underneath that,

"A NEW ERA." I spoke about my love for the university, its past glories, and its present challenges.

"Yet it is not our circumstances that define us," I added. "It is our choices. And we need to make some bold choices to move into our future together."

I led them through a PowerPoint presentation that sketched out our plans in broad strokes.

"Our university has compelling needs. Our business school needs a home. We need a new fitness center and a place for students to congregate. We need a new academic building for communication and another one for education, a new athletic building, new dorms.

"And it's not just buildings. We need funding for academic development, new programs, and more faculty. Our core curriculum was built in the 1970s; we need to bring our university into the twenty-first century. We need to be preparing our students for the world as it is going to be, not just for the world as it is."

The presentation did not load them down with details and specifics. For one thing, I didn't *have* detailed plans for achieving these goals—not yet. And besides, this wasn't about plans. It was about visioning transformation and impact. If we were to do great things together, it was imperative that we shared a similar vision for the university. This meeting was a crucially important step, because I needed everyone to know that we were a team. If we were truly going to be successful in this quest, we needed to build relationships of trust and honesty among all the constituencies on this campus.

Halfway through the presentation, I held up a big bar of Hershey's chocolate, and then a same-sized bar of Ghirardelli chocolate. I told them what each one cost and explained the difference.

"Hershey's chocolate is just fine. It's a perfectly acceptable chocolate. Ghirardelli chocolate, now that's different. Do you know why you'll spend four dollars on a bag of Hershey's chocolate, but ten times that amount for a Ghirardelli bar like this?"

No one answered, and no one needed to. These folks knew a rhetori-cal question when they heard one. Everyone leaned forward to hear what came next.

"Because," I said, "you buy Hershey's to eat. You buy Ghirardelli to give."

You could practically see the light bulbs popping on over people's heads.

I love this analogy, and I've employed it many times. Normally, I use Godiva as my example of premium quality, but in this case, I had a friend at Ghirardelli who had gotten me a good deal on a *lot* of chocolate.

As you'll see in a moment, a *lot* of chocolate was relevant.

"Both are good," I continued, "but only one provides an experience of distinction. The first is simply consumed and forgotten. The other is respected. The other is sought after, and once tasted is not forgotten. The other is exceptional—and *extraordinary*."

I then held up the Ghirardelli bar.

"This, this is what we are becoming. This is the journey we are on together. We are on a journey to reside in the extraordinary."

I paused. The room sensed a change in mood and became hushed.

I reminded the group of our pledge one month earlier to raise $10 million within sixty days. As if they needed reminding! It was not only those sixty or so community leaders who'd gathered over lunch on January 4 who knew about our ambitious goal. It had been written up in the area newspapers and circulated widely. *Everyone* knew about it, and no doubt every soul in that auditorium was wondering just how that effort was going now that we were halfway through the promised sixty days.

At this point, I confess, I indulged in a bit of showmanship. It was irresistible.

After a brief pause, I began.

"Well . . . what would be sweeter than ten million dollars? Eleven million?"

I looked out at the hall of people; the hall of people looked back. I smiled and shook my head.

"Because we didn't raise $11 million. Maybe $12 million?"

I could feel it, the realization starting to sink in. We had *already* reached the $10 million goal—and *exceeded* it.

I shook my head again slowly.

"No, we didn't raise $12 million. Perhaps . . . $13 million?"

I was teasing them now, and everyone knew it, but they couldn't help playing along. They were practically screaming with suspense at this point.

"Fourteen million?

"Fifteen million?"

Finally, I gave the sign, and a line of nine students filed onto center stage, each one holding up a sign three feet tall and bearing a single symbol or digit. The first student held a big zero, followed by another zero, and another, and then four more, followed by one holding up a big 2 and finally another sporting a big dollar sign. The nine stood in a line and spelled out:

$20,000,000

We hadn't raised $10 million in sixty days. We'd raised $20 million—in twenty-nine days. Twice the money, in half the time.

"What did James Taylor say?" I said over the raucous applause that swept the hall. "How sweet it is!"

And at that moment the title words of the famous James Taylor song "How Sweet It Is to Be Loved by You" came rolling out over the sound system:

How sweet it is to be loved by you.

How sweet it is to be loved by you.

I held up my big, monster-sized bar of Ghirardelli again as a prop for what came next.

"These changes will take time," I said after the applause died down. "But I can promise you the result, and the journey itself, will be sweet. And I mean that literally."

As I spoke, students began filing through the place handing out the gifts. I had arranged to have two tons of gourmet chocolate on hand for the event. Every one of the more than 600 people in attendance took home a ten-pound bar of Ghirardelli chocolate.

Do you know how big a ten-pound bar of chocolate is? It's like holding up a heavy laptop computer. I know, it sounds outrageous, but I was making a point.

Aim for the extraordinary.

"How sweet it is," I added, my voice rising over the music, "to be loved by the city of High Point and this wonderful community."

It brought down the house.

HPU's Springsteen Moment

A writer for a statewide business magazine attending the ceremony later wrote, "The last time I saw a crowd gasp, scream, and applaud like that, the man on the stage was Bruce Springsteen." I think that's what you call "adding journalistic color," because this was hardly a sell-out crowd at a rock concert. Still, I took his point: The mood in the place was pitched at a level of jubilation I'd match up against any musical event. The crowd responded as if we had raised $20 *billion*.

To put this in context, $20 million is not an outstandingly large amount of money for an institution of higher learning. We've now attracted close to a billion dollars without a campaign, committees, or consultants. But it wasn't really about the number. It was about the feeling it conveyed to those who supported the vision. It was about the sense of renewal, the *energy* of it. It said, "Hey, there really *is* an opportunity for something great to happen here."

It was a demonstration of *the art of the possible.*

The truth was, this $20 million was only the beginning. Our board of trustees had already approved a plan to raise more, and we would soon set a target for another $34 million. By that September, the target would be $60 million.

Over the years ahead, it would go into the hundreds of millions, heading fast toward $3 billion in investments generated from operating revenues, gifts, grants, and investments; our scholarship offerings grew with it. I've always believed that if what you are doing is worthy and worthwhile, you hang in there until it's done. And providing a solid, holistic education for our students in our ever-changing, highly competitive world is very worthy and worthwhile.

CHAPTER 3

Make Decisions with Your Head, Commitments with Your Heart

I almost said no.

Let me clarify that: I *did* say no.

In the spring of 2004, I was as busy as a human being can be. I was giving 100 speeches a year to corporate clients; running three companies, including holding the chairmanship of Great Harvest Bread Company, which had more than 240 retail stores across the United States; and running Creative Services Inc., a public relations firm I'd owned and operated since 1973. I was on the board of directors for a number of successful companies, including the La-Z-Boy Corporation, BB&T Bank (now Truist), and Dots, the women's apparel chain. Around the edges of that schedule, I also managed to fit in quite a bit of civic involvement, including heading up the High Point Economic Development Corporation and chairing the National Speakers Association Foundation.

That's how my life looked on March 17, 2004, when Dr. Jacob C. Martinson announced that after nearly twenty years of devoted service as president of High Point University, he was retiring at the end of the school year. He was a devoted president and a dear friend.

The university's board of trustees dutifully formed a search committee to comb the country for suitable candidates to be Jake's replacement. The core committee included Richard Budd, a prominent area businessman who was our board chairman; and Marsha Slane, a leading local philanthropist; among others. They placed an ad in the *Chronicle of Higher Education* and started putting out the word through our various networks. Applications and recommendations began coming in from around the country. Everything was going just as it was supposed to go.

Until one day in late May, when I had a meeting scheduled with Richard and Marsha to discuss university business, as I was slated to follow Richard as chairman of the university's board of trustees.

The three of us reviewed everything we had going on. Once we had finished and were about to break up the meeting, Richard and Marsha exchanged a brief glance, and then Richard spoke up.

"Nido," he said, "we've been talking with trustees and the search committee members [which included faculty, alumni, trustees, and students], and we believe the best candidate is YOU!"

"Well, Richard," I said, "that's nice of you to say. You think *what* should be me?"

"The position. President. We think our best candidate *is* sitting right here in High Point."

I distinctly remember both what I thought and what I said. What I thought was, *Me? What are you two thinking?* I was not an academic. Yes, I was on the school's board of trustees, but I was not involved in campus life and had no background in university administration.

That was what I thought. What I said was . . . nothing. For all of my adult life, I have made my living by talking. Over the decades, I've given more than 7,000 presentations. Ask anyone who knows me, and they will tell you I am never at a loss for words. But in that moment, I was stunned into silence.

Me? My alma mater's president? Right here in my hometown?

"Richard, are you serious?" I asked. "Of course, I am honored, deeply touched. But I couldn't possibly say yes to this. I've got a full speaking schedule, plus three businesses to run. Even if I were viewed as a qualified candidate, which is an entirely different discussion, how could I even think of taking on something like this?"

"Listen, Nido," he said. "Nobody's going to keep your time card. I'm sure you'd be able to do this, along with everything else you've got going on."

He made it sound easily doable.

"A Marriage Made in Heaven!"

That day, Mariana and I were holding an event for the local chapter of the United Way, and all the city leaders were coming over to our house. When I arrived home, my trusted and loyal friend Bill Horney had arrived ahead of me. He took one look at my face and said, "Nido, what's up?"

I told him about my meeting with Richard and Marsha to work on our search for a new president for the university.

"Bill," I said, "they wanted to offer the position to *me*."

Bill shook his head.

"Oh, Nido," he replied, chuckling. "You don't want to do that."

Bill was not the only one.

Over the next few days, I talked to a handful more people, and I got close to a dozen "no" responses back-to-back. I talked with a few friends and associates who were familiar with the world of higher education, and they all said the same thing: "Don't do it, Nido—it'll be a nightmare!"

In case I missed the subtlety of their point, they elaborated.

"Nido, you're at the peak of your career. Right now, you call all your own shots. You can do whatever you want. And you're thinking of taking this position where you'll have to deal with a whole bureaucracy, and faculty, and a board of trustees, and everything moving along at a glacial pace. You with your entrepreneurial nature and fast-paced style—are you utterly insane?"

Aha. So, not possible. No way.

And yet . . .

And yet there was something nagging at me, something that made me keep turning the question over in my mind. On the face of it, it seemed like a wildly impractical idea. Richard's assurances notwithstanding, I knew that if I were to take this position, even if only for a few years, it would need my full-time attention. That would put a significant crimp in my speaking schedule and require that I turn over the reins of my other businesses to someone else.

And anyway, would I really be the right fit for this situation? Most of the institution's past presidents had, like Jake Martinson, been ministers (High Point College was created by and affiliated with the United Methodist Church), and the few who weren't ministers were academics. I was an entrepreneur. I knew how to take bold steps and make meaningful change in a business structure. But I also knew enough about the academy to know that in an institution of higher education, things don't typically work that way. The academy is different. Would the institution and its constituencies embrace the kind of strategies and tactics I would want to bring?

I talked with a few more friends, but this time I reached out to other professional speakers I knew around the country and to trusted corporate chief executives, people who knew me well. Every one of them said the same thing: "Do it, Nido! This will be a marriage made in heaven!"

What if they were right? What if this was not a distraction from my "real" career at all, but was in fact the whole point of that career? What if this was exactly what all that other work had been preparing me for? I knew this was a big decision, and at fifty-six, I knew this would be one of the biggest in my life. How could I know which way to go?

Like I often do with any big decision, I looked within and asked, "What is God's plan for my life?"

He has always had a plan for me. I do believe that. I've seen it over the decades through so many signs. When I arrived in North Carolina as a college-bound teenager, He placed in my path someone who would become one of the most influential people in my life.

And I never knew their name. Even to this day.

My Mentors, My Hope

When I speak to audiences of entrepreneurs and businesspeople, I like to give them questions to ask themselves. For example: "If I could have everything the way I wanted it, what would my world look like? How would those conditions differ from my actual present conditions?"

This is not an exercise in escapism or futile fantasizing; it is a *clarifying question*. Having a personal vision sets up a creative tension between the world as it is and the world as you would like it to be. That creative tension provides fuel and leads you onto a path of accomplishment and fulfillment.

When I ask myself that question, the first answer that comes to me is this: "In my ideal world, I would have a father."

I was the youngest of five children, and shortly after I was born, my father became ill. When I was six years old, he died. If I had the power to turn back the clock and change anything in my life, I would much rather have had a father who would seat me on his lap, read me a book, sing me a song, take me to the circus, throw me a ball, or just talk with me, man to man. But that was not my fate.

So, my two brothers and two sisters and I grew up with a single parent.

A talented seamstress, my mother worked two jobs to keep us fed and clothed. While she provided for our basic survival needs, she also brought us up with a lasting sense of values. Her academic career did not go past the fourth grade, but she possessed the wisdom of the ages, a wisdom that she shared with us generously, giving us precious lessons for life and a very loving home.

"You may be poor in your pocket," she told us, "but you can always be wealthy in your heart."

My mother insisted that her children become educated, and one of her greatest wishes was that her youngest son pursue an education in America. So, I did. When I arrived on the shores of the United States in 1966 at the age of seventeen, I had about $50 in my pocket, the guidance of my older brother, and a firm commitment to get a good education.

I enrolled at Mount Olive Junior College (later renamed University of Mount Olive) in eastern North Carolina. I chose Mount Olive for two reasons. First, the name reminded me of the Mount of Olives of scripture, which reminded me of my home in the Middle East, and frankly, I was homesick. And second, they accepted me! For which I was (and still am) extremely grateful.

I went to Mount Olive for two years to earn an associate degree in business. Toward the end of my second year, as I was about to wrap up my final courses there, the president of the school, Dr. W. Burkette Raper, requested that I meet with him. When I arrived at his office, he congratulated me on my fine academic work and said, "Nido, I know that you *think* you paid your way through college last year."

What did he mean? Of course I had. I had worked very hard, seven or eight hours a day, while keeping up my course load. I'd found jobs at the school and in the city, and I spoke at churches, making maybe $10 a speech. I put every penny beyond my bare living costs into tuition.

"The truth is," he continued, "there was a gap between what you paid and what you owed."

He paused.

"A significant gap," he added.

This startled me. The idea that I had not fulfilled my obligation here was deeply troubling. Before I could say a thing, though, he continued.

"And I thought you might like to know, a doctor who lives nearby, in Goldsboro, picked up the tab for the difference."

I was stunned. Someone I didn't even know had paid my tuition deficit for me?

"Sir, who is this doctor?" I asked. "I'd like to express my gratitude for his or her kindness and generosity."

"Well, Nido, I can't tell you that because this person prefers to remain anonymous," Dr. Raper told me. "I just thought you'd want to know."

What would you have done, hearing news like that?

I'll tell you what I did: I went back to my dorm, knelt by the side of my bed, and cried my eyes out. Right then, I made a commitment to God and to myself. As soon as I was able, the moment I began earning money beyond my own tuition and basic living expenses, I would help other people go to college, just as I had been helped.

In the spring of 1968, with my associate degree in hand, I left Mount Olive and moved about two hours west to High Point College and earned a bachelor's degree in human relations. I then went on to the University of North Carolina at Greensboro, enrolled in the Bryan School of Business and Economics, and earned a master's degree in business in 1973. Because of what that doctor from Goldsboro did for me, one of my first actions upon graduating was to take the first $500 I could scrape together and start the Nido Qubein Associates Scholarship Foundation.

I'll never forget that doctor.

At the Qubein Foundation, we never saddled our grant recipients with burdensome contracts or obligations. Our only stipulation upon awarding someone a scholarship is that they use their education and good fortune to help others like themselves. To date, that fund has invested millions in scholarships to hundreds of students. I am eternally grateful to all my friends who pitch in annually to make it all possible. Like me, they believe fervently what Scottish theologian William Barclay once said: "Always give without remembering, always receive without forgetting."

The Heart's Path

In the spring of 2004, as I sat at home pondering this entirely unexpected job offer, I thought about the doctor and about that commitment I'd made so many years earlier to do my best to support the education of others. It occurred to me that, despite my own protestations to Richard Budd that I did not come from an academic background, I had been working in education for decades.

My first job upon emerging from college was as a youth director in a church, which led directly into my first business, selling leadership materials to adults who worked with young people in schools, churches, and camps. I worked on that business seventeen hours a day, seven days a week, and over time built up a clientele of thousands of customers in thirty-two countries. Many people started inviting me to come and speak to their groups. Soon thereafter, I became a motivational speaker, then a leadership speaker, then a business speaker. I was booking more than a hundred dates per year across the country. I taught courses on decision-making, problem-solving, and strategic thinking to millions of people and gave advanced coaching to CEOs.

More than anything, though, I had worked with young people.

Perhaps growing up without a father heightened my sense of appreciation for the mentors I'd been fortunate enough to have. It could be that my wish for a father of my own to guide me while growing up fueled my desire to work with young people later in life. Whatever the reason, the education of youth had always been a burning interest.

There was something here that felt like it was more than the call of civic duty. This felt *personal*. Yes, I was grateful to the city of High Point and felt a strong bond with my adopted home. The university, though, that was something different. These students were here to learn, looking to mold themselves into the leaders of tomorrow.

One day, as I thought about all this, I got in my car, drove over to campus, parked, and started walking around. None of the students passing me on those sidewalks had any idea who I was. I was just some guy walking around the campus, maybe a prospective parent or visiting professor for some class. I took it all in anonymously. As I walked, I wondered if that nameless doctor, my anonymous benefactor, had ever walked the campus at Mount Olive and watched me at eighteen walking by, lost in my own thoughts, entirely unaware of who was observing me.

Could I make a difference in these young people's lives?

I thought I'd been wrestling with a big decision, but that wasn't what was happening, not at all. This wasn't about a decision; it was about a *commitment*—and I knew the difference.

You make a decision with your head.

You make a commitment with your heart.

That's why commitments are long-lasting and why they are much harder to break.

Right then and there, I knew: If I followed my head, I'd say no. But if I followed my heart, I'd say yes.

The Big Decision

I asked Richard Budd for some time so I could think and pray about the opportunity. A few weeks later, I met with Richard again.

"Rich," I said, "I've really been chewing on this. I got a lot of feedback from my family, friends, and colleagues. I have prayed about it and thought about it. And to be honest with you, while it feels like this is, in a way, against my better judgment, I'm leaning toward saying *yes*.

"There are three conditions, though, and the only way I can even *consider* saying yes is if we can meet all three. Okay?"

"Shoot," said Richard.

"First, every single person on the board has to be in favor of this. It would have to be unanimous."

"Got it," said Richard, nodding in a way that said, *No problem.*

"Second, I wouldn't be able to start right in September. It would have to wait until January, because if I did take this on, it would take a few months to reorganize the leadership and management of my various businesses so they wouldn't suffer as a result of this career change on my part."

Another nod.

"Got it," he repeated.

"Finally," I said, "I could not consider accepting this position without having the opportunity first to meet with the entire faculty together, as a group—and if there is a single faculty member who doesn't want me there, then that will be that. I will not be able to accept."

Richard looked at me and just said, "Huh."

No nod this time.

Getting two dozen or so trustees, most of them businesspeople themselves, to sign on to my appointment as president seemed to be a breeze. No doubt they were all already on board with this idea. But 100-plus faculty members? This was no small feat.

There was good reason to expect that the faculty might not be altogether wild about my candidacy. I was an unusual choice, to say the least. I was an entrepreneur, a businessman, and academics are not typically enthusiastic about the idea of businesspeople being put at the helm of their institutions.

There is a phrase that has been used a good deal in recent years, the *corporatization of higher education*, and it is not meant as a compliment. Typically, it is used to express the concern that the academy is being run more and more by the forces of competitive economics and that institutions are looking for "return on investment." Just like a corporation. As a result, the academic program suffers.

I could well imagine what the faculty might think of their new entrepreneur-turned-college-president—storming onto campus using terms such as *branding*, and *marketing*, and *service* that we would *promote*. Such terminology horrifies some academics. "The university is not a business!" they would say.

And you know, there is significant merit to that objection. The business of higher education does exist. However, the university is *not* a business. Its purpose is not to produce a product or service that generates a dividend to shareholders. Its purpose is to bring learned and experienced educators together with young people to research and produce increased knowledge and wisdom for the betterment of society.

Nevertheless, I also knew the reality of the marketplace. As important as it was to be sensitive to academic traditions, I also knew that our university's future was in trouble, and it needed to do a significantly better job of positioning itself in a cluttered marketplace. If I were to become their president, I would in fact use terms such as *branding, marketing,* and *service* that we needed to *promote.* Would the academic community be willing to address both the *scholarship* of higher education and the *business* of higher education?

I knew I needed to find out. Later in my tenure, I realized that some would endorse it (as evidenced by 400 university presidents and their teams who visited campus to discover and learn our strategies) and some would resist it (as evidenced by a few critics who would opine about our ways, sometimes disrespectfully).

There was one more thing that made my third condition a challenge. Since most of the faculty were off for summer recess, we wouldn't be able to host them all in one room until August, nearly two months away.

This added a whole level of drama and suspense to the situation. By this time, it was already widely known around High Point that I was being considered for the position, and the possibilities and implications of my appointment were being openly discussed and debated in the local press. One talk show host started taking a daily poll of his listeners: "Will Nido take the job?" Needless to say, this lent something of a carnival atmosphere to the whole proceeding—something which I did not expect would do much to help the situation.

Richard handled my first condition on short order. He and Marsha talked with every single board member, and sure enough, each gave consent with enthusiasm. The second condition was also no problem. Four months' delay was no big deal, the board said. The university could get on fine waiting until January for their new president to take office. Besides, Jake (President Jacob Martinson) was gracious enough to stay on another semester.

Now all there was to do was wait for the faculty to return.

"I *Am* Your Guy"

August arrived and it was time to hold our meeting. We assembled in the great room at Slane, the student center that I was already thinking needed complete renovation. Every one of the roughly 100 members of the HPU faculty was there.

Richard, as chair of the board, introduced me. Then, it was my turn.

I started by telling the faculty how deeply honored I was to be offered this position—and then went right to the heart of the matter.

"I want you to know, I am not an academician. If you want me to be the president of High Point University, I need you all to know this. And if you *don't* want me to be your president, I need to know that, too. Because I am not going to leave behind what I am doing now to jump into this role if you don't want me here. So, I wanted to meet with you in person, all together, to make sure you understood. If who you want is an academician, a person who is familiar with how the university works and has been around higher education all his life, then you need to know, *I am not your guy.*"

There were more than a few startled looks in that hall. I don't think anyone was expecting me to say that. I continued.

"But let me tell you a little bit about who I *am.*"

I told them my story. I talked about how I left my homeland and resettled halfway around the world for the sake of the best possible education; about how I got into business and how I spent the first formative decades of my life; about some of the adversities I had overcome and some of the successes I'd been fortunate enough to have. I told them that, while I might not know everything about how a university worked, I had developed skills and core competencies in my business career that could definitely help. And that I was not only a proud alumnus of this university but also a loyal and longtime citizen of High Point, a city that I had come to love as my own. And finally, I told them I had been someone who believed passionately in the value and impact of education all my life.

"You know," I said, "my family was not in favor of this, not at first. In fact, just this morning, I was having a cup of Turkish coffee with my wife, and she said, 'Nido, just be sure this is really something you want to do.'

"So now I am saying the same thing to you. *Just be sure this is really something you want to do.* Again, if you're looking for someone who's an expert on curriculum and other aspects of the academy, I am not your man."

There was a brief silence.

"Though I am a quick study," I added. "I mean, hey—I don't want to sell myself short here."

They laughed.

"With your help, in time, I'm sure I'll learn whatever I need to know. And I do have a vision for what I believe High Point University can become, and I believe it can become something truly extraordinary. So, if you want a businessman with experience in how to grow businesses and make them thrive, someone who believes in our university and its future, then I *am* your guy—and with your help, we will make great things happen here."

At that, the entire body of faculty, down to the last person, stood and applauded. They were kind. I appreciated their hospitality.

As I told Richard, if a single faculty member opposed my appointment, I would decline the position. What I did not know at the time of that meeting was that there *was* in fact one person there who was dead set against it. Her name was Mary, and when our meeting began, she was adamantly opposed to the idea of this businessman sweeping onto campus, taking over the president's chair, and upsetting the way they did things. By the time the group was standing and applauding about one hour later, Mary was standing and applauding with them.

To this day, I do not know exactly what it was I said that changed her mind, but whatever the words were, I can tell you this: They came not from the head, but from the heart. And honestly, throughout my tenure at High Point University, the faculty have been collaborative, cooperative, and professional. I count myself blessed indeed to be a colleague to such a stellar family of accomplished educators. At times, I'm sure I made their lives somewhat uncomfortable. But I always had their best interests at heart! I never expected unanimous approval. I always appreciated their honesty and thoughtful discourse.

CHAPTER 4

Put Yourself in the Shoes of Your Client

It was January 2005, not long after I started as president, when I pulled into a dimly lit parking lot at least an hour after midnight, shifted my car to PARK, and shut off the engine. As I sat in my silenced car, I wanted to get the full late-night experience, and I imagined myself as a nineteen-year-old student coming home from some late-night event.

I'd driven in the main entrance and parked on the south end of the campus, in the lot just behind our old science building. To reach my dorm room, I would need to walk off the lot and around the science building, across the darkened promenade toward Roberts Hall, and circle Roberts before I could reach the residential buildings.

I closed and locked my car, stepped out into the cold, and began walking. My footsteps echoed into the pitch-black recesses. There were a number of public streets that traversed the campus, and anyone could be there. The bushes, full and close to the windows, blocked the view everywhere. I couldn't see past the trees. As I walked, my pulse quickened.

Of course, I reached the dorm without incident, as I fully expected. I wasn't genuinely afraid for my own safety. But when I put myself in the shoes of a young student? Terrified.

I turned around and retraced my path back to my car.

"Would I want my child making this walk?" I asked myself. "If not, then wouldn't every parent feel this way?"

We needed to make some changes. Fast.

Walking in Their Shoes

I was not alone in this thought. In their first January edition, the staff of the university's student newspaper, the *Campus Chronicle*, published an editorial on the front page with the headline "Some Suggestions for Our Incoming President." On their itemized list of issues, safety was at the very top. "Security," wrote the editors, "may be the most important concern on campus."

Also not surprising was the second item on their list of prioritized urgencies: improving the state of the residences. Here again, I agreed completely. The walk to the dorm was one thing. Once you arrived at your destination, the dorms themselves were in pretty rough shape, too. Many beds consisted of mattresses sitting on bare wooden boxes. There were stained and cracked bathroom doors, cracked tile floors, cracked chairs, cracked everything.

In one large bathroom in one of the women's dorms, there were no doors at all on the toilet stalls, just cheap vinyl shower curtains. One dorm lounge had a broken window "repaired" by the addition of two big strips of strapping tape applied in a large X. No exaggeration. I'm sure the deferred maintenance happened slowly and cumulatively until the university could no longer afford to fix it all.

This was more than a question of aesthetics. For the university itself, this was an economic issue, even an existential one.

Strategically speaking, if we wanted to put this institution on a solid economic footing and ensure its future, our first priority had to be increasing enrollment with a diverse student body while raising academic standards. More specifically, we needed to raise enrollment of students who *wanted* to be here, not as a backup school but as their preferred choice. And if we received enough students whose parents could help with tuition, we could assist more of those who needed aid. That was not a goal we could meet simply through more aggressive recruiting or clever marketing. If we wanted to attract more students, we had to *become* the place they wanted to be.

Why would these students want to come to HPU? Yes, to get an education, but that's the end result. What about the *experience*?

They would learn in the classrooms, but they would be living in the dorms. This was where they would go to sleep and wake up, where they would shower and dress, where they would study and think and talk to their roommates and write emails home. They weren't just coming here to learn, they were coming here to *live*, and their residence hall—more than any other location on campus—was where they would be doing it.

That same *Campus Chronicle* editorial put it perfectly: "A positive living experience during the first year of college is key to maintaining impressive retention and graduation rates." To which I would add: "and increasing enrollment appropriately."

Completely renovating all the classrooms, labs, and dorms, from top to bottom, had to become our chief priority for the year. We wouldn't be able to take full action on that until the summer months when the students had gone home, but we needed to start the planning process immediately.

This was clear as glass to me and to a good number of others—but not to everyone. One day in an administrative staff meeting, when I brought up my plan to renovate a particular residence building, our chief financial officer said, "Why would you want to spend money on that? It's already been paid for."

My proposal made no sense to him, and on paper, I could see his logic. Yet, the lifeblood of the campus was not something that existed on paper.

"Let me ask you a question," I said. "When was the last time you were inside that building yourself?"

He said nothing. I looked around the table.

"Anyone?"

No comment. Nobody there had set foot in any of those dorms for many years.

"Then, please forgive me for putting it in these blunt terms," I continued. "If you haven't been there yourself, are you really qualified to judge?"

The old Cherokee proverb says, "Don't judge a person until you have walked a mile in their shoes." To put that in leadership terms: If you are in a position to make important decisions that will affect others, if you want to make positive changes in their experience, if you want to provide genuine value, then you first have to walk a mile in their shoes—at least a mile. Perhaps several.

Imagine, for a moment, that you run a company that produces automobiles, or manages a chain of retail stores, or runs a diner. Now, if you don't personally drive one of those automobiles, or shop at those stores, or eat breakfast at that diner, then how on earth could you expect to make clear, informed decisions about what takes place every day at those establishments? Or let's say you are in government, responsible for shaping certain policies, and you take no opportunity to talk face-to-face with the people whose lives are affected by those policies. Or you run a nonprofit serving homeless children and never spend any time sitting with those kids and hearing about their experiences from their own lips. How can you possibly make sound choices on these people's behalf?

Unless you walk to the dorm building from a distant parking lot in the dead of night, unless you walk through that dorm's lounge, see the broken furniture in the bedrooms, investigate the rust around the showerhead, then how can you know where you need to spend your money?

Meaningful, effective change has to begin by walking in the shoes of the client.

A Leadership Secret

On Monday, January 11, a few days after my late-night walk to the dorms, the students returned to campus from winter vacation. When they went to lunch that day, there was someone new joining them—me. It still makes me smile to remember the students' faces as they sat at the cafeteria tables with their new president sitting next to them, laughing and joking and joining them in the Caribbean-styled theme luncheon as a steel drum musician played onstage.

For most of them, it was their first time meeting their new president. Most, but not all. On at least a few faces I saw startled looks of recognition, looks that said, *Oh,* that's *who that guy is!* Because a few of them had, in fact, talked with me before.

For months before taking office, I'd been conducting clandestine research. Three or four times a week, I'd drive over to the campus, park, and walk around. I just strolled the grounds, striking up conversations with everyone I met. I didn't identify myself, just introduced myself as "a visiting parent" (which, technically speaking, was true: I am a parent, and I was visiting). I even used several different cars to avoid standing out or being noticed. I didn't want anyone to make a fuss or change their behavior because the incoming president was there. So, I became "Nido incognito."

Mostly, on these campus walkabouts, I'd stop and talk with students, asking them questions about life on campus. I asked what they thought of the current president and whether they had ever engaged in conversation with him. I asked them what they thought of the incoming president. The conversations were always interesting, especially one I had with a particular young man.

"Yeah, apparently he's some successful businessman, so we're pretty excited about that," he told me. "You figure he must know *something* about how the world works."

Every time I made one of these anonymous visits, I came away feeling better and better about this choice I'd made. The idea of being part of these students' lives was thrilling to me. I got such a wonderful vibe from them—so open, so honest, so full of life and hope and promise.

I knew one thing for sure: Once the year began and I was officially on campus, no matter what other demands were placed on my time and focus, I had to keep these channels clear and wide open.

And we did. Today, more than nineteen years later, I still eat regularly at one of the many restaurants on campus. Could I eat at home? Of course, and in some ways, that would be a more efficient use of my time. Still, I eat breakfast and lunch where the students eat on campus, and I do it on purpose. I want to see the quality of the food. I want the people who work there to see me appreciating their service. Most of all, I want to mingle with the students. How could I lead this place effectively if I don't know how the students are experiencing it?

Out on campus, if a student walks past me without stopping to say hello and chat, I'll call out, "Hey! You didn't say good morning! What's up with that?" They'll laugh, come over, and talk. When I go from Roberts Hall over to another nearby building, that two- or three-minute walk typically takes me fifteen or twenty minutes because I'll have four or five conversations with students and faculty along the way.

Right in that first month, I also began freely giving out my email—and students used it. They would email me about a plumbing problem, a question about career options, or just to say how much they enjoyed a particular professor. People told me I was crazy to do this.

"How will you ever get anything done if you have students constantly emailing you?" said one.

"How can I get anything meaningful done if I *don't* have students constantly emailing me?" I responded.

To learn the pulse and the culture of an organization, the leader must be informed and involved, engaged and accessible.

The Case for Rocking Chairs

By February 2005, the whole city of High Point was abuzz with the news. The university had raised $20 million in a single month! Big changes were coming! Transformation was in the air!

The reality was that these big changes would take some time to put into effect. Twenty million notwithstanding, it wasn't as if we could snap our fingers and—*presto!*—just make it all happen. Buildings not only take time to construct, but they also take time to plan. Even putting in that big fountain I'd envisioned for the entrance was something we wouldn't be able to do right away. And while we were planning major renovations to the existing dorms from the moment I arrived, you can't renovate a residence hall while it's filled with students who are actually living there, going back and forth to classes every day. That would have to wait until summer when the campus cleared out.

In short, an awful lot of that forthcoming change was still many months in the future. But change itself could not wait. We needed to do something tangible, something that would begin changing students' experience right now.

So, we started in small ways.

During those anonymous visits to campus in late 2004, I had noticed that for much of the day, the campus had the feel of a ghost town. The only time you actually saw students out and about was during the few minutes between classes. Suddenly, there would be a flurry of students walking to and from classrooms or their residence halls, and then, all at once, it would go still and silent again. Other than those brief moments, there was hardly any pedestrian traffic.

How could we change this?

High Point was *the* Home Furnishings Capital of the World. Naturally, our thoughts turned to furniture. What would happen if we put out some rocking chairs around the campus? What would students do? Perhaps it would change the way the campus felt.

We secured half a dozen large white rocking chairs, placed them strategically in spots where we thought students might enjoy sitting outside . . . and waited to see what would happen.

Within a few days, it was impossible to find an empty chair. Students loved them.

We brought in 100 more rockers and spread them around the campus. Soon, every porch of every building sported rocking chairs. Like old folks in a small-town community, students were sitting out on their front porches and all around the campus, rocking and chatting with each other.

There was a method to the madness here; it wasn't just about putting chairs around. The idea was to foster more active *engagement*. We didn't want our students sitting in their rooms all alone, hunched over their computers all day. We wanted them integrating with other human beings. That's how you grow, expand your mind, build friendships, create a social experience.

What else?

Not Just a Cafeteria

In the spirit of walking in the students' shoes, I looked at where they actually walked. The HPU campus was bisected by a long, bland strip of grass and sidewalk, starting from the main entrance in front of Roberts Hall and running southwest to another entrance on the west side of campus. To me, it looked like one of those places cities everywhere like to call "parks." But in truth, these "parks" were not much more than spits of patchy grass and gray concrete.

How could we inject some energy, color, and personality?

At the time, we had some international students at HPU representing many countries. Why not put up a flag for every country and every state that had a student here? Soon, country flags and U.S. state flags hung from the lampposts, interspersed with our own purple-and-white HPU banners. Suddenly, the lawn—now rechristened the Kester International Promenade—was filled with color.

We installed a series of curved, cast-iron benches along the whole promenade. Now, instead of simply trudging down the path from one class to the next, students began strolling through, enjoying the walk, even sitting down and talking with one another.

What else?

We hired a photographer to spend time walking around the campus, taking pictures of students sharing animated conversations, playing Frisbee, engaging in various activities. After a few days of shooting, he had an impressive portfolio of shots showing happy, active students, laughing, talking, and playing together. We chose a selection of the best, had them framed, and hung them on the bare white cinderblock walls of the dorm hallways. A gallery of student life. Images of energy and engagement that engendered more of the same—a self-fulfilling prophecy.

What else?

There was no spot anywhere on campus that more sorely lacked engagement than the cafeteria, the only food service location on campus. The place felt stagnant and lifeless. You walked in, got in line, and passed behind a wall where two ladies behind the long counter would hand you your food on a tray, and that was that. You couldn't go back for more. You couldn't go fill up your cup a second time. You couldn't take more than the two cookies they gave you. You got what you got, and then you were out of there.

We conducted a survey and learned that the entire process of getting food, eating it, and then leaving took students on average eleven minutes. An eleven-minute drive-up fast-food window. Purely transactional.

This did not at all mesh with our picture of excellence. I wanted our cafeteria to be more than a fueling station. I wanted it to be an exciting, energetic environment where conversation would take place, where people would sit and talk, make friends, exchange ideas, compare notes, and dream about their futures. I wanted it to shift from being purely transactional to being relational, even transformational.

How could we bring some life to the place?

We made the entire cafeteria wireless (remember, it was 2005), so students could sit with their laptops and work on projects together. We did some modest redecorating, adding swatches of color here and there. And we added music. Not canned music. Real music, with live musicians. Starting with that Caribbean steel drum musician, we had live music happening in the cafeteria every single day at lunchtime with different musicians each day.

Suddenly, instead of being a glorified feeding trough, the café became a destination spot, a place where students actually *wanted* to go—and where they spent time once they got there. Before long, that average entry-to-exit time had nearly tripled, from eleven to thirty-two minutes. Now, our campus features twenty-one restaurants to host our 6,000 students and 2,000 faculty and staff. The restaurants have different menus and are located in various areas across campus. The students suggested themes and names.

Later that first year, we completely redesigned how the operation itself worked. We wanted students to choose their own food, instead of having someone hand it to them. We closed off those walls and brought the food out front, on long buffet-style steam tables. Now students served themselves the dishes they wanted in the amounts they wanted. We let them go back and get whatever they wanted, as many times as they wanted. We added an omelet station and a sandwich station, upgraded the quality of the food, and broadened the options, adding everything from vegan to gluten-free to all kinds of ethnic-themed dishes. We took it from boringly functional to extraordinary.

These changes all took time. But it started in January 2005 with live music and some splashes of color.

An Empathy-Intensive Process

Of course, none of this was as critical as the matter of security. HPU was actually a safe place. Yet, that was not the point. It *felt* unsafe. And while those crimes against person—assault, sexual offense, armed robbery, and the like—were not presently occurring, there was no guarantee they wouldn't.

We trimmed some trees and shrubs in spots where they hampered visibility to create a clear line of sight in every direction.

We added lighting everywhere on campus, from the dorms to Roberts Hall to the chapel garden to the parking lots. Suddenly every square foot was lit up at night.

We added video cameras to strategic locations, and more security staff to monitor them.

The existing security stations were squat wooden posts, each sporting a bright yellow box with a single button on it labeled HELP. They did not inspire confidence. We replaced these with new, redesigned security stations—tall, sleek, smooth metal mini-kiosks, bright blue with white letters saying HPU SECURITY, topped with a security light that would flash brightly if set off, and at waist level, a red button flanked by a two-way speaker system labeled EMERGENCY. The new stations were both more visible and easier to operate. We added dozens of these at key locations around the campus.

We also began a major project to build out the perimeter fencing. When I arrived, portions of our perimeter were framed by brick and iron fencing, but it was spotty and inconsistent. I wanted to circle the entire campus with beautiful fencing and elegant signage to give it a feeling of identity and distinction. Over the months of 2005, we built that perimeter out to become one single, continuous, well-defined boundary fence.

The effort continued over the years. Today, there is an ample supply of video cameras placed around the campus. As the size of campus grew, so did our security. At campus entry points, we've built eight Welcome Centers, all fully staffed, all the time. In 2020, *Security* magazine surveyed 500 college campuses across the U.S. to rate them on security, and HPU was ranked No. 12 safest in the nation. We've made the magazine's top twenty the past seven years, even though we're an urban campus.

Compared to the massive transformation that would come in the years ahead, the changes we made in the spring of 2005 were quite modest. It's easy today to look back at flags, rocking chairs, and music in the café and minimize their significance and forget how people reacted. At the time, though, the impact was enormous. It wasn't just the physical changes themselves, but the message they sent, the values they conveyed, and the feelings they created.

The truth is that it does not have to take huge amounts of money to make a profound shift in people's experience. The process is not capital intensive; it is empathy intensive.

There is a strategy for this that I've used for years. It revolves around two simple questions. The first of these has to do with *friction*.

Adding "Wow"

One day, a student emailed me with an observation. He had a medical issue that had forced him to take a semester off. Now, when he applied for readmission, he had to walk from the admissions office to the registrar's office to get registered, then to the business office to deal with tuition and financial arrangements, then to the health office, and then to the student life office. Wherever he went, he had to carry a card around from place to place to have it filled out by the agent in each of those offices.

I brought up his story at our next staff meeting.

"Let me get this straight," I said. "This young man wants to pay us $35,000, and we're making him walk around to eight different locations to have a piece of paper signed? Who came up with *that* plan?"

I call this an *irritant in the system*. A friction point—which is the first of my two strategic questions:

Where can we remove irritants in the system?

The cumbersome process this student described to me served the convenience of those who worked here, but it was clearly an inconvenience for the person it was supposed to serve. It was unproductive and inefficient. This sort of bureaucratic irritant is typical not only in most schools but also in many companies and, indeed, in most large organizations. In any of those situations, you could probably remove that irritant by doing something very much like what we did.

What we needed was a central place where this student could get all his questions answered and his issues handled. So, we created a concierge service with a concierge desk, a concierge's telephone number, and a concierge's email. It is mostly run by students as experiential learning for hospitality and event planning majors.

Our concierge service worked so well that we also made it available to parents. Now, when they come for Family Weekend, parents don't have to run all over the place looking for which hotel to book, where to make a reservation for dinner, where to get a car to the airport, where to get dry cleaning or a nail appointment while in town, or where to buy extra batteries or find supplies their child might need. They go to one place—the concierge's desk—to get answers to all their questions. In fact, parents query our concierge service on many topics, and they receive their answers almost instantly, seven days a week. What a service!

Irritant removed. They loved it.

Friction points are often easy to spot if you just open your eyes and look. The audience you serve will show them to you.

One day, I took our head of maintenance and groundskeeping with me for a walk around the campus. We noticed a spot where the students had cut across the promenade so often that they had worn a path right through the grass, exposing the dirt. He shook his head.

"Gotta be some way to stop them from doing this," he mused.

I saw it differently.

"Look at it this way," I said. "This is obviously where they want to walk. They've already shown us where we need to put a path. All we need to do is pave it for them."

It's not that the "customer" is always right. It's that they are always *worth listening to* because they will often show you solutions you hadn't thought of yet.

Talking with parents, I soon spotted another friction point: fees.

When you send your child to a private university, you are investing a significant sum of money. Parents understood and expected that. The problem was, it didn't stop there. In addition to the tuition itself, there was also room and board. And books to buy. And then, within weeks after the semester began, they would start getting calls from their kids asking them to send more money. Money for snacks. For movie tickets. For the copy machine. For any special event. It seemed like they were paying extra for *everything*, and they didn't like the feeling of being nickel-and-dimed.

This was a major irritant. So, we removed it. We designed a comprehensive fee that included everything. *Everything*. Once that fee was paid, that was it. No added costs.

We created a special card, like a credit card, that we called the HPU Passport, and set up everything on campus that used to cost money so that it now ran on the Passport. You want to pay for a snack from our on-campus Starbucks or buy a book at the campus bookstore? Use your Passport as a debit card.

By this time, a few years after I arrived, we had a range of food establishments beyond the cafeteria, some pricier than others. However, I didn't want our students to have to pay more to eat in one place over another, so we built our food model around the idea that you could eat anywhere. We called it a "Magic Meal," and the magic was, it was all included in your comprehensive fee, no matter what you ate or where. Just use your Passport.

We had bicycles you could take out and ride anywhere for no cost. Go, ride, have fun! On many campuses, you have to pay extra for parking. Not at HPU. No charge.

I still remember the very first time I told a pair of parents about the comprehensive fee and HPU Passport. In unison, they both said, "Wow!" The next set of parents to whom I described the HPU Passport also said, "Wow!" You'll never guess what the third set of parents said upon being similarly informed the third time I had this conversation. You guessed correctly: "Wow!"

I was sensing a pattern here.

In fact, this was when I knew that we had found an answer to not just Strategic Question No. 1: "Where can we remove an irritant from the system?" We also found an answer to Strategic Question No. 2: "How can we add WOW to the experience?"

A *Wow* is something that goes so clearly beyond the realm of the ordinary and the expected that people cannot help but be impressed. It is a gesture, a service, or a feature that embodies the idea of *distinction*—an experience that makes people say, "Something extraordinary is happening here!"

The comprehensive fee and HPU Passport system were an indisputable *Wow*. So was the HPU Concierge (a glorified name for the Student Help Desk).

This, by the way, was one reason I had driven so hard to reach that

$20 million figure by February 3, 2005. Even those who might have been skeptical of our vision of where we were headed—and there were skeptics among us, no doubt—I knew had to be impressed with a number like that. You could argue with what we said, you could argue with what we proposed and projected, but you couldn't argue with the fact of raising $20 million in less than a month. No one could hear that announcement and not say, "*Wow!*"

That was the reason for the ten-pound Ghirardelli chocolate bars, too. The crowd that day wasn't leaving the theater with lollipops. Most of the people in that theater had never seen a ten-pound bar of chocolate in their lives, let alone a ten-pound bar of *high-end* chocolate. It was impossible to walk out of that auditorium and not be thinking, "*Wow!*"

To be clear: A genuine *Wow* is more than a gimmick. You could set off firecrackers or hire a team of jugglers and get a "*Wow!*" But those are gimmicks. To me, a genuine *Wow* is an experience that is both memorable and powerful, because it is *meaningful*.

Every single innovation we made on campus—from those modest changes in the spring of 2005 to the more dramatic transformations coming in the years ahead—was designed not only for its own sake but also to communicate a specific value. Rocking chairs and live music in the café were about *social engagement* and *fellowship*. And all the free extras we added into the Passport? That modeled *generosity*.

Those state and country flags on the promenade were not there purely to add color. They were there to send a message from us to our students. We wanted to create a feeling of warmth in them when they saw the flag from their own state or country flying. I wanted them to know this wasn't just an institution. This was personal. This was a place where cultural diversity could open minds and heighten awareness of other experiences and backgrounds. This was an inclusive community where every person was valued.

A true *Wow* is something that impresses not because it is showy or flashy or razzle-dazzle, but because it taps a vein of the extraordinary in a way that touches on one or more significant values.

Those gestures and displays were an expression of the values of *honor* and *respect*. And this was the real point of the whole exercise: to model those values that we wanted our students to learn and absorb—and not because we were telling them to, but because they were experiencing them.

To be effective, to be a genuine *Wow*, the feature doesn't necessarily have to be something big. Sometimes, little gestures generate big meaning.

There is a small visitors' parking lot just inside the main entrance with space for some thirty cars. I thought it would be a nice gesture if we put up little signs bearing the visitors' names. Reserved parking. Make them feel special, like we were expecting them.

At first, we used simple real estate signs. Every morning, someone in Admissions would write all the morning visitors' names on the front of these signs with an erasable marker, and afternoon visitors' name on the backs. Shortly before noon, someone would go out there and turn all the signs around.

We weren't satisfied with this. After a while, we asked our director of information technology (IT) to have some electronic signs made that we could operate from a single command location. Now, when you drove in through the Welcome Center and gave your name, the security officer on duty would nod and greet you and say, "You can park right over there—we have a spot reserved for you," and when you drove around the circle and into the lot, there would be your empty parking spot waiting for you, with an electronic sign displaying your name and your city.

Your name in lights.

So many students talk about pulling in and seeing their name and state in lights as a memorable touch that sets their visit apart from any other college and university they see. So many say that.

Like Zachary Wymer, a history major and business minor from Columbus, Ohio, who graduated in May 2023.

"I tell other students to not make High Point their first college visit because High Point sets the bar really high," Zachary says.

Today, the first thing most visitors do when they park in one of those spots is get out of the car, walk around to the front, and have someone take a snapshot of them standing by that sign.

The Laundry Lesson

Every *Wow* creates unanticipated benefits.

For example, not only did our parents love the comprehensive fee, but before long we discovered that it also changed their behavior in an unexpected way. They started donating more money to the school. We weren't asking for more; they were just giving more—a development I attributed to the fact that we were no longer irritating them with ask after ask. Because of this, they felt better about the school, and therefore they felt better about participating.

Ironically, we eventually had to back off the comprehensive fee idea somewhat. The problem was that families in their college search would compare our comprehensive fee to other colleges' tuition numbers. Since we were no longer breaking out tuition as a separate cost, they didn't have a specific number to put against other colleges' tuitions. We were giving them no way to compare apples to apples. People would go online, look at our fee, and freak out because they didn't understand that this one number included *everything*.

This is the challenge of innovation: Sometimes you go too fast or too far for the world around you, and the gain isn't worth the dissonance.

It wasn't an easy decision. We loved our single-comprehensive-fee model, and so did our existing parents. Unfortunately, it was too confusing to prospective parents, so we went back to a slightly more conventional model with two figures: one for tuition, and another that covered room and board and everything else. The HPU Passport, however, we retained, so that for the student, the one-fee-pays-all experience is still there.

Here's another example of an unanticipated benefit: One day, as I walked across campus, a student stopped me and asked if I happened to have any quarters. She was looking to change a few dollars.

"Well, I might have some in my office," I said. "What do you need the quarters for?"

"For the laundry machine," she said. "I'm trying to do my laundry."

This didn't sit well with me. I went back to my staff and asked about it, and what I learned disturbed me. If you wanted to do your laundry on campus, you had to go to this machine in the dorm and insert a bunch of quarters. Sometimes, it worked. Sometimes, it didn't. We had a lot of maintenance issues with our washing machines.

I'd been a college student myself, and I knew what this meant. It meant students were trekking back and forth from their dorm rooms to the laundry rooms to see if their stuff was dry yet, and they wanted to make sure someone else didn't take it out first and leave it somewhere. Those back-and-forth trips were a major interruption and distraction from their studying or socializing or whatever else they were trying to do.

An irritant in the system. What to do? Simple. Remove it.

When we created the HPU Passport, we revamped and computerized all our laundry machines. Now, you go to the laundry site on your laptop (or, as in later years, your iPad or smartphone) and it brings up a picture of the laundry room in your building, showing you all the individual machines and which machine is going to be available in how many minutes. When one frees up, you go down there with your laundry and swipe your Passport to unlock the machine. You put in your clothes and leave. That's it. The system notifies you by email when your laundry is three minutes from being finished, so you don't have to stick around and wait. And with the machine locked, you don't have to worry about someone taking your laundry by mistake.

This translated into more time for studies, more time for social hour, and more time for what's important. No distractions. No irritant. All that, we expected. But there was an unforeseen result, too.

In the old system, there was an incentive to do as much laundry as possible with the quarters you had, so students were stuffing too much laundry into each load. This move put enormous strain on the machines, which translated into more frequent mechanical breakdowns and higher maintenance costs for us. In the new system, now that the machines were essentially free, the students stopped overloading them. They could do as many loads as they wished, as often as they wished, and with the washing machines being more time efficient (since they could check on them from their laptops or smartphones), students started using them more sensibly. We ended up with far fewer maintenance calls, which meant lower costs and fewer complaints as well as better service for the students.

I'm sure you know what I said when I heard about this result.

Wow.

A Major *Wow*

There is one thing guaranteed to add *Wow* to any university campus: bringing in a commencement speaker with national star power. We have, and they come to our campus through all kinds of avenues.

An example is Steve Wozniak, the co-founder of Apple. I ran into him during a conference where we both spoke. I introduced myself and I told him, "Woz, it would be great if you could come to HPU. They'd love you." In May 2013, he did. He gave the commencement address, and nearly three years later, he came back to our campus as our Innovator in Residence. Visit our website and you'll see him taking questions from students onstage inside the Hayworth Fine Arts Center and sitting in a golf cart smiling, surrounded by nearly a dozen students. Every semester, he works with our students on various projects. That includes a driver-less golf cart created by HPUMinds, a group of students like Kelsey Quinn. She was a part of HPUMinds since her sophomore year. In May 2020, she graduated with a double degree in computer science and mathematical economics and walked straight into a market data analyst job with Bloomberg. That interaction with Woz, she says, helped her get her job.

"One hundred percent," Kelsey says. "It was brought up in every single interview."

Meanwhile, wherever Woz goes, he champions High Point University.

"HPU graduates will be builders who discover new ways to solve the old problems," he says. "That's what innovation is all about."

With Gen. Colin Powell, we first met in 2006 when I was inducted in the Horatio Alger Association for Distinguished Americans in Washington, D.C. Gen. Powell was inducted into the same association in 1991. We were sitting at the same table at the State Department sharing our immigrant stories. His parents came from Jamaica. At the time, I had just become president of High Point University and I invited him to come to campus to speak to our students. I told him his values were our values.

In 2014, on a Saturday in May under a beautiful blue sky, he addressed our graduates. He called them "my young friends." He talked about love of country and the importance of civic involvement. But before he started his speech, he told our graduates that they needed to look out over the crowd, find their family, blow them a kiss, and say, "Thanks, Mom!"

And he laughed. Then, he started.

"Go forth and raise strong families, and remember all you can leave behind is your reputation, your good works, and your children for the next generation," he told them. "Let your dreams be your only limitation."

The last time I saw Gen. Colin Powell in person was a year before he died. We had dinner together before he gave the keynote address at the induction celebration at the American Home Furnishings Hall of Fame Foundation. At our table, we laughed and shared stories about our grandchildren, our lives, and our passion for living.

Our friendship grew over the years. He was a loyal friend of HPU until the day he passed away in October 2021. He became one of the founding members of the National Board of Advisors at High Point University. He was a giant of a man, a grand gentleman, a servant leader, and the embodiment of the American Dream. I was proud to call him my friend.

Attracting Dr. Rice

Like Woz, Gen. Powell supported HPU in every way he could. He helped convince Secretary of State Dr. Condoleezza Rice to come to our campus in May 2016 to do exactly what he did—give the commencement address and inspire an audience of 10,000 on the expansive lawn in front of Roberts Hall. With the help of Gen. Powell, we at HPU worked for a year to bring Dr. Rice to campus.

It started with a video on an iPhone.

After more than forty years speaking in front of audiences everywhere, I had learned that it's not about what you're saying, it's about what audiences are feeling. I put myself in the shoes of Secretary Rice and thought about her life growing up in Alabama during the age of segregation and what she had worked hard to accomplish in her life. So, without notes, I began.

"Secretary Rice, you have spent a lifetime helping to make the world a better place, and here at High Point University where we are a God, family, country school, we know you'll enlighten our young people and be the hero, model, and mentor they need to allow them to compete in an ever-competitive global stage."

But I knew I couldn't stop there.

I contacted members I knew at the Augusta National Golf Club, the home of the Masters tournament in Augusta, Georgia. I asked them to put in a good word for us with Dr. Rice. I knew she loved golf, and she was one of the first female members admitted to the Augusta National Golf Club. I did the same thing with members at the Horatio Alger Association of Distinguished Americans because I knew Dr. Rice had received the Horatio Alger Award in 2010.

One of the lessons I've learned in life is that your connections, your relational capital, will help you achieve your goals. They believe in you, you believe in them, and they will work on your behalf with no questions asked. In any situation, great or small, that holistic approach can make a difference. It did for us at High Point University. Condoleezza Rice came in May 2016 and delivered an impactful speech at commencement *and* engaged in an illuminating hour-long conversation with me in front of a live audience for a program broadcast a few months later on UNC-TV, now known as PBS North Carolina.

The night before commencement, she shared her incredible story in front of an audience inside Hayworth Fine Arts Center. I've often told our students that a good story is to a speech what a window is to a house. It lets in the light. And Dr. Rice let in the light that night.

She talked about how she grew up in the segregated south, the only child of a teacher mom and a minister dad, and how she lost a classmate in 1963 when members of the Ku Klux Klan planted a bomb in a church in her hometown of Birmingham, Alabama. Growing up, she found herself surrounded by what she called "unspeakable violence."

But she always had discipline. When she was three, she began taking piano lessons from her grandmother. The cost? A quarter. Rice loved playing the piano, and she told her dad, a Presbyterian minister, that she wanted a piano of her own. Her dad had an idea.

He told her that she could get a piano when she could play, "What a Friend We Have in Jesus" without missing a note.

The next day, Rice practiced. She practiced for eight hours. She even skipped lunch. When her parents came home from work and picked her up at her grandmother's house, Rice could play that hymn.

Her discipline helped her get a piano. It also helped her get an education and earn a string of accolades, including becoming the first female and first Black provost of Stanford University as well as the country's sixty-sixth secretary of state.

"In my family, starting all the way back to my grandparents, education was core to everything," she told me. "My parents really believed that if you had a high-quality education there is nothing that you couldn't do. You would be armored against segregation, armored against hatred, armored against prejudice.

"So, the idea was that you couldn't control your circumstances, but you could control the response to your circumstances, and education gave you a way to control that response. It was core to who we were."

We later talked for an hour in my office during her two days on campus, and we chatted about everything. She had accomplished so much, and she was known worldwide for her intelligence and her leadership. But what I came away with was how humble she was in front of an audience, with our students, and with everyone she talked to before, during, and after commencement. Dr. Rice is a teacher at heart.

At commencement, she shook the hand of every graduate. During her speech, she gave our graduates—and their families sitting and standing behind them—reason to believe that one person can change the world.

"When you find your passion, it's yours, not what someone else thinks it should be," she told our graduates. "There's no earthly reason that a Black girl from Birmingham, Alabama, should be a Soviet specialist. But that's what I wanted to be. Don't let anyone else define your passion for you because of your gender or the color of your skin."

Before she left, she found me and smiled. She had a message.

"Nido, please come see me at Stanford," she said. "Let me know any time when you're in the area."

For me, my time with Dr. Rice was one more confirmation that you can accomplish virtually anything—provided you put yourself in the other person's shoes.

CHAPTER 5

Build a Culture of Growth

It began on a Monday, January 3, 2005, bright and early.

I climbed the stairs to the third floor of Roberts Hall and made my way to the boardroom for my first day in office. I was about to hold my first official staff meeting. In the entire eighty-one-year history of the school, I didn't think the administrative team had ever been called to a meeting at 7:00 a.m. This, however, was the start of a new era.

I entered the boardroom, took out a canvas bag I'd brought, and began moving around the table, carefully placing several objects at each place.

My vice presidents filed into the room along with the directors of the various departments—director of athletics, dean of the graduate school, chair of the faculty council, and so forth. The group totaled about a dozen. They were the president's cabinet.

As they assembled themselves around the big table, they noticed the three objects set before each of them: an electronic gadget of some sort, a small clock, and an oddly shaped fragment of a photograph mounted on stiff cardboard backing. One by one, they picked up their photo fragment and realized what they had in their hands. Each of them had been given a single piece of a puzzle.

I thanked them for coming and invited them to enjoy the breakfast available. I told them how much I appreciated their joining me for this early meeting.

"Before we begin our conversation, let's see if we can put together this puzzle that is in front of us."

It didn't take long for the picture to take shape. Once the pieces were all assembled correctly, we were looking at a beautiful photograph of Roberts Hall, the very building we were sitting in.

In the fall of 1924, when High Point College opened its doors for the first time, the entire campus except for two unfinished dorms was contained within these walls. Roberts Hall included offices, classrooms, laboratories, a bookstore, a library, kitchen and dining hall, and a small auditorium that served as chapel. Even now, eight decades later, the building whose picture we'd just re-created symbolized High Point University itself.

"Wonderful," I said.

I placed both hands on the table and looked around at each person.

"Now that we've done that," I continued, emphasizing each word, "let's see if we can put together this puzzle that is in front of us."

Meaning, the future of this university.

One by one, I went around the table, highlighting the critical significance of the role each person there played.

"Taken all together," I said, "we make up a wonderful picture. Yet, this can happen only if each individual does his or her part to a T."

The Game Plan Unveiled

As I talked, I began weaving a picture of what High Point University would become, a place where the extraordinary became the standard we expected of ourselves each and every day. I sketched in broad strokes some of the changes we needed—the new buildings, the expanding campus, raising the bar of excellence in all our facilities, from athletic arenas to academic specialties to student career labs. It would become a shining academic community on a hill.

At first, I think they were hearing all of this in the context of what they had always known. Change would occur gradually, over a span of decades. As my descriptions unfolded, though, I could see it in their eyes as it dawned on them: I wasn't talking about decades. I was talking about months. I was talking about starting *right now*.

I gestured toward the second object arrayed in front of each of them: a beautiful Waterford clock.

"This small gift is the reason we are meeting so early today," I told them. "This morning we are not merely starting a new semester; we are initiating a new relationship with *time*."

I spoke about working with a sense of urgency, about working with velocity, about not rushing things or being careless but acting boldly and with confidence.

"As we move forward, I want you to think about what impediments are keeping you from being extraordinary. Let's identify them and remove them from your path. And let's do so swiftly, without delay."

I directed their attention to the last object in their collection.

"This," I said, "is a telecommunications device—a telephone—called a BlackBerry. You can make calls, keep a calendar, and do your email right here, from anywhere, whether on campus or off."

No one on campus owned a BlackBerry. In fact, not many were even aware of exactly what the device was. In January 2005, the smartphone industry was still in its infancy, BlackBerrys had been on the market only a few years, and the first iPhone was still a few years away.

I told them we were instituting a new communications protocol: Feel free to communicate directly with me and with each other.

"I want to keep us all on board, all moving in the same direction," I said. "I want you to know that I'm here to respond to any and all questions, any time. So here, let me give you my direct email. If you ask me a question, I'll respond right away."

By the looks on their faces, I could see what I said surprised them. They were not accustomed to working this way. They were used to operating fairly independently, which had generally worked quite well because, in truth, very little change had happened in the past. People didn't run ideas past one another because there was really no need. Communication tended to be more hierarchical, with each person reporting to their immediate superior, and the idea of anyone and everyone communicating directly with the president was . . . well, it was different.

"So, if we email you," said one department head, "you'll respond right away—that same day?"

"No," I said. "Not the same day. I'll reply that same *minute*."

So help me, the man's jaw actually dropped open.

They walked out of that meeting at an altogether different level of energy—an energy level, as a few later confided, that many of them had never seen or experienced before.

And that, more than anything we actually put into words, was the real message and meaning of that meeting. It wasn't about policy or procedure or how I wanted them to communicate with me. It was about a fundamental shift that needed to happen—not in the HPU campus or program, but in the people there.

It was our new culture.

Yes, a wave of transformation was coming, huge changes in both the college's physical space and its academic offerings. We would establish entire new schools, dramatically expand our property lines, and make thousands of innovations and improvements in what we did and how we did it. Yet, none of this could occur without an internal, invisible shift taking place first. To embody fully the new vision for the university, new patterns of thinking had to be introduced and allowed to take root. Before we could do new things, we needed a new way of doing.

And a new way of "being."

This is any organization's greatest challenge. Whether you run a division of a multinational conglomerate or the lunch counter of a local coffee shop, you cannot effect meaningful change unless the underlying culture changes first. All other transformation starts here.

What exactly *is* culture? You could define it as a shared set of values. A culture is defined by what people hold as important, or to put it more accurately, by what they hold as *most* important. Your organization's everyday fabric of decisions and actions is woven from the priorities and sensibilities that define who the people there are and how they operate together. It is the *who* that defines the *what*, never the other way around. And ultimately, it is the *why* that matters the most.

Culture, in other words, is not an idea, a slogan, or mission statement. Culture is made of *people*. If you want to transform your organization, you first must decide what kind of culture you want it to be. You want it to live and breathe. Then, you need to identify your key team of people who will help you establish and promulgate that throughout the organization.

This, I knew, was my greatest challenge in the days and months ahead. Not raising money. Not boosting enrollment. Not renovating old buildings and constructing new ones. All of that was ancillary. The central task was to instill a new spirit and vision into the culture and, along the way, identify my key lieutenants. And it began on Day One. There had to be a shift in culture, and it had to happen right away—or it would never happen at all.

HPU's Mission

During that first week, we held a staff meeting in a large science room filled to its 100-person capacity. After greetings and introductions and opening remarks, I began.

"Let me share with you an operational philosophy that has helped me enormously in my life, both in business and in other endeavors," I said. "It's something I call *primary and secondary*.

"Identifying something as primary means it comes first. And it *always* comes first. With every decision you make, you first ask yourself, 'What's the primary here?' Because you can never let the secondary rule the decision. Here is this philosophy in a nutshell: *The secondary must always serve the primary—never the other way around.*"

I saw plenty of heads nodding. They were with me—so far.

"So, we have to ask ourselves: What is our *primary* here at High Point University? Why are we here? What is our central purpose? Well, the question practically answers itself, doesn't it?

"We are here for the students. Our primary concern, in other words, is whatever serves the learning interests of the student. All other considerations—logistics, costs, convenience, convention, and so forth—these are all secondary. Not irrelevant, but secondary. Of course, we cannot ignore questions of cost or convenience.

"Yes, these have to be considered, but they cannot be the determining factor. The determining factor must always be whatever serves the interests of the student, principally their academic journey."

I saw no heads nodding now. Everyone in that science room was thinking hard. I could practically see the wheels turning as people began sorting through the implications of this idea.

"For me, there is nothing more important, more urgent, or of higher priority than when I'm communicating with a student or a parent," I said. "There is no meeting I won't interrupt, no task I won't postpone, when I get that call."

Now I was getting some reactions. This was fairly radical stuff.

Any student or parent could interrupt the *president*? While he was in a *meeting*?

I continued.

"Whether I'm meeting with someone from the city council, or the chairman of our own board of trustees, or the president of the United States, or even someone more important than that."

My eyes grew wide, and my voice dropped to a whisper.

"And yes, even a *donor*."

Laughter rippled around the room. I knew I had their attention.

"No matter who it is," I said, "I'll apologize, put that meeting on hold for a moment, and take the call. Because if there's a problem on campus, no matter who we are or what we're doing, we have to get to it and fix it, right now.

"And this doesn't apply only to our people in the Student Life office. How we treat visiting students isn't just up to Admissions. Admissions is *everybody's* job. Student Life is *everyone's* job.

"Retention is something on which any and every one of us has an impact. If a student needs help, help them. Rather than simply pointing them to the building where they should go, walk them to that building, talk with them. Make them feel welcome in this home of ours.

"They are not an interruption in your day—they are what your day is all about, no matter what your formal role or title. They are why we're all here."

Finding Our Primary

There were three specific ways that we needed to shift the culture at HPU, and in that initial meeting, our administrative staff heard all about the first of these three:

We had to become a *student-focused culture.*

To be clear, it's not that the people there didn't already care about the students. They did. And it's not as if the university staff were not friendly and helpful. They were. Students were being considered—of course they were—but that consideration was not necessarily always *primary.*

This is not an issue that applied only to HPU, nor indeed only to the academic world. It speaks to something I've observed throughout my professional life.

There is a tendency in any organization for it to become self-serving. The larger the organization grows and the older it is, the stronger this tendency expresses itself and becomes this kind of inertia, a growing gravitational field if you will, that pulls everything into its orbit. Whatever its stated goals or original mission may have been, the organization's everyday purpose becomes more and more about the perpetuation of the organization itself. This is the essence of the term *bureaucracy.*

Here is the question every organization needs to ask itself: Are we here to serve our constituents—or has it become the other way around?

As for us at HPU, we had to ask ourselves two key questions: Was the university here to help nurture the students? Or were the students here to help nurture the university's employees?

You could say, "Well, both are true," but that is a nonanswer, because while both may very well be true, *one has to be primary.* In order to operate effectively, in order to make clear decisions, you first have to know what it is you're seeking to achieve. If you don't know your destination, how can you possibly choose the best route?

For some faculty, this might take some getting used to.

It's natural for an institution of higher learning to evolve a culture that revolves around the faculty. Students, after all, don't stay at the university for long. They pass through, stopping for only a few years to learn and move on. The faculty stays. To the student, it is a brief chapter in their life as they prepare for a career. To the faculty member, it *is* their career. Faculty provide the teaching and the curriculum. Key administrative posts are often filled by former professors. It is by nature an academic culture.

Now, I have to take great care in how I express exactly what we sought to do here because it's not as simple as saying, "We changed the focus from faculty to students." When I say "a student-focused culture," it would be easy to interpret this as meaning we wanted to diminish the importance of the faculty.

Not at all.

Our claim to be extraordinary had to rest first and foremost on the quality and integrity of the core academic experience. That academic experience is the reason we exist. And it *is* the faculty who provide that core academic experience, it *is* the faculty who embody and pass on that knowledge and wisdom that we are here to impart. So, the traditional importance that the academy bestows on its faculty is not at all misplaced.

But what's the reason for creating that academic experience in the first place?

The students, of course. No students, no university.

In a word, the students had to be our *primary.*

This shift in priorities was not easy for everyone to embrace, but in time, it would become our signature trait. Today, if you ask HPU parents or alumni to identify what they credit most for why they are so devoted to this community, it would be this: Every last person at High Point University genuinely cares about the students and considers them first in every decision, at every level, without exception. That doesn't mean students always get what they want! HPU is a serious academic institution with a rich legacy and high standards. It simply means our faculty are mentors to our students. It means we care a lot about each other and we march forward with a common goal.

Talk to any student, and they'll have a story. Here is one.

"A Role Model for Me"

Dr. Meghan Blackledge, an associate professor of chemistry, turned her whiteboard in her office into a road map for Rebecca Ulrich, one of her students. For two weeks, Rebecca and Dr. Blackledge thought it through.

They compared the long-term benefits for each of the post-grad opportunities Rebecca had stacked up. And those opportunities were stellar. She had been selected for the prestigious Oxford-Cambridge Scholars Program where students can pursue a research-based doctorate at Oxford or Cambridge University in the United Kingdom while conducting research for the National Institutes of Health in the United States. Only twelve applicants worldwide are accepted, and Rebecca was one.

Since her freshman year, Rebecca always thought she would pursue medicine. But she changed her mind. She spent months talking with Dr. Blackledge about her future, about what to do and where to go. In the end, Rebecca followed her heart. After graduating in May 2018 with a degree in biochemistry and a minor in physics, she began pursuing a PhD in organic chemistry at the University of Illinois at Urbana-Champaign.

"Dr. Blackledge's office is always open, and she has spent countless hours giving me advice about life, my career, my future aspirations, and about how to succeed as a woman in science," Rebecca says. "She knows when I need tough love and how to challenge me and push me to grow, but she also knows when I need someone to be kind and empathetic and lets me vent. She has been a role model for me."

At High Point University, students find heroes, models, and mentors among the faculty and staff. Dr. Blackledge is one.

Two Challenging Days

Later in January 2005, I brought a half dozen of the senior staff and faculty leadership on a two-day retreat at the Grandover Resort in Greensboro, fifteen minutes from campus. This was the kind of high-end executive retreat you might see at a large corporation, and none of the people present had ever experienced such a thing. Yet, that was exactly the point. This was not going to be just another staff meeting, and I needed to create an entirely novel context.

Their charge was simple: Spend these two days talking about the future of High Point University, without any reference to encumbrances of the past or limitations of the present.

Open our minds wide and dream.

Offer new ideas, without interjecting any reasons why it "could not be done."

No negative statements were allowed. No whining.

It was a two-day deep dive into the art of the possible. This is not easy to do, and I acknowledged that.

"Look, I know that each of you knows an enormous amount about how this university works, and you know what you know," I told them that first day. "For now, however, I want you to forget what you know. Don't be constrained by the limits of your present knowledge. And forget about asking, 'How do we make this university *better*?' Instead, ask yourself, 'If we were going to make the greatest university in the world, what would we do?'"

"You want us to think outside the box," offered one.

"No, please don't think outside the box because when you do that, you're still using the box as your frame of reference," I responded. "Let us throw the box out the window."

A few people chuckled, but I paused because I wanted that image to sink in. It has. It has become a tactical catchphrase here on campus that has persisted to this very day: *Don't think outside the box—throw the box out the window!*

"Really," I continued, "what we're talking about here is having a *growth mindset*. A *fixed mindset* says, 'This is how we've always done it, so this is how we should keep doing it.'

"A *growth mindset* says, 'In the most ideal world, how might we do this?' and then works from there. A growth mindset doesn't rely on what's been done in the past or what others are doing. A growth mindset doesn't tweak; it reinvents. It explores, expands, and inspires the organization to become radically better in every way, on merit and by design."

I looked around the room. I could tell I had their attention.

"A growth mindset asks these three questions. No. 1: If we could start over, with no limitations, what would that look like? No. 2: How would that be different than what we're doing right now? No. 3: How can we make what we're doing right now more like that?

"We're not interested in making incremental improvements. No one will notice that. We're interested in asking ourselves, 'How are we going to take huge steps in the direction of the extraordinary?' Let's look at this HPU world completely differently, and let's do it together."

I then looked at each person in the room. I paused. I wanted to make sure my next point would sink in.

"And let's not just do *something*. Let's do something *significant*."

If making students' best welfare primary in every decision was the first fundamental shift in culture we needed at HPU, this was the second: I was asking them *to embrace an entrepreneurial spirit.*

To think like entrepreneurs.

This, I knew, could be an enormous challenge.

"This Is Who We Are"

First of all, the idea of approaching a university through the eyes of business is a controversial notion. In the academic world, there is great sensitivity to the idea of operating by business principles like the logic of profit and loss, of balance sheets and efficiencies, of cost-cutting and economies of scale that pay allegiance to the fiscal bottom line rather than the academic furthering of the students. Some refer to it, wrongly so, as the "corporatization" of the university.

I am completely sympathetic to that concern. This is why I am so emphatic about this philosophy of primary and secondary. Make no mistake about it, we are an academic institution. Our entire purpose for being here is to resource our faculty so they can prepare students for careers of success and significance. This is why we exist. Of course, we care about faculty research and how it can improve our world. But without students, that world would not even be possible.

Yet, this does not preclude the need for employing smart business principles in our operation. We are not a business. We are a nonprofit organization. But we do face business challenges in the higher education landscape that require business solutions. If we didn't pay attention to the fundamentals, we couldn't have resources to enhance academic performance. We could even shrink and disappear as some colleges sadly do.

For example, we believe in *branding* as one strategy of our larger vision. We started putting up "High Point University" banners all over the campus. Soon, you saw the purple-and-white HPU logo popping up everywhere—on coffee cups, T-shirts, notebooks, and buildings. We were saying, "This is who we are!"

Before that, there was very little expression of pride in our school. If we wanted to become a first-choice school, we had to start acting like one. We needed to shout from the mountaintop, "We're High Point University, and we're proud of it!"

Some people didn't like that because they saw it as too over the top, too much commercialization of the university. Yet, look at businesses. Look at well-run nonprofits, such as the American Cancer Society, the United Way,

or the American Red Cross. Look at churches that are thriving and growing. It's not a purely corporate, for-profit business concept. By definition,
as organizations grow and expand, there are core principles of operation
that you need in *any* context for things to go well.

Still, the idea of shifting their orientation to a model based on business
principles was a tall enough order on its own. And I wasn't just asking for
them to think like businesspeople. I was asking them to think like *entrepreneurial university leaders.*

This is very different. Not all businesspeople are entrepreneurs. In fact,
the majority are not. Which, in my view, is a big problem because they
should be. Even in the most established, solid companies and organizations, an effective leader will always retain an entrepreneurial edge and
outlook. Or to put it differently, the day you stop thinking that way is the
day the organization begins to die.

This is what that staff meeting was really about when I said recruit-
ment and enrollment were everyone's job, not just the people in the
Office of Admissions. In an entrepreneurial culture, everyone has a
shared sense of ownership over the whole. It's not only maintenance's job
to look for broken light bulbs out on streetlamps. It's everybody's job.
And it's not even a "job"; it's a cause, a calling. A meaningful investment
in the life of other human beings.

This is also what that first early-morning, put-together-a-puzzle
meeting was all about. Urgency, agility, action, direct communication,
and cooperation.

And this was what the two-day retreat at the Grandover was about, too.
It was about dreaming, brainstorming, innovating, looking vigorously and
creatively to the future.

These three traits, to me, comprise the essence of an entrepreneurial
culture:

- The willingness to take personal responsibility for any and every
  aspect of the organization.

- The willingness to move fast and stay in motion.

- The willingness to dream big and never stop dreaming, to imagine future innovations unshackled by the achievements, challenges, and habits of the past.

Be responsible.
Be quick.
Be bold.

That is how people behave in an entrepreneurial culture—and it would become a bedrock principle not only in how we operated at HPU but also in what we taught our students.

Four Essential Ingredients of Growth

They were not easy, these conversations at the Grandover. The men and women there had never been challenged in this way before. And it wasn't all coming from me, either. I asked them to challenge each other, and they did. Some were more resistant than others, and there were moments when the feeling in the room grew tense. I was pushing them—and they were pushing each other. Yet, it was exhilarating. It was like a locked cage had been opened. People began sharing their dreams and ideas for the university. They raised all kinds of concepts, strategies, and tactics, and no suggestion was too small or too large. A solid range of practical ideas emerged from that retreat that would become the seeds of new directions for that entire first year.

The two days both started early and ended late. At the end, everyone was drained and exhausted. At the same time, though, they were utterly invigorated by the possibilities we had all begun exploring together.

By mid-February, the preliminary work was largely done. We had raised nearly $30 million. We had sorted through priorities and identified key strategic areas where we wanted to effect change. And in getting to know and work with everyone there, I had begun getting a fairly solid sense of where the talent lay, where the strongest resistance might come from, and who my key leaders, my lieutenants of transformation, were.

It was time to *execute*.

During these six weeks, I also had shared with our team a set of principles I'd been using for decades in my business consulting as well as in my own businesses. To effect progress and growth in an organization, I believe you need four essential ingredients:

- A clear vision

- Solid strategies

- Practical systems

- Consistent execution

I'd been articulating the vision from the get-go. I'd described it hundreds of times to everyone I talked with, in meetings large and small. In those six weeks, we also had brainstormed solid strategies for turning that vision into prioritized plans, and we had mapped out practical systems for turning those plans into pragmatic sequences of steps.

Now it was time to get things done. We needed to create what I call a *culture of executional consistency.*

And Then Some

Everyone loves to talk about vision. Years ago, I wrote a book about high performance and visioning.

Vision is inspiring. When you create a vision statement, you get to use bold phrases and sweeping imagery. It's thrilling. Dramatic. Sexy. And, let's be honest, it's also *easy.* Because it's just words. Anyone can say, "We're going to make some big changes here." But at some point, you have to get down to the *doing* part.

In the term "consistent execution," I place particular emphasis on the word *consistent.* This is the critical element that so many organizations lack in their habits of execution. The reason *consistent* is so crucial is that the gains of doing things right 98 percent of the time are so easily undermined by that pernicious 2 percent when something goes wrong.

"Imagine if somebody in Student Life spends twenty minutes with a visiting family and does a fantastic job," I said at one meeting. "Then, the family walks out of that wonderful experience and across campus to another building—where they have an altogether lousy experience. Suddenly, it no longer matters how good that twenty minutes across the way was because they're going to walk away feeling lousy.

"We have to give not just excellent service but *consistently excellent* service—because in the final analysis, our chain of impression will only be as strong as its weakest link.

"Our weakest effort and best effort are only inches apart. So, our efforts across the board have to be very consistent *everywhere*."

This, too, entered the lexicon as an expression that is still used today at HPU: *The weakest effort and best effort are only inches apart.*

I also shared with our staff a principle I call "And Then Some," which refers to that extra mile, that beyond-the-call additional effort that so often makes the critical difference between *sufficient* and *exceptional*.

Think about water.

At 212 degrees Fahrenheit, water heats to a boiling simmer. Turn it up just one more degree to 213 and it gives you steam. Simmering hot water can make you a nice cup of tea, but steam can drive locomotives. It's that extra degree, that "And Then Some."

That makes bold things happen, and *that's* where success comes from.

I never leave my office for the day without first stopping and asking myself, "What's one more thing I can do?" It may be one phone call, one more letter or email. It may be leaving a note for my assistant about something we need to do the next day. It may even be a note to myself with an idea for a talk I'll soon be giving. It typically will not be a big, dramatic task, but whatever it is, it's that one more degree that keeps the edge of progress moving forward. Then, once I've identified that one more job, I do it.

I've done this every single day since I first walked into the president's office. Heating the water to that one last degree helps water transform to steam. That is the concept of "And Then Some."

It sounds so simple. It *is* so simple. Yet, tragically, it's so uncommon in people's actual habits of execution. What makes that kind of best effort so rare is that it is so easy to do the opposite—to slip into the practice of leaving a few minutes early, of doing just a little bit less. It is a type of gradual desensitization. Laziness creeps in. Without noticing, you become habituated to cutting corners, assuming things are right rather than checking on them one more time, and without realizing it, you have begun the lugubrious slide into mediocrity.

Why?

It's certainly not out of malevolence or an intention to create poor results. It's pure inertia. It happens because most of us would rather be comfortable than excellent. Because nobody has inspired us to become all that we can become. So, you cease doing everything you can possibly do. Instead, you start to settle for less from yourself. Who wants that?

Getting "On the Bus"

The first time I spoke with the faculty back in August 2004, I got a standing ovation at the end of the meeting. As long as I was talking about the extraordinary future, everyone was on board and excited. In 2005, when things were actually changing, that enthusiasm started to be tested. As we began to execute on these ideas, I began seeing some resistance.

When we started work out in front of Roberts Hall to prepare for building the first big fountain, someone said, "I don't understand why you're building that fountain. We need that money in the biology lab!"

When we trimmed some trees to improve security by opening up the field of vision on campus, we fielded an outcry of objection from some quarters.

When we transformed the promenade by lining it with colorful flags, we heard from a faculty member. She hated it. She preferred the bland "cemetery" look of the promenade the way it used to be. She was far from alone. Some faculty felt threatened by all this talk of change, and they worried everything seemed to be moving so fast. They had questions. Here are a few:

- Why are we suddenly talking about tearing down this building and pouring money into putting up a new one?

- Why are we talking about radically boosting enrollment and drastically lowering our tuition discount rate?

- What is this talk about building a "national brand"?

It was not the change itself, I believe, that felt threatening, so much as the perceptions about how that change might affect them. After all, people resist change, but they embrace progress.

I knew I needed to proceed with caution and due respect here. A new corporate CEO can come charging in like a bull and tear everything up. A university president is not like that. He or she is not the owner of the academy. My employment contract identified me as CEO, but I never refer to myself using that title.

There is a system or process in the academic world called "shared governance," which refers to the idea that the different constituencies of the university—faculty, student body, staff—all have a voice. It's the administration's job to balance and integrate those various points of view. A university is a more collaborative ecosystem than your typical business, although in my experience, the most effective business leaders are precisely those who foster that same kind of collaborative environment.

My approach at HPU was to be as transparent as possible. I didn't do as some business-minded college presidents might, marching in, closing departments or reducing the number of faculty as cost-cutting measures or declaring that we needed to abolish tenure. When we needed to do something, I told the faculty exactly what it was and why we hoped to do it. I told them what I saw as the challenges we faced, what I saw as our best strategies, and how we could overcome those challenges and why. I listened, compromised, and collaborated. And honestly, our faculty were always thoughtful and responsive.

Still, my first season as college president was tough for some, not only on the faculty but on the administration side as well. College campuses traditionally serve as a place of calm, a world apart. Change normally occurs at a very gradual pace.

That spring, I had an excruciating decision to make. I had to let someone go. And not just anyone. One of the top people on campus. We had to part ways with our chief financial officer. He was the same person who'd said, "Why would you want to renovate that building? It's already paid for!" He was a fine person and competent, but he didn't want to take any risks and was resistant at every turn to the kind of culture I was working to create. For the first few months, I'd hoped we could work it out, but we didn't. Now came the hard part.

He had given twenty-two years of his life to this campus. So, it was one of the toughest days I've had in my time at HPU when I told him his services would no longer be needed.

It sent shock waves throughout the university. He had been, in many ways, the person running the place. To learn that I was letting *him* go shook up quite a few people. Yet, it also sent a message. I hadn't come here to fire people, but we had to have the right team or we were not going to succeed. We needed, in Jim Collins's famous words, "the right people on the bus," and it was a very different bus than the one they'd all been riding on for years.

Others left too. They weren't people I let go, but they were people who simply moved on of their own accord. Our faculty have contracts that renew every year at the end of May, and when their contracts came up in May 2005, some opted not to renew. And yes, the one who had objected to the flags on the promenade was among them. There were some in the administration who left too. It all showed me what I had learned throughout my career: You can't change things without changing things.

Finding Talent

By the time that first semester ended, we hadn't put up a single new building or renovated a single old one, and we hadn't expanded the campus or enlarged the student body or opened any new academic programs. We hadn't done anything, really, that looked terribly dramatic to the outside world. But we had effected the most crucial change that we would ever make in my entire tenure as president.

We had shifted the culture at High Point University.

Of course, it would take years to fully inhabit this new skin of ours. An organization's culture is like a new pair of shoes. It takes some breaking in. You have to walk some miles in them before they feel comfortable on your feet. Yet, High Point University had become accustomed to its new pair of shoes. It became a community of people who placed our students' interests first, who embraced and embodied an entrepreneurial spirit, and who exhibited a passion for consistent executional excellence.

Most importantly, I had also identified the key talent and capacity within the team. These talented, energetic, extraordinary people were among the staff I found in our midst when I arrived. They became team members who would become my most trusted lieutenants. And they are still my most trusted lieutenants to this day.

Back in 2005, at the end of that semester, I knew who they were; they knew who I was. We were truly ready to work together to build something extraordinary.

There will come a day when I finally leave this post. Lord willing, that won't happen for a long time. But I'm realistic enough to know that it has to come eventually. When that happens, I'll leave content, knowing that the vision of HPU is in good hands, and our extraordinary faculty and staff are the people who give me cause to feel that way.

The world is rich in exceptional talent. There are good people everywhere. You just have to be on the lookout for them, and when you find them, give them the opportunity to grow and exercise their own excellence.

CHAPTER 6

Take Calculated Risks, Make Controlled Explosions

The fall of 2005 began with a fanfare. I don't mean that as a figure of speech.

On Tuesday, September 13, community leaders walked up the path toward the Hayworth Fine Arts Center and discovered three trumpeters welcoming them with a royal refrain.

They could not help noticing a few changes since that first breakfast meeting eight months earlier. The big fountain I'd envisioned now graced the main entrance—thirty-six feet in diameter, geysering gallons of water along with its message of energy and vibrancy. We'd also built two more, one at the west entrance of campus and the other in front of Smith Library. Roberts Hall itself had changed, too. We had installed four gigantic clock faces on each side of its tower to honor the service of Dr. and Mrs. Jacob Martinson. They reminded me of those little Waterford clocks I'd given my cabinet members my first day in office—only these were fifty times larger, backlit and clearly visible, day or night, from every point on campus.

As our guests turned the corner and approached the Hayworth entrance, they stopped to read a series of display boards, ten feet tall, leaning up against the building's brick façade. These display boards showed artistic renderings with text descriptions detailing the flurry of projects we were about to launch:

- A new building for our business school

- A brand-new, full-featured athletic complex

- A brand-new track and soccer stadium

- A massive 45,000-square-foot expansion of the Slane Student Center

- A beautiful new park behind Slane with streams, bridges, and walking trails; a large waterfall; and an amphitheater

- A comprehensive, top-to-bottom renovation of the women's dorm complex

- A brand-new 240-bed freshman residence building

"Oh my," one guest exclaimed. "Change is in the wind."

"That's no wind," her companion replied. "That's a hurricane."

Inside, as the guests took their seats at the special breakfast meeting, I outlined our $60 million plan to create a world-class campus that would capture the student experience normally found only at the best universities.

"Of course," I said with mock seriousness, "we considered moving at a more *reasonable* pace."

The guests laughed, but they all knew me well enough by now.

"We could put up one new building, say, every few years," I said. "That in itself would be ambitious. But there's no distinction in that. We didn't promise the city of High Point *ambitious*. We promised the city—and you—*extraordinary*."

By now, most guests had noticed the single fortune cookie sitting in front of each place setting, and a few had cracked their cookies open out of curiosity. Inside each was a strip of paper that read CHOOSE TO BE EXTRAORDINARY, and on the reverse side, HIGH POINT UNIVERSITY and our new website's URL.

"We invited you all here this morning in part to let you know, there *is* method to this madness," I said. "All this effort is aimed at achieving two specific, pragmatic results. For these improvements to pay off and our budget to remain intact, High Point University needs to attract at least 500 new freshmen every year, with at least 2,000 students in residence overall.

"When we reach those two milestones, we will know that the effort was worth it, that our growth is on track—and that the vision is real."

Today, we have 6,000 students, including 1,500 freshmen who come from all 50 states and 50 countries. And of those students, 5,000 live on campus. But back in 2006, we were only just starting to see our student numbers trending back in the right direction. In the fall of 2004, our freshman count had dropped to a dismal 370. Two years later, though, our freshman count had climbed back to 413, and the total residential student headcount had risen from 950 the previous fall to more than 1,000.

"This is a start, and a good one," I said. "But we have a long way yet to travel."

After the meeting, we held a second, similar meeting for the faculty, and then one more for the students. I needed everyone on board—students, faculty, and community members alike.

I needed everyone to know exactly what we were about to do. I needed everyone to fasten their seatbelts.

Because this was not going to be easy.

The Building Begins

Over the summer, in addition to the fountains and clock faces and other touches around the campus, we'd given every residence hall a basic makeover with fresh paint and general repairs, new carpets and furniture, new lighting inside and landscaping around it. All told, we'd spent some

$4 million. Yet, these were cosmetic changes. The real change, the transformation—the *explosion*—was still to come. And it had to be founded in academics and life skills.

Perhaps the most significant change we'd made all summer was the least attractive. We'd torn down several old structures like Harrison Hall, creating gaping holes in the campus landscape, to set the stage for the wave of new construction ahead.

The centerpiece of the whole plan, in many ways, was the new student center. During my campus visits in the months before I took office, one theme I heard over and over was the crying need for a decent recreational center. Students didn't really have anywhere to gather. The current student center was woefully inadequate, and the gym was a disaster. When it was finished, the new Slane Student Center would feature a student wellness area complete with weight room, aerobics room, and cardiovascular center; an outdoor pool; and a basketball court with indoor track suspended overhead. On the other side of its forty-foot glass atrium would be an on-campus post office, a 450-seat cafeteria, and a Barnes & Noble–managed bookstore, along with a Chick-fil-A, a Subway, and a Starbucks.

A decade later, the college rating organization Best College Values would name Slane the No. 1 student union complex in the nation.

No one had any doubt that our students would absolutely love it. First, though, we had to get from here—to there.

Building the new student center meant not only demolishing the gym, which we'd done over the summer, but also tearing up the street that ran by the current student center. And this was not somewhere on the fringes of the property, like the athletic complex and stadium we were building off to the north. This was right in the center of campus, with jackhammers and dust and noise and everything else that goes with major roadwork.

Step out the back of Roberts Hall and you were staring at a massive amount of construction. We wouldn't even break ground on the structure until early 2006, and it would not be completed until August of 2007. All that meant months and months of construction to endure.

And that was just Slane. Then there was the new freshman dorm we wanted to build.

That brings me to the donor who underwrote the project and made it happen. When she handed me her check for $5.75 million—then the largest single contribution we'd ever received—she told me she wanted to remain anonymous.

"For me," she said, "it's a blessing just to be able to do this."

She thought for a moment, and right then, she had an idea.

"You know, that's what I'd like you to call it."

And so we did. Blessing Hall.

Blessing Hall would be a magnificent apartment-style facility with private rooms around a shared bath and shared kitchen. It was located to the right of the current Slane Center, a few dozen steps from Roberts Hall, and directly next door to the Women's Complex, a series of four connected buildings that would be undergoing a total renovation at the same time. That renovation called for taking it right down to the studs and joists, which meant even more demolition and construction.

And that new building for the business school? Right between two other student residence halls, just west of Slane and a few dozen steps from Roberts Hall.

No matter where you lived on campus, there would be no escaping the sound and fury of construction for the next two years.

Deciphering Bold Moves

Everyone left those September meetings in a state of excitement bordering on euphoria. The students, in particular, were charged up about the prospects of all these fantastic improvements on their campus. However, as they settled into the daily routine of classes and study, the reality of what was happening started to sink in.

Their new president was tearing their campus apart.

Demolition is a messy, noisy, chaotic business, and the work we were doing was happening everywhere at once, with demolition and construction crews around every corner.

We ripped up the parking lots.

We left gaping holes in the middle of campus.

We filled the air with dust, noise, debris, and chaos.

It was hard to teach, and even harder to study. Sometimes, it was hard just to walk from one building to another. I knew these conditions would come, and I knew they would be neither easy nor popular. It was risky, taking on so many major projects at once, and when the students had first returned in late August, I'd done my best to prepare them for what was coming.

"No great accomplishment comes without some degree of discomfort," I wrote in the *Campus Chronicle*, the student newspaper. "There will most certainly be some inconvenience in parking and moving around campus as major construction gets underway. Please be patient with this temporary situation and know that you will be watching history being made."

It was not the last time I would take to the pages of the *Campus Chronicle* asking for their patience. Not the last time by far.

By early 2006 the campus was, as an editorial in the *Chronicle* put it, "a giant mud pit."

I knew I had to do something, so we set up a free student-run car wash. The university paid students to wash their fellow students' cars, and we set up a university-run valet parking service. Some critics made fun of us, saying we were squandering money on frivolous luxuries and treating our students like spoiled kids. Yet, there was nothing frivolous or spoiled about it. Their cars needed washing because *we* were covering them with dirt and dust. The reason they needed valet service was that *we* had demolished their parking lots. Now, students were parking far away, and it was both scary and uncomfortable to park and walk back to campus, especially at night. We knew we were making their lives incredibly inconvenient, and the least we could do was to work hard to compensate them for the annoyance. Today, we have neither valet service nor car washes. We don't need either one.

"What Is on My Heart"

The chaos and inconvenience of the construction itself, bad as it was, was not the topmost concern. Discontent also began bubbling up over the fact that many of our current students would never get to enjoy these new buildings. The new student center would not be finished until the fall of 2007, which meant that our current juniors and seniors would see the completed complex only *after* they graduated.

And Blessing Hall? That was especially controversial because it was designed exclusively for freshmen, which meant that of all the existing students on campus, not even one would ever have the opportunity to live there. And this, frankly, made some students feel resentful.

That decision to give our first new dorm building to freshmen was an especially tough call. It appeared to fly directly in the face of our student-focused philosophy because it made our current students feel they were being cheated. And in a very real sense, they were right. I knew it was important to acknowledge this, and not simply try to gloss over it or put a happy face on the reality.

In January 2006, once everyone had returned from winter break, I called a gathering of the entire student body.

"Let me tell you what is on my heart," I said. "This is my own alma mater, remember, so please don't take offense at what I say. But our school is not as strong as you may think it is. Oh, I know, looking at things day to day, everything seems like we're doing fine. Fiscally speaking, though, we have been living on borrowed time. We have not been growing—and we need to do so. We need to proactively create a picture here, a *reality* here that will take us somewhere new, somewhere great. Somewhere extraordinary.

"To do that, we have to make some bold moves. We have to build some new buildings. And buildings do not go up in a matter of weeks. It takes eighteen months to put up a decent structure that's going to last a hundred years.

"But think with me for a minute. We've got to grow enrollment. You may have better ideas for me on how to do this. But this is what we've come up with thus far. If we build this beautiful residence hall and make it available to new freshmen, that gives us a little bit of a carrot to hold out for people. Not that this would be the singular reason they will choose High Point University—but it is an attractive benefit. It tips the scales a little bit, and it moves us a little way out of the ocean of sameness."

I paused. I noticed their body language, their eyes, their energy, and I could feel they were getting what I was saying. Not liking it. But getting it.

"And let me add something here," I said. "Someday, you're going to look back, and because this university is going to be nationally known, because its reputation will have grown so strong, you'll find that your degree has continued to appreciate, that your diploma will have become a long-term investment worth significantly more than you expected. Because our brand will be strong, *your* brand will become even stronger—and you're going to thank us for this."

These students were smart. They knew there was likely a good deal of truth to this. They also knew I was leveling with them and genuinely sharing my own thought process.

"In the meantime, all I can do is beg your forgiveness. Because I don't have any other answer for you. Except to say: This is the temporary stage for suffering."

That got some laughs, even though they knew it was true. The students did their best to stay positive about these stresses, and by and large, they succeeded. Still, their patience continued to be tested throughout that semester as the pace of construction only intensified.

"We Will Accomplish Great Things"

Thankfully, they were spared the worst of it—the summer of 2006. This, we knew, was our only chance to carry out the brunt of the work on Blessing Hall and the Women's Complex, when the students were gone for the summer. The only feasible way to accomplish that task would be to have workers staffing three eight-hour shifts, around the clock, seven days a week, for three months. During those weeks, some existing structures would be torn down to make way for everything we were building anew.

Our commencement speaker that year was Her Majesty Queen Noor of Jordan. On that first Saturday in May 2006, she stood under a wide canopy on the green directly in front of Roberts Hall and addressed a record crowd of 6,000.

She started by describing the world's troubles and conflicts. She then talked about what caught her eye on campus.

"What encourages me today," she said, "is the sight of fifty international flags and more than forty state flags on the promenade behind you, symbols of diversity of cultures that make this campus and your experience here unique.

"Your generation must be the one to ensure that the voices of understanding in our world conquer the forces of intolerance. I truly believe that in our hearts and souls, in what we fear, and what we seek, and what we need, and what we love, there is much more that unites us than divides us. This understanding is nurtured on this campus, and it is pivotal, because it holds the key to the peace we seek in our own lives, in our communities, and in the larger world.

"The world waits today to see what contribution you will make. Make it extraordinary."

She was magnificent. After she finished, she shook hands with every single graduate, one by one. A day or so after her address, the bulldozers rolled in and a ninety-day blitz of demolition, renovation, and construction commenced.

Over the next three months, there were hundreds of workers on campus on any given day. We completely gutted the four buildings of the Women's Complex: walls, windows, roof, floors, and doors. Everything was removed, readying it for new air-conditioning, new utilities, new bathrooms, new laundry facilities—new everything. The deeper we got into the structure, the more new issues presented themselves. We found eighty-year-old steel supports that were rusted and on their last legs. Key architectural components had to be replaced. Rooms were redesigned and then redesigned again. Anything that didn't work out on the plans, we had to make instantaneous decisions to adapt and do differently. We *had* to have the buildings ready for occupancy by the end of August. Once the dust had settled—again, in this case, not a figure of speech!—that renovation alone had cost us about $10 million.

By August, we had finished the Women's Complex renovation, the Finch Hall (freshman dorm) renovation, the Norcross Hall (graduate school) renovation, and the construction of Blessing Hall. The first crop of new freshmen moved into their new digs in the newly constructed Blessing Hall—and the din and dust of construction bulldozed onward.

Now, the new Slane Student Center construction proceeded at full volume, along with work on the Phillips School of Business, the Steele Athletic Center, and more. In November, we broke ground on York Hall, yet another residence hall we dubbed "Blessing II" because it would be every bit as wonderful as the original Blessing Hall. And York Hall *would* be open to upperclassmen.

That fall, I again took to the pages of the *Campus Chronicle* to address the theme of patience and perspective.

"Impatience with the process," I wrote, "sometimes causes people to give up on their goals before they have had a chance to bear fruit."

I again promised students we would continue making every effort to make this transformation as painless as possible and asked them to keep the long view in mind.

"When complete, your university will have successfully traveled the road from ordinary to extraordinary," I wrote. "Keep your thoughts in perspective, and together we will accomplish great things."

Some had a harder time holding this positive view than others.

"I think Nido is treating the freshmen like this for a reason, but he's taking away from the whole college experience," said one senior interviewed in the *Chronicle*.

Another, a junior, was more blunt: "Nido is giving the freshmen too much. He will have three years of alumni [current sophomores, juniors, and seniors] not happy with him."

A January 2007 *Chronicle* editorial put it this way: "Students seem to be losing faith and questioning just how 'extraordinary' this university really is . . ."

And then, just as everyone's patience seemed to edge toward the breaking point, the end came into view.

In the April 2007 issue of the *Chronicle*, I penned a column. It came nearly two years after the first flurry of demolition and construction. I wrote:

"For all of us at HPU, it is the end of a demanding year and transformation at every level. Clearly, we've inconvenienced you with construction projects. Forgive us, please, but also know that in the long term you'll be so proud of your alma mater. I defer to your good judgment, your warm heart, and your sense of school spirit to continue to cooperate with us as we come close to the finish line."

It was the last time I would feel compelled to ask students for their patience over the pain of improvement. It had been a difficult year of dodging construction workers, tripping over dirt piles, and walking around yellow caution tape. It now was coming to a close.

By May 2007, the worst was over. In future years, we would continue building, but those projects would occur mainly at the periphery of the property or on newly acquired property. Never again would we have to go through the upheaval of tearing things down and building things up right in the heart of our campus.

"This Is Your Home"

In retrospect, it's remarkable that we didn't have more complaints and pushback than we did. Yes, there was discontent, but it never reached the level of being outright nasty or adversarial.

There was no student rebellion in the streets, no mass protests or revolutions, as some feared there might be. By and large, the students exhibited a stunning capacity for patience, empathy, and long-range vision. Rather than becoming the aggrieved victims of a difficult situation, they remained able to see their role as partners in the process and, ultimately, as beneficiaries. And while that bond of partnership was at times stretched and tested, it never broke.

And faculty, too, were magnanimous in their attitude and response. Their lives were inconvenienced, but they never wavered in their acknowledgment that we must transform our campus. I will be eternally grateful for their cooperation.

I believe there are two reasons it all went as smoothly as it did.

First, we kept an open dialogue about what was going on. At every step of the way, the campus community knew everything we were going to do before we did it, and in each case, we did just what we said we would do so there were no surprises. Change, even the best of change, often poses pain and hardship in the short term. Effective leaders confront that challenge with transparency and open communication.

Yet, I believe there was another reason we had as much support as we did, from students and faculty alike, and that reason had to do with the *relationships* we had established.

When we started building our fountains in the summer of 2005, I heard some predict that the students would vandalize them. When we renovated the dorms, putting nice furniture and big-screen televisions in the lounges, I heard others say the students would wreck them in no time. I didn't think so. I thought they would rise to the occasion. More importantly, I said, these students knew this wasn't just some anonymous campus they were living in.

"This is your home," I said often. "Take good care of it."

From my first day as president—actually, before that—I made it my business to get to know our students. Not just as an administrator, but as a friend. And since they were my friends, it was only natural that they would want to take good care of our place.

I have always viewed the concept of capital as having six distinct layers. There is *financial* capital, of course, which was as critical to our task as oxygen. There is also *physical* capital, which is what we were investing in with these new buildings. There is *reputational* capital, *educational* capital, and *relational* capital. They're all important. But the most important of all is the sixth: *spiritual* capital—a belief system that God will bless High Point University. We are grateful that we had ample relational capital with our students, staff, and faculty, and those relationships carried us through a time that could easily have become a crippling crisis of dwindling morale.

As we ignited our explosion of development, the students and faculty were not the only ones who experienced some growing pains. There were also the people around us, the residents of the city of High Point.

One of our biggest impediments to growth was the fact that our campus was effectively landlocked. We were spread over a tight ninety-one acres with nowhere to go. We needed more space. We needed it to house our growing student body, add classroom capacity, and expand parking facilities. We needed it to add new academic buildings.

Which meant we were now in the real estate business.

Our campus was situated in a fairly dense residential area. A number of public streets crisscrossed the campus at different points, and the houses on these streets, as well as those of the adjacent and neighboring streets, were what you would have to call substandard. Many of these were being rented to students, owned by absentee landlords who frankly didn't keep them up that well. It didn't look good.

We instituted a new rule: All freshmen, sophomores, and juniors had to live "on campus." Many studies show that students who live on campus tend to do better socially and academically.

Over the next few years, we would buy dozens of houses. Some we restored or improved, painting them bright colors and creating charming, distinctive new *de facto* neighborhoods. Others we demolished and replaced. But make no mistake, every one of them was an individual purchase that had to be negotiated. Many of those doors, I knocked on myself.

"Hello," I would say to the person who came to the door. "My name is Nido Qubein; I'm president of the university. Would you consider selling us your house at a price higher than market value?"

We negotiated these purchases as generously as possible. We didn't want families to feel displaced. We wanted them to feel honored and respected.

We paid top dollar for their properties, prices that nobody else would have paid. In some cases, particularly with the more elderly residents, we helped them find new homes (typically, a significant upgrade from where they had been) and moved their belongings ourselves.

There was one gentleman who lived on a particular corner property who was the last holdout on his block. He absolutely would not move. I met with him thirty-two times before he finally relented and said yes.

One day, another man who owned one of the homes we were trying to buy came by to meet with me. When he walked into my office, I couldn't help noticing that he had brought a big stick with him. It frankly looked a bit scary.

"Uh-oh," I told myself. "This was stupid of me."

I wondered if perhaps this guy was going to hurt me. I wondered if perhaps I should not have agreed to meet with him alone, here in my office. Oh well, not much I could do about it now, one way or the other. So, I started the conversation.

"Hello."

"THIS IS MY HOUSE!" he said. "YOU CAN'T BUY MY HOUSE!"

"Well," I said, "let's talk about it."

We talked, and we worked things out. We bought his house—and he did not hit me with the stick. It was a fair transaction, paying him a multiple of the tax value. He actually thanked us later for helping him to improve his lot in life.

By March 2007, we had bought more than seventy homes and parcels of land around the perimeter of the campus and expanded our acreage by 40 percent, to about 130 acres. Health Sciences programs couldn't have happened without this. Today, we are grateful for our 550-acre campus and 128 buildings with 6 more under construction. We have entire residential neighborhoods that are university owned, served by university-run shuttles, with HPU security call boxes everywhere and our HPU security officers patrolling the streets.

But the more we grew, the more challenges came along. It wasn't simply a question of finances, because amassing the cash to purchase these properties was a relatively straightforward matter. Managing the politics and personalities, though, was quite another dynamic.

As the explosion continued, some neighbors and city residents began complaining that we were growing too fast. Construction noise, heavy machinery, more student activity. They were not wrong. The way some saw it, we were gobbling up property, shutting down streets, and absorbing neighborhoods.

People started getting nervous, saying, "Where is Nido going to strike next?" almost as if it were a foreign invasion.

When I first arrived, the university did not have a bad relationship with the city, but it didn't have an especially good one, either. The truth is, it really didn't have *any* relationship to speak of. The campus had no bearing on the city's life, and one of my overarching goals, as I'd said right in my first public meeting, was to become High *Point's* university.

This sounded wonderful . . . in theory. Now we were going through the growing pains of actually developing that relationship. As an article in the *Chronicle of Higher Education* put it, "While [HPU] contributes immensely to High Point's economy, its appetite for growth unnerves some."

The *Chronicle* was accurate.

This was one of the most challenging aspects of our growth, perhaps *the* most challenging. We were moving so fast, and at first, I did not do an adequate job of bringing key people in the city along with me. As one city council member said repeatedly, "I want to see the master *plan* of this university! What is your future *plan?*"

But I did not show them our plan. The truth was, we *had* no plan.

We had a philosophy, and yes, we had a general direction. We knew where we wanted to go. But a detailed, sequential plan? No.

For one thing, we never knew where the next available parcel of land was going to come from, so we needed to be prepared to go wherever the opportunity presented itself. If we'd had an orderly, predetermined master plan, the campus today would probably look a good deal more orderly, with built-in quads laid out the way you find in Washington, D.C.

Instead, our campus looked more like Boston—something that appears to be less perfectly drawn because it grew organically. And to be honest, we prefer that because it's more interesting and has more character.

In the long run, every party involved benefited from the transformation. The owners we bought out did very well. We paid typically 150–200 percent or more of their properties' tax value, and they were able to move to nicer homes than the ones they left. Meanwhile, with all the business brought by our growing student population and their visiting families, we built a significant income stream for the city.

Still, suspicion, apprehension, and opposition were slow to abate. As I said, change—even of the most positive and beneficial variety—easily makes people feel threatened. People resist change, but they embrace progress. That's what HPU demonstrates every year: progress.

Patience, a generous spirit, and above all, open and consistent communication are paramount.

Taking Extraordinary Steps

There was one more challenging aspect to all this explosive growth: It cost an enormous amount of money.

Yes, by then we had secured tens of millions of dollars in donations. However, the bulk of that was in pledges and installment arrangements that would flow into our bank accounts only over time. In addition to the generous donations and appropriations from our operating budget, we needed to access some immediate cash. And time was not our friend.

This put us in the classic growth-versus-cash-flow dilemma that every businessperson knows only too well. A business needs financial capital to build inventory, inventory that will in turn generate the cash flow that will repay the capital investment. For us, space in our new residence halls was our "inventory." We needed to fund it.

So, we needed to borrow money—and this worried some people a bit.

At that September 2005 trumpet-fanfare meeting where I described our goals and milestones and timetables, I also told community leaders that we would be taking on $15 million in bond debt. To some, that seemed like a lot of borrowing, yet that number would grow considerably as the growth rolled on.

Again, this is a common tactic in the business world, where it's usually referred to as *leverage*. In higher education, though, especially at small private colleges and universities, people don't typically think this way and tend to take a much safer, more conservative route.

That normally is a fine path to take when you want your numbers to stay fixed and are not pursuing robust growth. But when you're seeking to do something extraordinary, you have to take extraordinary steps.

This, by the way, was one of the major sticking points between me and our CFO. He had a fixed mindset; I had a growth mindset. His mindset said, "Why would you *borrow* money to renovate these buildings when they're already paid for?" My mindset said, "We cannot grow and improve this school with facilities that are substandard. And we can't raise all the money we need to fix them from our best source, which is operating revenues. Without growing our operating revenues, which means bringing in more students, we can't improve anything."

It was, in a sense, a chicken-and-egg situation. Our CFO wanted us to sit on the eggs we had. I felt we needed to grow a bigger, more valuable chicken.

Was it a risk? It was—but it was a *calculated* risk. The buildings we were putting up were well worth the investment as long as we maintained them and did not let ourselves fall into the deferred-maintenance trap that had snared the university in the past. Our new buildings would pay us back dozens of times over as class after class of new students passed through our campus.

During those first three or four years, we did a fairly hefty amount of borrowing to finance this burst in growth. However, I viewed this from a long-term perspective. I knew that over time, the fruits of our growth would pay back that debt and bring the scale into balance. And that is exactly what happened.

In the long run, the amount we borrowed added up to barely 7 percent of the total amount we invested, the rest coming from donations and appropriations from our constantly growing influx of tuition payments from our expanding student body. It was, mathematically speaking, like buying a home for $100,000 and having to borrow only $7,000 of the total purchase price. Today, we have assets of $1.3 billion and a low-interest bond debt of under $90 million—and that is being reduced by $10 million annually.

Still, it didn't look that way, not in those early years.

Thankfully, our board of trustees understood what I was suggesting, and they supported the mission to make it happen. With every significant move we made, I would first present to them exactly what we wanted to do, why we wanted to do it, how we planned to do it, how we would measure its success *and* mitigate its risks. I was always careful to keep them fully informed.

Still, it took some courage for them to continue providing such unblinking, unwavering support, and I will be forever grateful to them for their faith and their courage. Many of them stepped up with generous donations themselves.

When I think about what we have accomplished, I can't help but think of Ecclesiastes 3:1–2: "For everything there is a season, and a time for every matter under heaven: a time to be born, and a time to die; a time to plant, and a time to pluck up what is planted."

To which I would add, there is a time to spend, and a time to refrain from spending.

Looking at our campus today—at the beautiful buildings and the inviting landscaping, at the imposing fountains and exquisite appointments, at the top-tier academic schools and award-winning student facilities—anyone might be tempted to draw the conclusion that we are so flush with cash that we happily throw money at anything we want. It's natural, stepping into this culture and this environment for the first time, to assume that we're going to buy ten-pound Ghirardelli chocolate bars for everyone, in every situation, and that our budgets are unlimited, and this place is paved with gold bricks.

The fact is, it took rigorous fiscal discipline to grow as we did.

Yes, we erected beautiful buildings, founded eleven academic schools, and moved from Level III to Level VI in accreditation. For every capital improvement we made, though, we secured multiple quotes and negotiated the costs as carefully as possible, and we watched our ongoing operational costs with the eyes of an eagle. It is that kind of discipline on the everyday operational end that allows us to be exceptionally generous on some of these other features.

It's not a matter of penny-pinching or being stingy. Nor, however, is it a matter of fiscal carelessness.

I call it being *selectively extravagant* and *prudently frugal*.

When we began, I knew we could not afford to be extravagant everywhere, but we also couldn't afford to be inappropriately frugal everywhere, either. Blessing Hall ended up costing closer to $11 million than the $6 million we had projected. (That same donor's family increased their contribution accordingly. Bless them!) Our $60 million plan had soon become a $100 million plan, and as we started leapfrogging over previous estimates and leaving our more conservative projections in the dust, some of my cabinet members would start to get a little nervous.

"Nido," they'd say, "we're going way over budget!"

"Yes, but do you see how fantastic it is? This is no time to be prudently frugal," I'd respond. "We're putting up a building that's going to last for 100 years. Fifty years from now, no one's going to care whether we spent another $6 million or another $11 million."

What I knew about this building was that because of it, we would begin drawing new freshmen who would very possibly not have come otherwise. This building, as expensive as it was, would help pave the way for a bright future—an extraordinary future.

Moving Forward

By the fall of 2007, the Slane Center was complete. The thoroughly renovated Women's Complex and freshly constructed Blessing Hall had both been lived in for a year. York Hall ("Blessing II") was complete and filled with students, and every other student residence building had gone through a comprehensive upgrade. Phillips School of Business was open for business, as were the Steele Athletic Center, Vert Track and Soccer Stadium, and Williard Baseball Stadium.

So far, our calculated risk appeared to be paying off. Freshman enrollment had more than doubled, from its 2004–5 low of 370 to an all-time high of 749 in 2007, meeting and blowing well past our target of 500. Our goal for total undergraduate enrollment had been 2,000; we were now at 1,910. (Getting close!) Student reservations for October visits to the campus had more than doubled over the previous year, strongly suggesting that the numbers would continue rising. Today, we have 5,000 undergraduates and 1,200 graduate students, speeding toward our goal of 2,500 graduate students.

All of which now presents a challenge of its own.

When we announced this aggressive expansion at that September meeting in 2005, we anticipated that we would stay ahead of the growth rate. We were wrong. The surge in student interest and enrollment was even greater than we expected. Suddenly, High Point University was being regarded as something of a hot school, not only in our region but also nationwide. If we didn't keep building, we would soon have ourselves a crowding problem.

That October, we bought eleven more homes to pave the way for the Wanek Center, a massive student services center. It would feature a learning commons and a suite of counseling and career training resources, along with more dining options and a 200-seat theater. Also, in its two four-story wings, the Wanek Center would have the capacity to house more than 500 additional students. Its 277,000 square feet would make it more than triple the size of the Slane Center, and at a price tag of $70 million, it would be far and away the most expensive project we'd yet undertaken. Ron Wanek and his son, Todd, contributed $30 million to our work.

Yet even that wouldn't be enough, which was why we wrote a $900,000 check to purchase fifteen acres just north of the campus, to become the site of our first experiment in building our own off-campus housing, an apartment complex for upperclassmen, a sort of mini-campus with its own basketball courts, dining facility, satellite security station, and study spaces.

The explosion was just getting started. That $100 million plan had now blossomed into a $225 million plan.

Before long, it would be well edging toward $2 billion. But I believed we could do more.

Knowing Our Why

On a Tuesday afternoon in September 2019, I stood in front of a big crowd inside Hayworth Fine Arts Center. At least 600 regional leaders came. With my hands steepled as if in prayer, I walked to the edge of the stage and began. My voice was barely above a whisper.

"Ladies and gentlemen, in all my life, I understood the words of Victor Frankl were so, so poignant. He once said, 'When you know your why, you can always, always figure out your how.'

"At High Point University, I do believe we know our why—to admit students and educate them, guide them, model behaviors for them, and to pray that their careers and their futures will be filled with success and framed with significance.

"And I believe we High Pointers know our why—to build our city, to make it a better place for everyone who lives here, everyone who visits here. Folks, you have to stand up. You have to be counted. You've got to step out; you've got to step up. We've got to make sure people in this community can access all the goodness that we can provide."

That day, I announced HPU would invest $1 billion in new construction, new academic programs, new student scholarships, and faculty support over the next decade. We would invest $300 million to start a School of Nursing, expand graduate programs significantly, and initiate a half dozen new programs including hospitality and event planning. The investment would also be used to build a new library, a new admissions center, and a new academic building.

The remaining $700 million in scholarships would focus on making college more affordable for the students who needed the help. HPU would award scholarships to veterans, students of diverse backgrounds, and children whose immediate family never went to college.

"Affordability is a major concern in America," I said. "We don't want this school to exclude anyone."

Our announcement grabbed headlines and TV time across central North Carolina. In an editorial titled "Nido's Golden Touch," a newspaper said of me, "He is that rare combination of a talker and a doer. A showman with substance." Interesting.

Leadership is not about lessons you learn or what you do. It's about who you are. It's about empowering others to reach their full potential. And on that Tuesday afternoon, I knew we could reach our goal of investing another $1 billion in High Point University and preparing students for the world as it is going to be.

More than seventy-five years ago, a small-time Missouri politician who hadn't gone to college became our thirty-third U.S. president. He helped rebuild Europe, stopped the spread of communism overseas, and turned Japan into a friendly democracy. Here in the United States, he dealt with defiant segregationists who resisted dismantling racial barriers and virulent red-baiters who were willing to sacrifice democratic principles in their zeal to exterminate communism.

That was Harry Truman, the man who once said, "America was not built on fear. America was built on courage, on imagination, and an unbeatable determination to do the job at hand."

He refused to underestimate himself, and I refused to underestimate High Point University and its supporters in our pursuit of excellence. On that Tuesday afternoon in September 2019, inside HPU's Pauline Theatre, I challenged our audience. I knew we could do it. Together.

"My prayer for all of us is that we invest ourselves in all that is good," I told them. "And my challenge to all of us, including me, is that we rise to the occasion."

I believe in the power of us. But I've been believing that for a long time.

We are, after all, a God, family, country institution. And we have faithful courage.

At High Point University every student receives an extraordinary
education in an inspiring environment with caring people.

Nido and Mariana Qubein Arena, Conference Center, and Hotel

Students learning in the state-of-the-art Culp Planetarium
inside the Wanek School of Natural Sciences

The Cain Conservatory

2005 campus map

High Point University, 2024

R.G. Wanek Center

Nido and Mariana Qubein Arena, Conference Center, and Hotel

HPU freshmen build 100 bikes annually for underprivileged children.

HPU's Chamber Singers, one of many talented groups on campus

Our students signing the Honor Code

Weekly service in Hayworth Chapel

Dr. Nido Qubein speaking to HPU families inside the Hayworth Fine Arts Center

My good friend General Colin Powell

UNC Hall of Fame basketball coach Roy Williams presenting me with a Tarheel jersey

Dr. Condoleezza Rice, former U.S. secretary of state, visiting my office

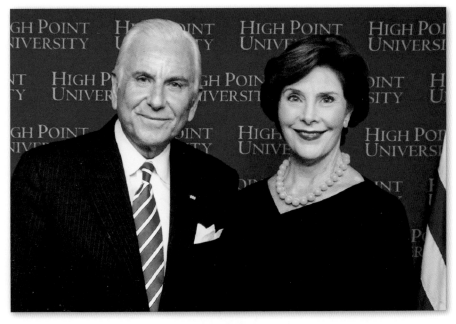

Former First Lady Laura Bush at HPU to speak at commencement

Forty-third United States President George W. Bush visiting High Point University

Queen Noor of Jordan prior to giving the commencement address

Supreme Court Justice Clarence Thomas before giving the
commencement address at High Point University

Bill Gates, co-founder of the software giant Microsoft

Presenting Steve Wozniak, co-founder of Apple,
with his HPU Innovator in Residence business card

Forty-second United States President Bill Clinton hosting me in his office in Harlem

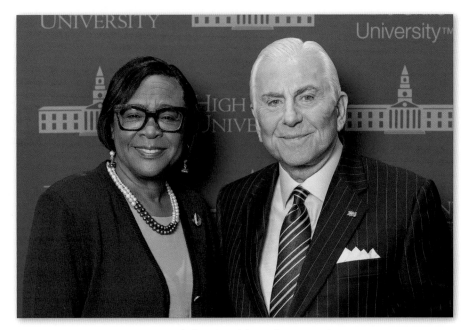

Cynt Marshall, CEO of the Dallas Mavericks

William Kennard, former U.S. ambassador and chairman of the board of AT&T

Marc Randolph, Netflix co-founder, on my PBS show

Dr. Ben Carson, former U.S. secretary of housing
and urban development, visiting campus

Michio Kaku, famed theoretical physicist and futurist

New York Times best-selling author Malcom Gladwell

Steve Forbes and me sharing the platform at a national conference

Interviewing Josh Groban for my TV show

My friend of many years Casey Kasem

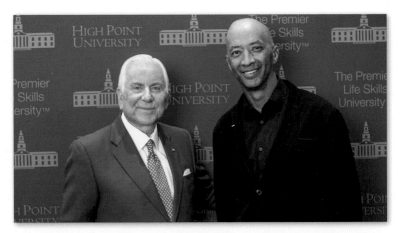

Byron Pitts, ABC *Nightline* news anchor

"Superman" Dean Cain

My dear friends Jim Millis, Jack Slane, and Bill Horney celebrating with
me in New York when I received the Ellis Island Medal of Honor

CHAPTER 7

Create a Brand of Appreciated Value

E arly one morning in the spring of 2006, as I was standing in front of the bathroom mirror at home shaving, I started thinking about everything we were doing at HPU. Today was the day we would begin commencement exercises that would mark the end of my first full year as president. The campus would be flooded with parents, many of whom would have exchanges and brief conversations with various staff members and administrators. That all got me thinking about our employees and how they talked to others about what we were doing on campus.

How would I get each member of our HPU employee family of 400 to understand, with total and unambiguous clarity, exactly what it is we're doing *and* to understand it so well that they can explain it, simply and succinctly, to anyone?

I knew I could paint a vivid picture for parents and prospective students when I met with them in person. I'd been doing that for a year and a half. I was about to do it again later that day for a large audience. But that was me talking. Could every one of our vice presidents do the same thing? Every dean, every faculty member, every person on the administrative staff? What about the librarian, the people serving food in The Café, the people cutting the grass or staffing the security stations?

We needed a simple mission statement, one that everyone here could easily grasp, internalize, and communicate to others.

It might surprise you to learn that at this point, a year and a half into my presidency, we didn't have a mission statement. After all, everyone talks about the importance of this. You've probably read a dozen books and heard hundreds of lectures that talked about how every company or organization needs a clear mission statement to be successful and to make sure everyone is on the same page. And you probably have read or heard that you *have* to do this before you do anything else.

In theory, this makes complete sense. In reality, though, it doesn't always work out exactly that way—at least, not right out of the starting gate.

The clearest articulation of a vision doesn't always come at the very beginning of the enterprise. For one thing, you often don't have the luxury of time. Circumstances are forcing you to act now, whether or not you've got your mission statement all nicely worked out. The realities of business are knocking at your door, the clock is ticking. "Ready or not," says the marketplace, "here I am!"

This was certainly the case for us. When I took office in January 2005, our institution was already up and running and had been for more than eighty years. I had to jump in and swim immediately, starting with the small matter of raising $20 million in a few weeks. And now here we were, eighteen months later, and yes, we did have a clear vision that we were following. And yes, we had articulated it hundreds of times in dozens of ways.

Yet, I still didn't think we had quite hit upon the most articulate, succinct, complete statement of what it was we were here to achieve.

Perhaps the closest thing we had to a mission statement was our rallying cry, "Choose to be extraordinary."

This phrase traces its roots back to my childhood, and specifically, to my mother. As I said, throughout those early years, my mother imparted jewels of wisdom to my siblings and me, and I count these pearls and rubies among my greatest treasures. One of these elegant little gems of understanding she gave us was this: "The choices you make determine the person you become."

At High Point University, we amplified this into a statement that you can still find today on posters everywhere on campus. The posters read: "It's not your circumstances that define the person you become; it's your choices."

Very early on, we had set our eye on the idea of extraordinary. It was the destination we consistently aimed for, and we married it with that proactive idea of choice: Choose to be extraordinary. That is how we aimed to get there. As a vision, it wasn't bad. With those four words, we had staked our claim, and in the past eighteen months, we had come far. Yet as strong as the statement was, I knew it ultimately was not clear enough or fully defined enough to carry us the full distance we wanted to go.

Choose to be extraordinary . . . Yes, but in what way? Extraordinary how? And what exactly should that look like?

When Google started out, they had a slogan, "Don't be evil." That's an interesting idea, but practically speaking, what does it mean? Their mission statement later became: "To organize the world's information and make it universally accessible and useful." Now *that* is a clear blueprint for action.

Our challenge of finding a mission statement occupied my mind that morning as I shaved. What was our blueprint for action? You could run a shipping business, a clothing outlet, a gym, a day care center, a coffee shop with "Choose to be extraordinary" as your slogan, and it would work just fine.

"We need something that more specifically defines *us*," I told myself as I looked in the mirror. "Who we are, what we do, and how we do it."

I rinsed off my face, set down my razor, and began dressing for the events of the day.

So what exactly, precisely, *was* our vision—not in a paragraph, not in a speech, but in a single sentence? I knew it had to fully describe our mission, and yet be simple. Two or three points, no more.

In twenty words or less. How?

Reshaping Language

I have always paid very close attention to language, not only at High Point University but also throughout my professional life.

They say one picture is worth 1,000 words, but this is not always true. Sometimes, a few well-chosen, expertly placed words have more meaning and impact than a thousand pictures, or even a thousand actions. The Sermon on the Mount, the Magna Carta, the American Declaration of Independence, the Emancipation Proclamation. Words can change how humanity sees things. Words can change history. Words are one of humanity's most powerful inventions—perhaps *the* most powerful invention.

In my President's Seminar on Life Skills, one of my favorite videos to teach students about life is about helping them understand the power of words. The video shows a blind man begging on the street with a sign by his feet that reads "I'm blind. Please help." A woman in sunglasses comes by, stops, pulls out her pen, and rewrites the sign.

"It's a beautiful day, and I can't see it."

She used the same thought—except with different words.

Change your words, and you can change your world.

At first, it may sound simplistic. It's not. Think of your language as the software of your brain. When we say something a certain way, we're predisposed to think about it in terms of what the words mean and how they affect us and everyone around us.

As I said, my relationship to words is informed by the fact that English was (and is) my second language. Because of that, I have an immigrant's unique appreciation for words and turns of phrase, their nuance and finer points, that a native speaker might more readily take for granted and thus gloss over or miss entirely.

When I began working with the staff at HPU, I soon discarded the term "problem-solving" in favor of the far more productive term "solution-finding." Yes, these two could be construed as meaning essentially the same thing. Yet they frame your perspective in opposite ways—and often lead to very different results.

I began teaching everyone around me the distinction between

having a to-do list and having a to-*be* list. Doing is transactional; being is transformational.

From my first season at HPU, even before we began reshaping the physical campus, we began reshaping the landscape of our language—the words and terms we used to describe what we were doing. If we wanted to differentiate ourselves, then we needed to start using highly differentiated language.

For example, like everyone else, we had a maintenance department. Put yourself in the shoes of the person whose job this is. When someone asks you what you do at HPU and your answer is "Maintenance," how inspiring is that? To "maintain" something means to keep it the way it is. Not only is that boring and uninspiring, but it's also not even accurate. If something in the campus is broken or dirty, or needs fixing or cleaning, then we don't want to keep it the way it is. We want to improve it! The whole point is to aim upward, to grow, to become better, to strive for the extraordinary.

So, we changed Maintenance to *Campus Enhancement*. We printed shirts and hats with CAMPUS ENHANCEMENT on them. From our landscapers and groundskeepers to our plumbers, electricians, painters, and housekeepers, nobody worked for Maintenance anymore. They all worked in the service of *Campus Enhancement*.

"What's the difference?" you ask. "Isn't that just semantics?"

Here is the difference: If your job is to mop the floor, then once you've mopped the floor, you're done. Your world is defined by whether the floor is mopped. However, if you work in Campus Enhancement, your world expands. Your task is now to improve this entire beautiful campus. You are not a manual laborer; you are an ambassador. Yes, you are an ambassador who happens to mop floors as part of your calling. But it *is* a *calling*.

"I'm Building a Cathedral"

On most campuses, people who work with food are known as "food service workers." That was not the message I wanted to send, so we changed the name of our Food Service department. We said, "Your job is not to slice potatoes. Your job is to make all your guests feel at home. You don't *work* in *Food Service*; you *lead* in *Hospitality*."

There's a reason a great restaurant identifies itself as being in the "hospitality business" and not the "food business." Because it's not really about the food. The word "hospitality" means "hosting." Serving. When you host someone, that means you put them first. It's an entirely different mindset. Today, we have twenty-one on-campus restaurants plus a full catering department, and all told, that's more than 500 staff right there—and they aren't there to serve food, but to serve and host *people*.

We took a close look at the word "teacher." Was that what we really wanted our academic faculty's mission to be? To teach? A friend once told me about a boys' prep school where he taught. There was an instructor there who was greatly admired by all his colleagues. "What a great teacher he is!" they would say. "Terrible with kids—but an incredible teacher!" What they were really saying was that this man was an impressive *lecturer*. He couldn't stand the students (and one suspects the feelings were mutual), but he was a heck of a talker, and he surely knew his subject.

Was that what we wanted? Of course not. Our academic goal was not simply to have our faculty *teach* but to have our students *learn*. Again, like "problem-solving" and "solution-finding," they may seem like two ways of saying the same thing . . . but are they really?

We began replacing the term "teacher" with the word "mentor" or the term "enabler of learning."

Perhaps you have heard the famous story of the three bricklayers. A boy was walking by a construction site one day where laborers were laying bricks for the foundation of a new cathedral. He stopped and asked one man what he was doing. "What does it look like I'm doing?" the man said. "I'm laying bricks!"

The boy walked another twenty paces and came to a second bricklayer. He stopped and asked the same question: "What are you doing?" The second man frowned and said, "I'm putting up a wall, son. It's hard work, and it's dangerous, no place for little boys. Now run along."

After yet another twenty paces the boy came to a third man. He stopped and asked once more: "What are you doing?" The man looked at the brick in his hands, then back at the boy, and smiled.

"I'm building a cathedral," he said.

At High Point University, we didn't want our people laying bricks or putting up walls. We wanted them building a cathedral.

The Rhetoric of a New Direction

There is a phrase sometimes used in the academy: a "gatekeeper course," referring to a course designed to identify high-achieving students and flush out the lower-performing ones, pushing them to reconsider their major. Typically, this is described as "weeding students out."

Now, we certainly believe in high academic standards and have zero interest in doing anything to undercut that core value. If anything, we aim to raise our academic standards at HPU (and in fact we did exactly that, as we'll see in the next chapter). Our view, though, was that once we had accepted a student here, it was our responsibility to support, build, and grow that student, not to view him or her as a weed.

One day, I was talking with the visiting parents of a prospective student, and the term "gatekeeper course" came up. I looked them in the eye and had a response ready.

"You will find no such thing here on our campus, not now, not ever," I said. "At High Point, we do not weed students out of the classroom—we *weave them into the family*."

I still remember their reaction. They literally stood up straighter, both of them at once.

"Wow," one of them murmured. "We've never heard anything like *that* before."

Later that day in another conversation, I said it again: "We do not weed students out of the classroom—we weave them into the family." And I kept saying it. If you spend any time at HPU, you'll still hear it said today. It has become part of the fabric of who we are.

In similar conversations with parents, faculty, staff, donors, and others, certain terms and phrases began emerging, and I began crafting them into messaging that we began using over and over. That messaging became a part of our core identity.

> *At HPU, we are planting seeds of greatness not only in the minds but also in the hearts and souls of our students.*
>
> *We are preparing our students for the world not as it was, not even as it is, but as it is going to be.*
>
> *At HPU, we are an extension of a student's home, and we underscore and feed the values parents have instilled in their children.*
>
> *HPU is a God, family, country school.*
>
> *We are graduating not simply "job takers" but "job creators."*
>
> *High Point University is the premier life skills university.*

Now, I don't want to give the impression of being cavalier or Pollyanna here. I was not so naïve as to think that changing a department's name or repeating a certain turn of phrase was going to transform our university overnight. Simply saying something does not, in and of itself, make it so. Still, this new messaging had an undeniable impact. As people began saying these terms and phrases, it began changing the way they thought, which changed the way they behaved. It penetrated our ecosystem.

One can scarcely overstate the power of language. Your words, and particularly those words and phrases that you repeat consistently, affect your thoughts, which in turn affect your attitude and intentions. And your attitudes and intentions are what direct your actions and outcomes.

Throughout that first year, I could see this tugboat of simple messaging slowly and cumulatively begin pulling the ocean liner of our university in a new direction, away from the harbor of sameness and out onto the open ocean of distinction.

Building a Brand

The landscape of language on campus was one thing. Then there was the question of our identity out in the world around us. We also needed to craft messaging that would go out into the community at large, that would spark new awareness of our existence, of who we were and what we were up to.

We needed to establish our *brand*.

"Right now, the HPU brand is not that visible nationwide." That's what I'd said during that first meeting of community leaders at the Sechrest Gallery on January 4, 2005. The truth was it wasn't even all that visible right here in our own city. We needed to start our branding journey by establishing the simple fact that we were here, that we existed. In other words, we needed to establish clear, strong *brand awareness*.

Our first step was to promote our identity in the simplest of all possible ways—by displaying our name appropriately, anywhere and everywhere we could. We codified the graphic look of the HPU logo in every aspect of color, typography, proportions, background color, and so forth. We did the same with the spelled-out version, "High Point University." And we started putting up banners everywhere—along the Kester International Promenade, on the facing of residence halls and classroom buildings, on lampposts, and on the walls of dorm hallways.

We instituted a plan for students: You can have free access to our airport shuttle, but you had to agree to wear some piece of HPU-branded clothing once you're in the airport.

We printed HPU bumper stickers, HPU buttons and pins. We produced HPU-branded T-shirts and sweatshirts and hats in great numbers and made them freely available to all our students, and faculty and staff members, too.

"You know, if you put an HPU bumper sticker on your car, it may feel a little silly, but people will see it, and it will register," I started telling faculty and staff.

We still do this today. The other day, I happened to meet a professor as we were both walking on campus, and I noticed he was wearing an HPU lapel pin.

"Hey," I said, "I see what you're wearing. That's great."

"Oh, always!" he replied.

"No, no," I said, holding up one finger. "I saw you a couple of times without it."

We both laughed, and I went on to tell him how proud I was of all the creative practices he'd been doing with his students. All of which were absolutely true. But he also got the message: I do genuinely appreciate it every time anyone makes an effort to wear the HPU brand.

It makes a difference.

"That's Our University!"

I have mentioned that one of our early projects was to build out the existing perimeter fence, but I have not really explained why this was so important to us. It was, more than anything else, an expression of branding.

Like most every aspect of our growth, this effort met with some community resistance. There were some who felt that we were seeking to separate ourselves from the community, that we were saying, "Stay out." But this was not a security fence, and it wasn't going to physically prevent anyone from entering the grounds if they wanted to. That was not its central purpose. Its central purpose was to create not separation, but *distinction*. Not to cloister or sequester the school but to frame it, just as you would frame a piece of art when you put it on display.

The real message of the fence wasn't about separation or security. It was about promoting awareness of our work. We didn't want people to drive along the adjoining streets without ever even noticing that they were passing our campus. We wanted people to drive by and say, "Wow, they are really doing something special in there." We wanted to inspire civic pride.

Happily, it worked. For every one person who objected, there were four or five who loved it—and those four or five became ten or twelve and then twenty. Soon people were driving by and saying to each other, "Hey, there's HPU—that's our university!"

The other day, I was driving along a main street in the city of High

Point, a mile or so from the campus, and I noticed a large sign posted in the front window of a local restaurant. It said, "We ♥ HPU."

There are so many of these signs all over our city. *That* is an expression that appreciates our university. Obviously, these businesses know they get a lot of business from HPU—including the more than 100,000 visitors we host each year.

The Workings of a Wraparound

In the fall of 2005, just as we were launching our explosion of construction across the campus, we also launched an explosion of words and images into the world beyond our walls. It was our first major branding campaign. We called it "Are You Extraordinary?" The strategy was to draw people to a website, AreYouExtraordinary.com, and have them discover all that was happening at HPU, contact us, and/or leave their contact information to receive future updates.

Soon commuters throughout the region were seeing billboards that read:

Life is choice.
CHOOSE to be EXTRAORDINARY.

And underneath that headline were the "Are You Extraordinary" URL and HPU's name. In addition to the billboards, we put up a back-lit diorama at the Piedmont Triad International Airport that was eight feet tall, thirty-eight feet long. We also ran ads everywhere—in local and regional publications; in *Money, Fortune, Forbes, Inc., BusinessWeek*, the *Business Journal, BizLife*, and *Fast Company* magazines; and on NPR and in all major regional newspapers.

My philosophy is this: If you're going to put some energy and resources into doing something, do it on a scale that has impact. You don't have to do it forever. Choose your time and hit hard. If you're going to mount a marketing campaign, don't do it in bits and pieces. Go all out and get your message out through multiple channels.

If people just hear it on the radio, they'll forget it. Even if they're just driving in the car, it's no more than background noise. But if they hear the radio ad, then they see your ad the next day in the paper, then they hear about you in an interview on TV that night, then they find your full-page ad in their business journal, and then they see your poster at the airport on their next business trip—they're going to remember, all right.

The magic is not only in the message. *The magic is in the mix.*

In our ads, we featured designs of all these buildings we were going to build, along with full narrative descriptions of our plans for the years ahead. The ad agencies told me this would not work. "That's way too much copy," they said. "Nobody will read it!"

"We don't need them to read it all," I said. "I just want them to see that it's all there. If they just read the headlines and see the pictures, that's okay." I knew there would be people who would read the details, and people who would just take in the headlines and photos. We didn't need them to grasp all the details. We needed them to know we were here, we existed, and that *something* was happening—something big, something exciting. We needed to create brand awareness.

Since then, we've mounted campaigns like this numerous times.

One year, we thought about advertising in business journals across the country. But everyone does that. We asked ourselves, "How could we do that better, take that idea further and take it to a place of distinction?" We came up with the idea of packaging a whole magazine of our own together with every business journal, every publication. Our thinking was you might easily skip over an ad, but if you have an entire magazine in your hands, you're going to browse through it and read at least something in there.

By this time, we had significantly improved our semiannual university magazine by taking it to a professional standard of production. So, we did an extra print run of our latest issue and polybagged it in along with issues of *Business North Carolina*, *Speaker* (the magazine of the National Speakers Association), and business journals in thirty cities across the U.S.

Another year, we ran stories about HPU in all the major airline magazines. Then, a few years ago, we started interviewing major thought leaders, such as Colin Powell, Condoleezza Rice, and Tom Brokaw, in a series of one-hour conversations that the promo describes as "about achieving success, overcoming adversity and preparing a new generation to move the world forward in positive ways." The program aired every Monday night at 7:00 p.m. on one of our local television stations for ten straight weeks. Now, I have my own regional primetime PBS show interviewing interesting and fascinating guests every week.

This is good, but this is only one channel. The magic, remember, is in the mix. So, every Monday morning, we also run full-page ads in all the area newspapers under the headline "High Point University presents *Access to Innovators*," featuring full details on that evening's guest, along with a listing of all the other speakers in the series.

The idea is not just to get you to watch the program on television. If you do, that's great. However, even if you don't, our goal is that you will *know* about the show and be *inspired* by the idea. I imagined the conversations over morning coffee: "Wow, this High Point University place is really doing great things! Look at the amazing lineup of speakers they're having in to address their students."

This sort of thing really works—but only if you execute with consistency. If you run an ad only once, you're just wasting time and money. If you run it every Monday for a period of ten weeks, then it begins to register, and it soon starts creating some dialogue. People start saying to each other, "Hey, did you see the Colin Powell interview?" "Did you see who's coming up next Monday?" It has a cumulative effect.

I call this a "wraparound," and it's a concept I have used in business and taught my clients for years. Wraparound simply means you can multiply the value of an event by wrapping around it a multitude of offshoots. It is tremendously valuable in business, because a business is always looking for ways to amortize the cost. You may think a certain event or contract I propose is expensive, but if I can show you six or seven (or better yet, a dozen) ways you can leverage the fruits of that investment well into the future such that it effectively amortizes that cost, now it is not merely *affordable*, it is invaluable.

For example, when we had a Colin Powell or a Condoleezza Rice come to speak, or a Steve Wozniak or a Byron Pitts, we could think of that as a singular isolated event. We announce it, people come hear them speak, and that's that.

The wraparound idea says, "How can we be creative with this event?"

So, we might have a little reception beforehand with a group of our students where they can meet and get pictures taken with this famous person. After the event, we could have an event for our major donors.

We can videotape the event, and with the speaker's permission, we can send a link to alumni, friends of the university, donors, and others in positions of influence. We can link to the video on our website. We can quote the speech in places around campus. We can display the speaker's picture in our buildings, alongside photos of our other famous guest speakers, and tell visiting parents, "These are the kinds of speakers we have come talk with your children at our university." We could select a short clip of their speech and insert what they say into various presentations we do. We can use their name, photo, and an excerpt of their talk in promotional materials.

We can even, as I mentioned previously, create a broadcast television event that airs locally—and then promote that event in multiple ways, in effect wrapping around the wraparound!

One event. Dozens of ideas and applications.

Understanding Intentional Congruence

Here I have to clarify a central point about branding. Everything I just described, from that massive fall marketing campaign to our hats and bumper stickers, was *ancillary*. Yes, it was effective, but in the big picture, the marketing tactics toward the goal of establishing our brand were all secondary. None of the effort was primary.

Why not? Because *a slogan is not a brand*.

Putting "Extraordinary" on a sign is all well and good, but for that to mean anything, you need to *be* extraordinary. And not just now and then, or even often, but *always*, each and every time.

A brand is not something you can simply cobble together in a marketing brainstorming session. To reach people, to be effective, to have an impact, a genuine brand has to spring from something deep inside, something primal. A brand has to be an expression of your values, of who you genuinely are.

At its heart, a brand is a promise. If your promise is a valuable one and you deliver on it, then you are golden. But if you break your promise? You are history.

If our brand is, say, that we serve fresh, hot, high-quality bread products, and you go to our store one day and experience something completely different from that, then we have destroyed our brand. FedEx did not become a hugely successful global brand because it *promised* overnight delivery. It became a hugely successful global brand because it *delivered* on that promise.

This goes back to consistent execution. No matter how lofty your intentions, if your organization's execution is inconsistent, you cannot maintain a brand. In turn, that means you do not have a sustainable product or service. Bic pens would never have achieved global dominance with a slogan that promised, "Writes most of the time." No, it was that slogan, "Writes first time, *every* time," coupled with the fact that the pen in fact did what it promised to do.

This is why a real, living brand is not something you can create on a billboard or in a magazine ad. *Your brand is a promise*, and you breathe life into your brand through the day-in-and-day-out fulfillment of that promise, in the delivery of your product or service, in how you treat your customers and clients, in how you treat your employees and staff in everything you do. A targeted marketing campaign can create a burst of awareness and give your promise a shot of adrenaline. But the truth, vibrancy, and vitality of a brand must be maintained over the long haul by consistent execution that is congruent with your values.

This creates something I call *intentional congruence*. Intentional congruence means that everything you do, every gesture both large and small, expresses the same set of values.

In that sense, everything we were doing was marketing. From the quality of our academic program, the construction and renovation of new buildings, to the execution of hospitality in our café and campus enhancement on our grounds, it was *all* marketing. It was *all* branding, because it was all an expression of our values and a fulfillment of our promise.

Rather than simply creating marketing on its own, we were creating an experience that served as a marketing function in itself. People were talking about it, and *that's* what was getting other people to come here. Then, they went back home and started getting the message out. That was our strongest marketing—people's experience of HPU when they came to visit or when they enrolled.

The Essential Core of Effective Branding

Right now, you may be wondering, "If what really creates my brand is our client experience and how we deliver on our promise day in and day out, then why not just do that? If all that marketing and branding business is ancillary, why bother? Why go to all the trouble?"

The short answer is this: *Because people are busy.*

Everyone's lives are already full. Everyone is engaged with their own thoughts and tasks, their own needs and stresses, their own missions and goals, and their own careers and families. You don't have the luxury of hoping people will take the initiative to come figure out what it is you do, because they won't do it. They're too busy. So, remember this: *Nobody will notice the value you provide unless you tell them.*

Creating value is essential to establishing your brand, but it is just as essential that you continually *interpret* that value—not only to your clients and potential clients but also to your staff, investors, board members (if you have them), and every stakeholder connected with your enterprise.

In our case, it was not enough to create something extraordinary at HPU. It was not enough to put live music in The Café, to build a beautiful new student center, to have exceptional thought leaders come speak to our students. We also had to communicate to our students, to our parents, and to our community why we were doing that and what difference it made *to them.*

Even today, in every talk I give, whether it's a speech to a few thousand people or a chat with a student on a brisk walk across campus, I always consider who I'm talking to and what is meaningful to them. When I talk with parents, I remind them of the value their children are getting here and why they are investing the money to send them here. When I talk with faculty, I remind them of what we are achieving here, and why they are investing their energy and effort into these young people. When I talk with donors, I remind them not only of the impact their contribution is having today but also of the impact it will have for generations to come.

That is called *value interpretation*, and it is what lies at the core of all effective branding. It was the goal not only of all our marketing but also of every event, every meeting, and every conversation.

Now, to that elusive mission statement I was looking for. I found it as I prepared for a day of commencement exercises on that spring morning in May of 2006.

The Big Deal of a Brand

I tucked into my jacket, slipped on my shoes, and went downstairs to my car, thinking about everything we had accomplished in this year and a half—all the language, the words, the messaging, all the interviews and meetings and phone calls and visits. All to communicate our message. Now, as we wrapped up my first full academic year at HPU and prepared for the whirlwind of construction that would transform the campus over the summer, I felt we needed to take the next step in branding to harness the power of our words. We needed a single, clear, compelling, comprehensive statement of our vision.

I slipped behind the wheel of my car, turned the key—and then I had it! Our mission, in three points, and less than twenty words.

Really, seventeen words, to be exact.

That afternoon, I spoke to a group of 1,200 parents and students at our 2006 commencement luncheon. It was Friday, May 5, the day before Queen Noor would give her commencement address.

"You may have noticed a banner," I said in my remarks, "up by the Admissions building. 'Choose to be extraordinary,' it says. If you've lived on this campus for any length of time, especially over the last fifteen or sixteen months, you've heard the word *extraordinary* over and over again . . ."

I spoke a little about what that word meant and why we loved to use it, about our quest to exit an ocean of sameness and swim into a pool of distinction, uniqueness, and excellence. I spoke about the importance of language and establishing a clear brand. About six minutes into my talk, I paused, then said, "Our own branding statement goes something like this—" and spoke the seventeen words that had come to me that morning as I turned the ignition key in my car:

"*At High Point University, every student receives an extraordinary education, in a fun environment, with caring people.*"

As it turned out, our branding statement went almost exactly like that. We soon recognized "inspiring" was much more accurate to our vision than the word "fun." Aside from that single alteration, our verbal blueprint was born on May 5, 2006. Today, almost two decades later, you will find these seventeen words on the back of every business card of every member of the HPU family:

> At High Point University, every student receives an extraordinary
> education, in an inspiring environment, with caring people.

That statement would give us a comprehensive framework, a road map that showed every single member of the HPU community where we were going and what we were seeking to achieve. Those seventeen words— and especially their three central descriptors, *extraordinary, inspiring,* and *caring*—would guide our every choice, every decision, every action.

A brand is a promise. In those seventeen words, we now had a succinct, comprehensive, crystal-clear statement of exactly what our promise was.

CHAPTER 8

What Is Your Promise?

A t High Point University, every student receives an extraordinary education in an inspiring environment with caring people.

These seventeen words would serve as our blueprint. Yet, they are more than simply a road map to our own success at HPU. This seventeen-word statement can serve as a blueprint for *any* business, once you translate it into terms and particulars that suit your own situation. Let me show you what I mean.

Extraordinary education is about the distinction of your product, the core of what you do and why you are in business. For example, let's say you own and operate a restaurant. In that case, in place of "extraordinary education" you might say "exceptional food." If you are a museum, then this part of the statement is about the art hanging on your walls.

Inspiring environment is about the quality of your clients' experience. If you are a restaurant, then "in an inspiring environment" is about everything *except* the food you serve. The tables, the place settings, the art on the walls, the air quality, the ambient music, the acoustics, the signage outside . . . *everything*. If you are a museum, it is about everything that *surrounds* the art hanging on your walls: the architecture, the arrangement and sequence of exhibits, the lighting.

Caring people is exactly the same for you as it is for us—because all businesses, all organizations, all endeavors are always, at their heart, about people. If you are a restaurant, then "caring people" refers to your servers. If you are a museum, it refers to the docents and other staff who help visitors experience the art. It is about the human experience your clients have as a result of how you and your staff treat them.

Any business, any organized endeavor, is going to be composed of these three critical elements: the product, the context in which it is delivered, and the people who deliver it.

That is your *promise*.

To show you how we approached all three elements at High Point University, let me share with you the stories of several High Point students. At some point (perhaps at many points) you may see in our experience a reflection of your own business or organization or find strategies and tactics we used that may have relevance to your situation.

An Extraordinary Education . . .

Today, we welcome 1,600 new students each fall. But in the fall of 2005, my first autumn as president, we welcomed just 412 new freshmen. Among those freshmen was a quiet young man named Justin Handy. Justin had already decided on a psychology major, but when he walked into Dr. Kimberly Wear's psychology classroom, he found his exact calling.

When the students were assigned to write a paper on a topic of their choice, Justin picked "emotion and memory." Justin says he'll never forget what happened next. Dr. Wear walked over to his desk and plopped down a stack of review articles for him to read.

"You know, this particular topic is one I spent a lot of time on myself in grad school," she told him.

Justin took it as a challenge and immersed himself in the literature. He was hooked.

"I came to High Point with a lot of aspirations," he says, "but no real target to direct my energies. My professor was very nurturing as a mentor, talking with me not only about science and psychology, but about life in general. I've always been kind of shy. Having a forum where I felt comfortable enough to express myself was instrumental in my experience there."

He took all Dr. Wear's classes in cognitive psychology, even one class she wasn't offering but which they did as a directed study. They met together once a week to go over what Justin was reading in the field, how it connected to his other coursework, and what directions the field at large was taking.

Justin says Dr. Wear struck the perfect balance between scientist and educator, and that she was exceptionally patient and generous with her time. What's more, she set a tone of academic excellence that Justin thrived on. As he puts it, "The coursework was geared not just toward making the grade on a test, but also toward teaching us to push the boundaries, to ask questions—to be *scientists*."

Justin and Dr. Wear collaborated on a research project, and after they finished writing up their results, they collaborated on a few more.

"It started out as a mentorship," Dr. Wear says, "but soon became more of a partnership."

In Justin's sophomore year, when they learned that NCICU (North Carolina Independent Colleges and Universities) was offering research grants for undergrads, they submitted an application. Justin was one of only seven recipients. The following year, Dr. Wear brought Justin to the annual Psychonomic Society Conference in Chicago to present the results of his research. While there, they got in a conversation with a Texas A&M professor, Dr. Steven Smith, whom Dr. Wear had known from her own grad school days in Texas. At one point, she took Dr. Smith aside and said, "Steve, you know, Justin is looking for a graduate program."

Smith's reply spoke volumes about how Justin presented himself.

"You're kidding," replied Smith. "I thought he *was* a graduate student!"

Graduate school is incredibly competitive, and Dr. Wear makes it her business each year to talk with people at the schools where her students are applying, so when her students' files and application hit their desk, they already have a connection.

Justin ended up pursuing his PhD at Texas A&M, and Smith was his graduate advisor.

As I write, Justin—Dr. Handy, I should say—is working as a research psychologist at the Naval Submarine Medical Research Laboratory. He has worked with active-duty military and first responders to deepen his understanding of post-traumatic stress disorder (PTSD) and mild traumatic brain injury, "taking incremental steps . . . to address the problem from diverse perspectives."

The Football Player from Sutton Springs

As Justin Handy was finishing out his first year at HPU, a student named Zach Jones was preparing to graduate.

When Zach started his freshman year, you'd be forgiven if you'd thought he was not a terribly promising student. Zach hailed from Sutton Springs, a tiny little North Carolina town with a population of eighty-six. No one in his family had a college degree.

"The idea of grad school or a master's degree didn't really register," Zach says.

Zach planned on getting an undergrad degree and a teaching certificate, moving back home, and teaching high school math. And maybe doing some coaching. Zach had played football at Garner High because Sutton Springs was so small it didn't exactly have its own school system.

However, Zach had a passion for computers.

Professor Roger Shore remembers Zach walking into his Intro to Computer Science class that first day. It was a big room, computers all around the perimeter, a group of juniors and seniors all sitting together over in one corner. Shore and his colleague Bill Hightower were both concerned about finding ways to make sure interested freshmen could integrate themselves into this well-established group.

In Zach's case, they needn't have worried.

"You know how wrong first impressions can be," Shore says later. "I could see some people in the room thinking, 'Here's this football player from

Sutton Springs, what exactly is *he* doing in computer science?' Oh, so wrong! It didn't take everyone long to realize what a bright light this kid was."

A few weeks into the class, Shore was talking about how to solve a programming problem, and all at once something clicked for Zach.

"The way Professor Shore described it, and his excitement not only about the problem we were solving but also about the tools we were learning in the process," Zach says, "it just triggered an epiphany."

In high school, Zach had tried to teach himself with several programming books, but he had gotten frustrated. Now, he suddenly started finding solutions to problems that had eluded him before. From that day onward, he dove into computer science with unalloyed passion.

His professors were thrilled. With anything having to do with technology, Zach showed an uncanny ability to ask great questions and get excited about the topic, and that excitement was hugely contagious.

"He was an integral part of that group almost immediately," Shore says, "and by the end of the year he was having a huge impact on those seniors."

Just like what Dr. Wear did with Justin Handy, one of Shore's colleagues worked with Zach on a series of projects and brought him along to present his findings at conferences. When Zach applied for a graduate slot at Clemson University in his senior year, Shore contacted several faculty members he knew there.

"In all fairness," he told them, "I have to tell you, you'd be making a mistake if you didn't hire this kid as your department system administrator."

Sure enough, after they interviewed Zach at Clemson that spring, they put him to work that summer, even before he started classes there.

Once at grad school, Zach stayed in close contact with his HPU professors. Shore remembers a few times during those years when Zach started to second-guess himself.

"We would tell him, 'Look, Zach, you've got this. You have the ability. Don't let doubt keep you from getting that degree.'"

He didn't. With PhD in hand, Zach went through a succession of professional incarnations, expanding his horizons, or as he puts it, "looking for bigger problems to solve."

As I write this, Dr. Zach Jones is a performance and kernel engineer at Verizon Media, where he is in charge of troubleshooting and quality control for the conglomerate's content delivery network (CDN) worldwide—"on every continent but Antarctica."

He also is a regular fixture on the HPU campus. Shore invites Zach to campus regularly to talk with students about what he's up to and about current research and developments within the world of computer science.

"His ability to sit down, chat with you, and have you totally excited about something you're working on, it's just second to none," Shore says.

When I ask Zach why he does this, his answer is one I would have been proud to give myself: "I consider High Point home—and I have a serious definition of what home is. You take care of the house you live in. It's just what you do."

The Importance of Mentors

Outstanding as they are, stories like these are not unusual at High Point. I could offer hundreds of similar narratives—a thousand, really—and they all revolve around a student's experience with a *mentor*. This is not an accident.

To a great extent, an institution of higher learning is judged by its peers on the basis of its faculty. From my first season at HPU, we were already attracting new faculty, and our accelerated growth meant that we would be doing so almost continuously every year, sometimes bringing on as many as forty new faculty members at a time. One of our central priorities was to attract stellar faculty. The central question was, how did we define "stellar"?

Obviously, any new hire needed to be academically qualified. That was a given. This meant each new faculty member had to have an incisive and comprehensive knowledge of their discipline, had to be adept in the skills of delivering that content in a way that was both understandable and engaging, and had to be dedicated to the continuum of learning—attending seminars, doing their own research, writing their own papers, serving on boards and panels, expanding their knowledge in their field. We also sought a diversity of backgrounds and viewpoints to create a thriving academic environment. You don't want all your people to be duplicates of one another. Again, the magic is in the mix.

In our definition of "stellar faculty," these characteristics were necessary—but not sufficient. Once again, we wanted to create a student-focused culture. Yes, achieving and maintaining consistent excellence in our pedagogy was paramount, but the purpose of that excellent pedagogy was to create an experience of *extraordinary education* for our students.

Thus, as we grew our family of accomplished faculty, we also began looking specifically at candidates' ability to connect with students. Our goal was not simply to instruct students but to help each student bond with a major—and thus, with a profession and career—that he or she could be passionate about. We were looking for faculty who could be excellent coaches and mentors, professors who could help build our students' capacity in every aspect and not just academically.

Like Kimberly Wear, Roger Shore, and Bill Hightower.

At some universities, students hardly ever see their professors because they work through teaching assistants (TAs) or graduate students. At High Point University, we don't have TAs or grad assistants. We just have faculty, period. This means you'll *always* have a faculty member in the classroom, and most of our faculty have terminal degrees (doctorate degrees or the equivalent in their particular discipline). And this, in turn, means that every one of our faculty members needs to be an expert not only in their field, but they also have to be skilled at building and developing graduates of substance and character.

Justin is quick to point out that as influential as Dr. Wear was in the trajectory of his career, he had exceptional support from *all* his professors. This, too, is the rule, not the exception. Ask any HPU graduate what their greatest experience was in their years here and you will typically hear something along the lines of, "Well, the creature comforts were wonderful—but you know, it was that faculty member who mentored me that has really made a difference in my life."

Our Three Goals

Our academic program was already quite good when I arrived at HPU. Really, it could not have been otherwise. Given the realities of accreditation in higher education, you *have* to meet certain requirements across the board. (It's a bit like saying, "Our restaurant is clean." That's not a point of pride, it's just the minimum requirement for having your doors open for business.)

So yes, our program was good. But it needed to be more than good. For us to achieve our goal of becoming a premier institution for higher learning, it needed to be *excellent*. Thus, we had to ask ourselves, "Beyond stellar faculty, what exactly does an excellent education mean to us? What is our definition of 'extraordinary' here?"

Naturally, we continued to embrace academic excellence as measured in the traditional ways. We knew we needed to provide a *rigorous education*, one that was intellectually challenging and held our students to high standards and expectations. This is something you cannot achieve purely through rote memorization. It means students have to engage their critical faculties and judgment and develop the capacity not only to absorb a body of knowledge, but they also had to apply that knowledge creatively in a multiplicity of contexts and circumstances.

Yet, this definition of an extraordinary education, again, was *necessary but not sufficient*. From 2005 to 2010, scores of our entering freshmen rose from average to excellent. Yet, these scores could not be our sole parameters for defining excellence. In our admissions process, we were looking not simply for students with high SAT scores who could achieve academically, but for young people who had the potential to become leaders, who could be innovative, who could survive and thrive in the real world and contribute in a meaningful way. We wanted to focus not simply on the product but on the product of the product—not on the diploma, but on the life that a young person would go on to build with that diploma in hand.

This boiled down to three fundamental tenets: We wanted to offer a *holistic education*, rooted in *experiential learning* and *values-based living*.

Holistic education meant we believed our students needed to evolve and develop as total human beings. If you understand your subject but you don't know how to get along with people, how to write a decent letter, how to manage your time and energy, how to communicate well, how to be persuasive, how to guide and inspire others . . . then you've been *trained*, but not *educated*.

There is an enormous difference.

Experiential learning meant we wanted our students to be fully engaged with their major field, not only inside the classroom but outside as well, not just in theory but also in real-world application. I began regularly citing to our students the Chinese proverb: "I hear, and I forget; I see, and I may remember; I do, and I understand." We knew our students would see and hear plenty during their four years here, but if we wanted them to genuinely *understand*, then it was incumbent upon us to ensure that they also had ample opportunity to *do*.

Values-based living meant we wanted our students to have not only a holistic and engaged experience of their chosen fields, but also a deeply personal experience of a broad base of values that spoke to the core of the best in humanity. This meant doing what we could to instill such values as generosity, faith, caring, fellowship, inclusivity, patriotism, and service. We wanted to ensure that we were an institution that promoted not only higher learning but also *higher living*.

These three goals—holistic education, experiential learning, values-based living—were the three pillars upon which we would build that "extraordinary education." *That* was our definition of excellence, and we pursued these goals in a thousand and one ways.

Planting Seeds of Greatness

As soon as I arrived at HPU, I began offering a weekly class called the President's Seminar on Life Skills. This course was designed to help students learn how to manage their time and energy, understand the fundamentals of fiscal literacy and sound stewardship, and use essential communication and leadership skills to their benefit. These were basic life skills, tools that would assist these young people in their personal, academic, and professional development. They needed to learn how to shake someone's hand and look them in the eye, how to manage a conversation with someone they didn't know, from a part of the world they'd never been to. I saw it as instruction and inspiration on how to operate in the real world. The class continues today, more popular than ever with students and even parents. Today, some 1,500 freshmen and 100 transfer students attend one of the two sections on Thursday mornings in the fall.

This became the foundation of our *holistic approach* to higher learning and higher living.

We brought in world-class leaders to speak with our students—Tom Brokaw, Colin Powell, Condoleezza Rice, Steve Wozniak, and others—both in their commencement addresses and also separately in one-on-one interviews with me in front of our students inside the Hayworth Fine Arts Center. But once a year was not enough. Along with our distinguished annual commencement speakers, we began bringing in accomplished thought leaders to talk with our students year-round—Malcolm Gladwell, Seth Godin, Dallas Mavericks CEO Cynt Marshall, John Maxwell, Netflix co-founder Marc Randolph, Twitter founder Biz Stone, and a host of other CEOs, business owners, artists, journalists, authors, U.S. ambassadors, and other experienced and inspiring individuals. We wanted to give our students an enormous range of real-world perspective in a personal, intimate setting. Here is a partial list of the speakers we brought in to meet with our students:

Patch Adams, Mitch Albom, Buzz Aldrin, Ed Asner, Jennifer Azzi, Tom Brokaw, Pamela Brown, George W. Bush, Laura Bush, Dean Cain, Dr. Ben Carson, Richard Childress, Bill Clinton, Ken Dychtwald, Steve Forbes, Thomas Friedman, Chris Gardner, Rudy Giuliani, Malcolm Gladwell, Seth Godin, Stedman Graham, Lee Greenwood, Steve Harvey, Dr. Michio Kaku, William Kennard, Muhtar Kent, Dr. John C. Maxwell,

Governor Pat McCrory, Scott McKain, Wes Moore, David Neal,
Her Majesty Queen Noor, Colin Powell, Byron Pitts, Howard
Putnam, Marc Randolph, Condoleezza Rice, Cal Ripken Jr.,
Karl Rove, Bob Ryan, Robert A. Schuller, Sage Steele, Charles
Strouse, Clarence Thomas, Dee Ann Turner, Russell Weiner . . .

Companies pay millions of dollars to send their employees to conferences to hear the people we were bringing to campus. But at HPU, these thought leaders were interacting with students in Q&A sessions and in small groups purely as a bonus. In essence, we were giving our students a top-tier executive education in tandem with their regular college education. Like our professors, those thought leaders have become mentors to our students. And nothing makes me prouder than to hear what they have done with and for our students.

We have so many stories at HPU of our thought leaders from our in Residence program stepping up and stepping out to help our students. Here are three.

"HPU Opened the Door"

Caitie Gehlhausen arrived at HPU from Cicero, Indiana, with dreams of running her own company one day. She majored in entrepreneurship, and she kept thinking of what she could do with what she could create. Like all college students, she kept her iPhone close—and that gave her an idea. She dreamed up a product she calls Socket Lock-It, a smartphone card holder that's also a phone grip.

She started pitching her product during our university's business competitions. As a sophomore, she received $1,500 after placing second in HPU's Elevator Pitch Competition. As a junior, she received $10,000 in HPU's Business Plan Competition. She also received help from Marc Randolph, HPU's Entrepreneur in Residence and the first CEO of Netflix.

Caitie pitched the idea to Randolph that same year, and he told her he saw much promise in it. The two stayed in touch and traded emails as she continued to develop her company. In her senior year, she pitched to Randolph again and got more advice on how to start and run a business.

Socket Lock-It is now Caitie's business. Her products are now sold online and in 3,055 Walmarts nationwide. She's gotten help. Her mom left the fundraising company where she had worked for thirty-three years to help Caitie run the business, while her dad helped her with the legal side of things.

Caitie has grown. Her work with Randolph showed her how.

"My goal evolved, and my questions evolved," Caitie says. "I pitched to Marc twice, and we continued our exchange. He gave me awesome advice. I couldn't have picked a better place than HPU to pursue my goal."

Now to Grace George, a 2021 graduate from Wheeling, West Virginia, with degrees in sports management and political science. Her life changed in the fall of 2019 because of an email from her advisor, Dr. Jenny Lukow, chair of HPU's sports management department.

Dr. Lukow had big news. She emailed Grace and three other students about an incredible opportunity. Lukow wanted them to spend three days in Dallas with Cynt Marshall, the CEO of the Dallas Mavericks and HPU's Sports Executive in Residence. They just needed to say yes.

Lukow highlighted her email to get their attention. At first, Grace thought it was fake. So, she emailed Lukow. Grace was wrong. The email was real, and in October 2019, Grace went to Dallas. When Marshall met Grace and the three other students, she hugged them all.

Grace calls her three days in Dallas "magical." She and her classmates talked to Marshall and others in the Mavericks organization. They also sat down and asked Marshall questions about everything and watched her do her job from a few feet away.

Grace saw her first NBA game. The Mavericks played the Washington Wizards. She also firmed up her idea of what she wanted to do with her law degree—marry her love for sports and politics and specialize in sports industry law.

Her three days in Dallas solidified that.

"It's one of the intangible opportunities you find only at High Point," says Grace. "You can only learn so much in school, and with its Innovators in Residence program, High Point gives you access to real-life professionals, and they share with you what you need to know."

Then there's Joseph Maronski, who graduated in 2023 with a degree in journalism. He's from Miller Park, New York. As a high school senior, Joseph thought he was bound to a college in Boston. But on a trip to North Carolina, his dad convinced him to visit HPU. During an open house, Joseph's life changed when he listened to a Q&A session I held with Byron Pitts, the co-anchor of ABC's *Nightline* and HPU's Journalist in Residence.

Pitts's frankness about his profession and his life captivated Joseph. On his way to the airport to catch a flight home, who did Joseph run into? Pitts himself.

Joseph approached Pitts, introduced himself, and told him how much he enjoyed his talk. Without being prompted, Pitts gave Joseph his cell number and told him to call him anytime.

On his flight home, Joseph filled out his HPU application. He had found his school, and he had found his mentor. Later, Pitts came back to campus and worked with HPU students inside the university's TV studio. Joseph was one of those students. At the end of their session in the TV studio, Joseph asked Pitts if he could shadow him at ABC's offices in New York City. Pitts agreed, and Joseph got a tour from Pitts himself. Pitts introduced Joseph to everyone, and Joseph saw the studio—all thirteen floors.

But that was just the beginning.

At the end of his sophomore year, Joseph knew he needed to line up a summer internship and called Pitts for advice. Instead, Pitts guided Joseph through ABC's internship application. Joseph applied, and in the summer of 2021, Joseph received a ten-week internship with the team at *Nightline*. Pitts helped. So did one of Joseph's professors, Joe Michaels, the former director at NBC's *TODAY* show, who was now teaching video production at HPU as the university's Broadcaster in Residence.

"I used the connections I've formed inside the School of Communication to propel past the awkward, get-to-know-you part of my internship interview," Joseph says. "ABC got to know more about me faster. My hard work got me the internship, but HPU opened the door."

Holistic education, I believe, is not about simply offering information or even dispensing knowledge. Holistic education is about gaining wisdom. But where—and how—does someone gain wisdom? From investing time and energy with wisdom.

Like Joseph did.

And Caitie.

And Grace.

I often tell our students, people will use you and discard you if all you have is information. If all you have is knowledge, people will need you until such a time as their own level of knowledge is equal to yours. But if you have wisdom, people will respect you.

And respect is lasting.

HPU's Innovative Education

From that very first meeting at the beginning of January 2005, I had told our community leaders that we were High *Point's* University, and this was no idle promise. We made service learning a core part of the curriculum, through which we not only steeped our students in core civic values but also began steadily increasing the flow of services and value we rendered to the city of High Point.

We have a requirement that all incoming freshmen complete at least fifty hours of community service per semester. Most exceed that. Today, our students contribute more than 500,000 service hours a year. Their impact is impressive. We also created a required course in ethics, with a civic engagement element built into it. We built a civic engagement component into quite a few upperclassmen courses, too. Those courses could entail working with a refugee family, teaching children how to read, tutoring or working in a homeless shelter, or working at our local environmental center and helping to organize cleanups in the city.

Meanwhile, we made sure our students were prepared after graduation.

We established an Office of Career and Professional Development where we taught students everything from how to prepare a strong résumé and compelling LinkedIn profile to how to dress for an interview. Our students also went through mock interviews for internship or employment, which we videotaped and critiqued to help them hone their skills. Today, 99 percent of our graduates find a job or attend graduate school within six months of graduation.

That's fourteen points higher than the national average. And students notice. Students like Carter Lohman, an exercise science major from Louisville, Kentucky, who graduated in 2019.

"HPU's 99 percent post-grad placement rate is no joke, no small task," says Carter, a document management specialist with PharmaCord, a pharmaceutical company that helps innovative therapies reach patients. "I noticed a lot of students had jobs lined up very quickly, and not just any jobs, but ones that are instrumental in making career moves."

As for our faculty, we created a grant program known as the Think BIG (Big Innovation Grant) Award, which supports them financially in finding innovative ways to create depth of learning through unusual student experiences. One year, a team of professors took students to work for CNN and ABC News at both the Democratic and Republican conventions. Another year, a team of students designed a device to help NASA astronauts collect samples from the surface of asteroids and ended up spending four days with NASA engineers in Houston, testing the device.

We've ramped up overseas study opportunities, too. We send design students to study furniture design in Scandinavia, art students to visit Monet's personal art studio in France and Rodin's studio and gardens in Barcelona, and music students to perform choral works in the Esztergom Basilica (Hungary's most famous Renaissance landmark) and the Lobkowicz Palace in Prague (where Mozart's handwritten reorchestration of Handel's *Messiah* is housed).

One student, Hannah Bailey, received a Fulbright to work with high school students in Bosnia on a project using photography to better understand prejudice and ethnic identities. Another student, Britton

Nagy, traveled to Norway's Bastøy Island on a Pulitzer Center on Crisis Reporting stipend to investigate a controversial minimum-security criminal correctional facility that aimed to become the world's first "ecological prison" system. It's impressive today to see how many students qualify for Fulbright awards, among many more.

We also established a center for undergraduate research, through which any and every undergrad could become involved in meaningful coursework beyond their classroom instruction. Typically, you think of research at universities as something for graduate students, but we wanted all our undergraduates to be steeped in the experience of real-world application of their disciplines. To complement those opportunities, we created a summer program in which students could come and work in research for ten weeks, side by side with our faculty. (They don't pay for this; in fact, we pay their room and board.) And we encouraged the exploration of other venues for research as well, depending on the discipline, such as the NASA project, or the conferences where Justin Handy and Zach Jones shared their research.

We made technology a priority because exceptional education doesn't happen in a vacuum. In 2005, the HPU campus didn't even have Wi-Fi. Back then, if you wanted to use a computer, you had to go to the library. Not anymore. We executed an immediate upgrade in our phone and broadband system that brought Wi-Fi to every square foot of the campus. We built state-of-the-art technology, from communications to audiovisual to biomechanics, into every new academic building we built. We also put in a live stock ticker for finance students, medical simulation labs for health sciences students, and state-of-the-art film editing suites and a broadcast studio for media students. That's just to name a few. In all, we invested hundreds of millions in technology.

We also wanted to ensure that our students learned a strong entrepreneurial spirit and graduated with a solid sense of such entrepreneurial values as industry, self-motivation, innovative thinking, and excellent communication skills. We wanted to create graduates who were not simply taking jobs but creating them, not graduates who had learned but who could create knowledge.

We created the Belk Entrepreneurship Center, where students could brainstorm real-world projects and practice pitching their ideas, on the second floor of Cottrell Hall. That's where Caitie Gehlhausen got her start. From our entrepreneurship center spring all kinds of ideas. In April 2021, during the annual Business Plan Competition, ideas ranged from small drones to help students better understand science and technology to a step stool designed for women to make shaving their legs in the shower safer and easier. The contest winners took home valuable start-up funding.

Inside Cottrell Hall, we built three rooms to resemble offices in a financial firm, a tech firm, and a health care firm to give students experience in how to interact in different environments. We also built a mock airplane cabin, a cross-section with rows of actual first-class airplane seats, where students could sit and practice the skill of what one HPU professor calls "planned happenstance," or productive conversations with close encounters with strangers.

Also inside Cottrell Hall, every freshman will find their Success Coach. All Success Coaches not only guide freshmen academically but also help them transition into their first two years of college, assisting them in exploring clubs to join, professors to talk to, and careers to seek. They meet with the freshmen assigned to them at least ten times—nine more than the typical advisor at other schools.

Perhaps the most substantial academic change was one that was not apparent to the casual observer. We began a sweeping review and restructuring of our entire curriculum.

Our general education curriculum was the basic core education that all liberal arts students receive beyond their own particular concentration and electives. It had been developed back in the 1970s and hadn't really changed since then. What's more, up to this point, the various departments had essentially taught in silos—the religion department was not connected to the history department, which had little to do with the education department, and so on. We needed to integrate our faculty. We needed to renovate our curriculum. We needed to innovate in every way possible.

The trend at liberal arts colleges was four-credit-hour courses, but we were still based on a three-credit-hour system. A fourth credit hour would beautifully support our goals of holistic education and experiential learning. It could be applied as a lab or studio work, a series of seminars and evening films, or research, an internship, or a series of field trips.

Our faculty decided to make the change.

Going from three to four credit hours sounds simple: just add another hour, right? In reality, it meant this:

- Every single faculty member had to completely reevaluate everything they were doing.

- Every department had to revamp its curriculum in order to incorporate a valuable experiential dimension.

- We had to reduce the number of courses in order to keep our majors manageable.

- Faculty and deans had to write an entirely new syllabus *for every single course.*

It was an enormous undertaking, every bit as challenging as the explosion of renovation, new construction, and expansion going on around us physically.

This change also laid the foundation for more innovation and expansion of our academic protocol. As we grew, we began building out our catalog of course offerings, adding dozens of new programs in everything from Chinese to mathematical economics, international relations to actuarial science and interactive gaming.

We've also expanded our graduate studies and added doctorate-level programs for the first time. New academic schools include nursing, dental medicine, optometry, law, pharmacy, engineering, and health sciences.

We see our growth ushering in a new chapter of High Point University. But it's certainly not the last.

. . . in an Inspiring Environment . . .

One day at a staff meeting, I pulled out a letter I'd received from Christine, a recent graduate, and began reading it aloud.

Christine wrote about how being at High Point University had changed her life, and about how everyone at HPU had always been there for her, helping her in every way possible to make full use of her potential and chase her biggest dreams. When she wanted to graduate a year early, nobody stood in her way. When she wanted to work early or late, the campus restaurants were always ready to provide her something to eat. When she needed to study at odd hours, she could always find a quiet, clean place to study, including a library open 24/7. If she needed a suit dry-cleaned for an interview, the HPU concierge would take care of it.

She concluded:

> *High Point's students-come-first philosophy made me feel like everyone was there only to help me, to encourage me to succeed, to clear the way for me to shine. HPU gave me the positive outlook I needed to dream big dreams and reach my goals without being intimidated by life's obstacles.*

"Wow," I said to myself.

Even as I stood there reading her letter aloud, I found myself deeply inspired by this young woman's spirit. "To dream big dreams . . ." Then, a thought hit me.

Those chairs.

I'd seen them when I drove past an outlet by the highway a few hours south of High Point—two gigantic rocking chairs towering some twenty feet in height. Each seat alone was nearly six feet off the ground. I'd been so struck by the sight that I had pulled over and gotten the business card of the man who built them.

We needed those chairs. They belonged here on our campus.

We contacted the builder, procured the chairs, and placed them behind the new Slane Student Center, overlooking the pond at Hayworth Park

along with a bronze placard engraved with an excerpt from Christine's letter. They have since become quite the destination spot and one of the most
popular Instagram stops on campus. Visitors are always clambering up and
having their picture taken. Students climb up just to sit and read or study.
One freshman in the university's Marching Panthers band even climbed
up there once and serenaded everyone with his saxophone. Students all
seem to appreciate looking out at the campus from that rarified height.
The scale of the chairs is such that when you hoist yourself up there, you
cannot help but see things from a different perspective—just as Christine
says her university experience provided for her. You view the world with a
larger outlook.

We call them the Think Big Dream Big Chairs.

The education at HPU is based on a set of core values, but we believe
you can't effectively just preach values, you can only effectively *model* them.
The principal purpose of the campus environment is to model such values
as excellence, beauty, greatness, generosity, fellowship, joy, faith, learning,
patriotism, and service. These are not mere words. We at HPU want our
students to appreciate these concepts and see how they can use them in
their lives.

When we began thinking about how to change our campus environment, I purposely did not go visit other campuses. I didn't want to copy
what others had done. We were, however, keenly interested in looking at
what Howard Schultz had done to create Starbucks and what Google and
Apple and other forward-looking companies were doing to create their
own innovative environments. Over the years, in my travels as a speaker
and consultant, I had also become intimately acquainted with the interiors
of hundreds of convention centers, airports, and hotel complexes, and I
had paid close attention. Now, as we began renovating and redesigning our
campus, we reflected carefully on everything I had seen.

Early on, we had ripped up those generic cement sidewalks on the
Kester International Promenade and replaced them with red brick
walkways to match the beautiful brickwork of our buildings' Georgian
architecture. We wanted to give our entire campus a feel of *intentional*

congruence. Remember that phrase? And yes, just as I'd envisioned as I stood on the brick steps of Roberts Hall on that chilly day in January 2005, we made the sidewalks twelve feet wide. We wanted to see our students walking side by side, talking, laughing, and sharing their lives with one another wherever they went.

> *"If you want to be a great person, Nido, you must first walk side by side, hand in hand with great people."*

I can still hear my mother's voice saying these words. Like other life principles she taught me, this became a central philosophy at High Point University: *Who you spend time with is who you become.*

We sought to embody that principle in the heart of the campus.

We installed speakers atop a section of the promenade lampposts to play classical music softly throughout the day, from 7:00 in the morning until 8:00 at night. No student, we believe, should graduate from college having not been exposed to the finest arts of all time: music and dance, sculpture, poetry, and art.

We populated the walkway with the giants of history, creating life-size and strikingly lifelike bronze statues of great men and women. We placed them, one by one, on those iron benches from the promenade to the Congdon Hall of Health Sciences and Fred Wilson School of Pharmacy: John Wesley, Thomas Jefferson, Aristotle, Martin Luther King Jr., Mark Twain, Mother Teresa, Ronald Reagan, and dozens more.

With the strains of Bach, Beethoven, and Brahms in their ears, our students would now stroll down the broad brick pathway and settle onto a bench to study their history text—with Mahatma Gandhi or Rosa Parks sitting companionably next to them.

"You may not care about Mark Twain, but you need to know who he was and what he did," I've told our students. "And you may not be in love with Chopin—we're not saying you have to go out and buy his music. But as citizens of the world, though, it should at least be familiar to you."

Soon others joined this group of history's giants: Galileo and Lincoln; Leonardo da Vinci, Beethoven, and John Coltrane (a High Point native!); Helen Keller, Sir Isaac Newton, Sacajawea, Maya Angelou, George Washington, Sally Ride, and Teddy Roosevelt.

We asked students, staff, and faculty to submit their favorite quotations from people of significance, and we set into the brick walkway a series of special pavers carved with the most inspiring of those passages they selected:

"People grow through experience if they meet life honestly and courageously. This is how character is built."
—Eleanor Roosevelt

"If we ever forget that we are One Nation Under God, then we will be a nation gone under."
—Ronald Reagan

"He who passively accepts evil is as much involved in it as he who helps to perpetuate it."
—Martin Luther King Jr.

"I attribute my success to this: I never gave or took any excuse."
—Florence Nightingale

"The best way to find yourself is to lose yourself in the service of others."
—Mahatma Gandhi

"Be a yardstick of quality. Some people aren't used to an environment where excellence is expected."
—Steve Jobs

We placed these and other inspiring thoughts on posters around the campus, in The Café, and in the hallways of our residences and academic buildings, to create strong and positive messaging everywhere:

Grow

Be entrepreneurial

Be extraordinary

The art of the possible

We included inspirational quotes in our daily calendar. That brought so much positive feedback that we took the idea further. A few years ago, I filmed fifty-two brief inspirational messages and sent one every Monday morning via email and on social media—one for every week of the year. We called it "Monday Motivation." At least 100,000 people now enjoy those.

We even changed our street names. That road we rerouted to make way for the new Slane Student Center was changed to Extraordinary Way, and the little avenue on the other side of Roberts Hall that ran in front of the new Blessing Hall was renamed Blessing Way. That's not all. North Avenue became Alumni Avenue; Fifth Street became Founders Street; and Kirkman Drive became International Avenue.

We named our buildings after extraordinary people, people whose generosity had helped to fund their construction and whose own lives stood as testaments to the values we wanted our campus to represent.

Then there were the fountains and the bronze statue of Atlas bearing the globe on his shoulders at the campus entrance. We wanted our students to see Atlas as a symbol of the global citizenship they were stepping into, and our grounds, our architecture, and our manicured gardens—twenty-nine of them, as of fall 2021—as a reminder of the importance of being good stewards wherever they might land. My wife, Mariana, saw to it that our gardens were nurtured. With faculty and students together, she oversaw the creation of many botanical gardens, a conservatory, and an arboretum. For fifteen years now, HPU has been selected as Tree Campus USA.

And of course, the Think Big Dream Big Chairs.

By creating an environment of positive values, inspiring language, and breathtaking imagery, our students were steeped in the best that humanity has to offer. We created an environment that encouraged them to nurture a higher level of inner dialogue—a habit of thought and attitude that said, "Yes, I can do this!"

"But that's not realistic," a critic may say. "Aren't you creating a kind of bubble? I mean, the world isn't really like that."

I say, that is not my experience.

The world in which these students would enter—where they will go to work, create, raise families, and make their mark—they are going to *create* that world. Our job is to inspire them to make it great. After all, I tell students in my class: There are no unrealistic dreams, only unrealistic timelines. Mostly, we've been proven right. Our goal all along was to graduate students ready to tackle the challenges of our ever-changing world.

. . . with Caring People

In December 2007, a young student named Kylie Pinheiro went home to New Jersey for Christmas vacation. Though only a freshman, barely four months into her experience on campus, "Smiley Kylie" (as her friends called her) had already established herself as one of the bright lights of Yadkin Hall. She had an infectious laugh and could make anyone else laugh, too. A certified lifeguard and varsity swimmer, she had begun volunteering with the High Point Big Brothers and Big Sisters (BBBS) program. She was an only child, she adored the color pink, and she aspired to achieve a life of purpose.

A few days after Christmas, while Kylie was at home in New Jersey, her car was struck head-on by a drunk driver. She was pronounced dead at the scene.

Kylie's death hit me hard. It was the first time since I had come to HPU that one of our students died, and it felt like it was one of my own children who had so suddenly left us.

What could we possibly do?

We sent our director of Student Life and director of counseling (a position we had just created) with a group up north to attend the funeral. More than twenty piled into an HPU bus and drove the eight hours north to South Brunswick, New Jersey. When they got there, they found a massive crowd waiting to pay tribute to Smiley Kylie. It was an open casket ceremony. As our group approached the coffin, they saw that the family had put Kylie's HPU magnets inside her coffin, right above her head.

"She loved it there," her parents told them.

A handful of other HPU parents had driven in with their children from surrounding states as far away as Maine, making up a group of some sixty in all. After the service, they all went to a somber dinner together, and while they were there, they texted me.

"We're all here together," they wrote, "and we wanted to thank you for sending us."

Three years later, when Kylie would have been due to graduate, we flew her parents down to North Carolina, where they joined us for commencement. We presented them with a diploma for Kylie, an honorary degree from High Point University. From that point on, this became a tradition that we would follow every time we lost a member of our family.

It is a sad tradition, but one we are grateful for nevertheless, because it speaks to how much these young people become a part of our lives. I thank God these occasions are few.

Earlier that year, the students at High Point University compiled and published a list of the "Top 10 Reasons to Attend HPU." I was touched to see this item on their list:

No. 6: The president knows my name. He eats lunch in The Café. I can stop by his office and talk with him. He really cares about the students.

You cannot fake this. There have been stories about us in the media that talk about "HPU's charismatic president," but charisma is an over-rated quality. Authenticity trumps charisma every time.

When Gen. Colin Powell visited our campus to talk with the students, he said that every time he parked in the garage at work, the attendants always parked his car up front, so he could hop in and be off quickly when he left. One day, he asked the guy on duty why that was.

"You want to know why your car's always up front?" the man said. "Listen. Every day, when you come in in the morning, you roll down your window and ask me, 'Jorge, how was your weekend? How are your sons doing? You enjoying this beautiful day?' Every day. *That's* why we park your car in front."

And that is why Colin Powell has had such a stunning career. It's not simply because he was smart (although he certainly was that), nor is it purely because he was ambitious (though that's true too). It's because he created relationships. He cared. Whether you're a dishwasher or a billion-aire, here is the secret to success: You create relationships, and you take care of those relationships.

This is not something I "put on," like a costume or a script. I *am* their friend.

When parents and other visitors first arrive, they see the electronic parking signs greeting them by name and the meticulously kept grounds. They walk past the gigantic Atlas statue and the fountain at the Welcome Center entrance and walk along the Kester Promenade past international flags and iron benches with life-size bronze statuary and inspirational quo-tations carved into the path. They stop and read the quotes.

These are the sorts of things that first meet their eyes. But when the visit is over and they're preparing to leave, they don't talk about any of that. They say, "You know what's amazing? Everyone, from the pro-fessor to the guy who cuts the grass, is hospitable, kind, welcoming, helpful. *Everyone.* How do you *do* that? I want to do the same thing in my business!"

The answer, in part, is that you have to *build* it. Creating a culture of caring people doesn't happen simply by wishing it so. Articulating a philosophy is an important first step, but then you have to follow through with structural changes that implement that philosophy and inject it into the fabric of the operation—every day in every way.

For example, soon after I arrived, we began taking steps to elevate, expand, and empower the Office of Student Life. We created a vice presidential position over this department, doubled our new VP's staff, and empowered her to completely reinvent the office and come up with ideas for enhancing the lives of students on an inclusive and welcoming campus in every conceivable way. We put in place educational programs on substance abuse, set up a peer mentoring program, and boosted the counseling program from a few part-time to eight full-time certified counselors. We established a Care Alert Team. If a student missed a day of class or a professor noticed that a student appeared unusually disconnected, someone from the team would check on them confidentially. We wanted to ensure the student was okay, physically and emotionally, and if they were not, we got them appropriate support. We also took steps to model the values of caring and community with all our staff and faculty.

When we created the HPU Passport, we shared them with employees as well as with students and began putting money on every employee's Passport so they could eat for free wherever they wanted on campus and feel part of the community.

Every year, we gave our faculty gifts that would keep them at the edge of technology—the latest iPad, the Apple Watch, a GoPro video camera, a Bose recorder. In 2015, at our tenth anniversary of our transformational journey, we distributed $3 million in bonuses to staff and faculty as a way of saying "thank you" and to let them know we care about them. Then, on our fifteenth anniversary, we distributed $5 million in bonuses to the staff and faculty. Full-time employees received 1 percent of their salary times their years of service up to $15,000. The minimum bonus for full-time employees was $1,500.

"We wanted to reward the people who have helped us on this incredible journey," I told a local reporter. "It's that simple."

We still share bonuses annually at Thanksgiving. In August 2021, we even distributed $1.5 million to thank our team for doing an extraordinary job during the global pandemic. In 2022, the university allocated $3 million in appreciation bonuses.

We expanded our budget for faculty development so our faculty could attend conferences and present papers and grow themselves further in their field. We also built a beautiful faculty club on campus with complimentary food. Meanwhile, my family donated our home on Myrtle Beach so that faculty could go spend a weekend with their loved ones or go on a retreat for a week to work on a book. We treated them as we would treat our own family. They *are* our family.

These are some of the ways we adapted to ensure that the spirit of caring is in the fabric of our lives on campus. The bottom line, though, is how we all behave every day toward one another. You can't simply *say* you are a place of caring people. You have to *mean* it. You have to *live* it.

The academic program at HPU is excellent. The environment is extraordinary. Yet in the final analysis, these are not the only distinctions that differentiate us. What differentiates us is our culture. We get hundreds of letters from our graduates every year, and none of them say, "I want to thank you for that great dorm building" or "I really appreciate the millions of dollars you put into upgrading the labs." Like Justin Hardy, Zach Jones, Christine, and so many others since, they thank us for the experience they had with the people here. This caring culture is the touch point that has been the key to our success.

You cannot *design* this. You cannot package or manufacture it. There is no magical combination of words, no clever turn of phrase or master stroke of marketing that can produce the effect that springs from a simple human gesture or heartfelt expression. We do, in fact, care about the students who are given to our care—and their parents appreciate this.

That, more than any impressive feature of our campus or any aspect of our program, is *why* they entrust their children to our care.

Parents play a big role in our success. They advocate for HPU in their circles of influence. They contribute generously their gifts, time, and energy. They flock in huge numbers to our Family Weekend events. They love HPU.

And it shows.

A Letter to Remember

I began this section on *caring people* with Kylie's story, and I cannot leave it without also telling the story of a young lady from Hartford, Connecticut, named Alixandra Cascio. Ali struggled with cancer and heart and lung issues for two years here as she worked her way through her course of study. Her mother, Judith, moved down to High Point and stayed in the condo of a friend of the university so she could be near her daughter.

In May 2016, while Ali was back in Connecticut for treatments, her parents contacted Gail Tuttle, then our vice president of Student Life. Her parents wanted Gail to know that Ali's condition was rapidly deteriorating.

Gail texted back, asking what we could do to support her.

"Is there any way we could possibly get her a diploma?" Judith replied.

Ali was a junior, just about to enter her senior year. She was so close to graduating, and she had worked so hard to make it to the end of her academic race. There was nothing in this world that meant more to her than that diploma. We *had* to find a way to make this happen, and we had to do it quickly, because Judith had told us that the end was imminent. But issuing a university diploma is a serious matter, a certification of genuine achievement. Even in such an unusual issuance as this, there were procedures that needed to be followed; this is the nature of an accredited institution.

The provost and I both had to approve this to go forward—and it just so happened that when news of Ali's worsening condition came, we were both out of the office. Gail managed to get hold of us, and the moment she began explaining the situation, we each immediately gave our approval.

This was, after all, our promise.

The honorary diploma was created, printed, packaged, and shipped up to Connecticut by overnight express. The next day, Judith sent us a photograph of Ali in the ICU, sitting up in her hospital bed triumphantly holding her diploma, her sweet face beaming with pride.

She died a few hours later.

A few days after Ali died, I received a letter from one of Ali's cousins who had been there with her. Enclosed was a photo of Ali, sitting up in her hospital bed and holding her honorary diploma, flashing her big, beautiful grin at the camera. Here is what the letter said:

> *Dear Dr. Qubein,*
>
> *Last Friday, my cousin, Alixandra Cascio, passed away after a lifetime of dealing with heart and lung issues. Despite the many challenges she faced, she attended and loved High Point University.*
>
> *When I spoke to Ali's mom Saturday afternoon, she told me what you did. It's hard to put into words what an amazing act of kindness you showed to a girl with mere hours to live. Her mom sent me a picture of Ali in her hospital bed with her diploma and a graduation cap. She had a smile on her face and passed knowing she was a proud alumna of High Point University.*
>
> *I really want to thank you and to let you know that your act of kindness was recognized and very much appreciated. I hope someday I can perform such a meaningful act for someone in need.*
>
> > *Best regards,*
> > *Edmund*

I still have this letter. I'll keep it for the rest of my life. Let me tell you my favorite part:

I hope someday I can perform such a meaningful act for someone in need.

I cannot think of a more beautiful, more poignant, more perfect expression of the spirit we strive to impart to our students no matter what year they attended.

For instance, take Ammie Jenkins.

The Empathic Side of HPU

I called Ammie on her birthday.

She had just turned seventy-eight on May 28, 2019, and I called her because I heard from a researcher at our Smith Library that she was the university's first Black student. She enrolled in the fall of 1962, a time of racial tension nationwide, and she stayed two years. She left because she couldn't afford the cost of college. But that didn't stop her education. She later graduated from the Electronic Computer Programming Institute in nearby Greensboro and received a two-year associate degree in computer programming from Durham Technical Institute.

She went on to become a teacher and entrepreneur. She founded the Sandhills Family Heritage Association, a nonprofit organization that provides programs and services to help farmers and rural families in need of assistance in four counties in southeastern North Carolina. The organization also documents and preserves the history and heritage of the unsung Black heroes in the Sandhills region of North Carolina. She also has written two books and interviewed dozens of older people about their life experiences. From their stories, she has discovered the importance of learning from the past to understand the present and leave a legacy for future generations.

When I heard all about what she had done, I wanted to honor her in a way that is rare at HPU. I wanted to award her an honorary degree. But I wanted it to be a surprise. So, two months later, on a Monday morning in August, we picked up Ammie and twenty-two of her friends and family in one of the university's big coach buses and drove them seventy-five miles north to campus from their homes in Cameron, North Carolina. We served them breakfast, took them on a tour around campus, and escorted them to the Hayworth Fine Arts Center for the ceremony. As they all stood backstage, I called up Ammie to stand beside me.

"This is a precious gift from our hearts to your heart to show that you have been a champion," I told her, "and you have turned that into purposeful endeavors throughout your life."

The degree now hangs above her computer in her home office. She sees it as a constant reminder of her High Point University experience and the champions who helped her and taught her how to give back to the community and help those in need.

"When I received that degree, I was accepted by all of those people who had invested in me in one way or another," Jenkins told one of the university's writers. "They are people who impacted my life, and I've learned from them. When you see me, you see them."

I often tell our students that the dash between the day we are born and the day we die is what matters. That dash represents our life and how we can impact and effect change in the world around us. It's a wonderful responsibility to have because the happiest moments in our lives can happen when we do something good for someone and expect nothing in return. It will mean so much to them—you'll see it, guaranteed—and in turn, it will mean so much to you.

Every November, I see that appreciation when we invite at least 1,000 military veterans to campus for our annual Veterans Day celebration. I also see that appreciation every December when at least 30,000 cars drive through our campus to see Santa, gawk at candy-cane stilt walkers, and see a life-size Nativity scene outside Norton Hall during our Community Christmas celebration.

Then, there is that Friday morning in February 2019. That was special too.

"The Holy Spirit Is in This Place"

For the past month, I had been texting Dr. Phyllis Worthy Dawkins, sometimes as early as 5:00 a.m., because I wanted to see how we could help Bennett College, one of America's two colleges for Black women, whose survival was threatened. Phyllis was the president of a school of 465 women in Greensboro, North Carolina, thirty minutes north of High Point University, and she needed to raise $5 million in less than two months to hold on to Bennett's accreditation, which was in jeopardy after years of financial issues.

Both HPU and Bennett have some key similarities—two schools, both private, both in the same county, both connected to the United Methodist Church. And we at HPU all saw the need to help save a school from losing its accreditation and closing.

I also had been impressed by Phyllis's tenacity and the college's "StandWithBennett" fundraising campaign. From the hashtag on Twitter to the blue T-shirts, "StandWithBennett" led to thousands of donations. But Bennett had only raised $3.6 million, and I told Phyllis, "We have to do something." We teamed up with Dr. Harold Martin, the chancellor of North Carolina A&T State University, a historically Black university in Greensboro, and gathered other area college presidents to discuss what we all collectively could do. Meanwhile, I approached our faculty and the HPU Board of Trustees about the idea of a financial gift, and they overwhelmingly supported it. Our board and our faculty never cease to amaze me.

Then came the time for our announcement. So, on a Friday, the first day of Black History Month 2019, Phyllis, along with many Bennett students and more than a few professors, came to campus just like Ammie had—in one of our big coach buses—for our announcement in Hayworth Chapel. Bennett students, known as Bennett Belles, filled nine rows; their faculty filled three. I sat beside Phyllis in the front of the sanctuary, and after everyone settled into the pews, I stepped up to the podium to begin.

"You'll be telling your grandchildren, 'I was there when,'" I told them.

I announced HPU's $1 million cash gift to Bennett. Hayworth Chapel erupted in applause.

"Listen, I came to this country, and by the grace of God, they let me in, and they kept me in," I said. "I have faith. *We* have faithful courage that Monday at noon on the campus of Bennett College, she will be able to announce that she's got what she needs.

"This is Black History Month, and you can't mess with Bennett College during Black History Month."

That Monday in Bennett's Pfeiffer Chapel, I announced that we at HPU had collected another $357,000 from companies and friends. I spoke to students and families during Family Weekend, and they gave what they could and what they felt compelled to give because they wanted to help our sister school. On Monday, on the campus of Bennett College, we heard we had helped Bennett raise $9.5 million, nearly double what the school needed.

I was incredibly moved by what I saw that Monday, just the jubilation of students, faculty, staff, and supporters of Bennett. I sat up front in Bennett's historic Pfeiffer Chapel, and you could feel the revival spirit inside that place, of people waving white handkerchiefs and shouting, "Amen!" We all had come together for a common good—to save Bennett. I stepped up to a podium inside Pfeiffer Chapel and spoke from my heart.

"I believe God has ordained Bennett in a very special way—to say to the world that there is a reason why Bennett was founded and there's a reason why Bennett must continue to sustain itself with both success and significance.

"All of this speaks loudly to what Bennett represents. This is not a small thing. This is about the future of tens of thousands of young women who have entered these hallowed halls and departed to make the world a better place, planting seeds of greatness wherever they go. The Holy Spirit is in this place."

Our contribution caught attention nationwide from the *Washington Post*, the *Chronicle of Higher Education*, and many more news outlets.

"High Point's donation is a show of support not often seen in higher education," the *Chronicle of Higher Education* wrote.

Local leaders weighed in too.

"Dr. Qubein is extremely busy leading HPU and the downtown revitalization efforts in High Point, yet he saw a need to reach out and help a neighboring college in our region," Don Cameron, president emeritus of Guilford Technical Community College, wrote in the *News & Record*, the daily newspaper in Greensboro. "What we have observed from this tremendous fundraising effort is his servant leadership, a caring attitude and how, by working together in our Piedmont Triad region, we all can be stronger."

True stewardship is a gift, a gift of your time, money, and talents because you see a need and you want to help. Our value to humanity depends on how much of ourselves we give to make the world a better place. It's a rent we pay for the oxygen God gives us at no cost.

There is a verse from Corinthians that talks about how those who sow sparingly will reap little, but those who sow bountifully will reap much. God does love a cheerful giver. We *all* are here because He gave all of us the greatest of all gifts: life. So, as I tell our students—and I'll say to you—make the most of it.

Our Forever Promise

In 2005, as we set out to transform this university, we knew that every school offered *an education, in an environment, with people.* There was nothing special about that. Just like every restaurant offered food, every insurance company sold insurance, and every airline flew planes. Imagine how exciting it would have been if our mission statement were just this: "At High Point University, every student receives an education, in an environment, with people."

Not very exciting. Excruciatingly boring, in fact.

And it wouldn't even have helped much to elevate us to the level of *very good*: "Every student receives a *strong* education, in a *clean* environment, with *nice* people." Yawn. Simply improving in these areas, making them strengths, would not create anything very compelling. Because *you don't compete on your strengths; you compete on your differences.* On your distinctions. Which is why, of those seventeen words that constituted our mission statement, the real power and substance of our brand, of our promise, rested in these three:

Extraordinary.

Inspiring.

Caring.

These three words represented our future; they embodied the promise we were making, to our students and alumni, parents and donors, community, and the world.

That's a promise we will always keep.

CHAPTER 9

Facing Adversity with Faithful Courage

A ugust has always been the beginning of a new academic year and some important announcements. The president typically releases statements on new fundraising goals, construction plans, and the school's latest version of its three-year plan or five-year plan or ten-year plan.

August of 2008 was no different . . . except that it was.

For one thing, there was a bit of nervousness in the air. While there had never been a precise timeline for my term as president, I'd used the phrase "two or three years" fairly freely back in 2004 before taking office, and there was a general assumption that two or three years was about how long I would stay. Just enough time, in other words, to effect the beginnings of a turnaround, get things on a solid footing, and then ride off into the North Carolina sunset. Everyone knew I had other business opportunities that I'd put on hold to be at HPU, as well as an active speaking career that still beckoned impatiently. Now that I'd been at the university for three full academic years (three and a half, actually, counting from that first spring semester in 2005), the question hung palpably in the air: This September, would I be announcing a date for my pending departure?

Would this be an *outgoing* president's address?

The truth was, I really *had* planned for this to be something I did for no more than two or three years. But something happened along the way.

Over those past three and a half years, I'd spent hundreds of hours talking with students. I was a father myself, with four wonderful children, but through my experiences at High Point University, it was as though I got to be a father to *thousands* of young men and women. Every year, I would receive notes from students saying things like, "I've been out of school for a year now, and every day I remember what I learned in your seminar . . . It has changed my life." I had just turned sixty, and I had friends my age who talked about how they were starting to feel old.

Not me.

I have always been a high-energy person, but spending my days on this campus, with these remarkable young people, feeling their energy and curiosity, their ambition and appetite for life, and being a part of that, I was feeling positively younger than ever.

What happened was simply this: I had set out to do a job, and in the process, I fell in love. I fell in love with the students, and I fell in love with our faculty and staff. I fell in love with the environment, with the philosophy, with the purpose of what we were here to do, and with the fact that we were *doing* it. And doing it well. Our families appreciated our work and advocated the university to the world!

So, I was love-struck, plain and simple. I couldn't have left if I'd wanted to—and I clearly, emphatically did not want to.

So, that August, the board of trustees sent out a press release stating that I would be staying around for at least another three or four years. Maybe longer. *Probably* longer.

The HPU community breathed a collective sigh of relief. And I was thankful for the opportunity to continue my service.

And the very next week, all of Wall Street was rocked when Lehman Brothers' stock plunged 45 percent. By the following Monday, it had filed for Chapter 11—the largest bankruptcy filing in U.S. history—and the tremors were felt across the country and around the world.

The great collapse was underway.

A Sleepless Fall

As the next few weeks careened on, the economic outlook grew only more terrifying. On September 29, 2008, the Dow Jones plunged more than 777 points, the largest single-day drop in history at that time. And that was just one day. The week of October 6, 2008, was the worst week for the stock market since the 1930s. Stock exchanges around the globe plummeted, many experiencing the worst declines in their history. Merrill Lynch, AIG, Freddie Mac, Fannie Mae, WaMu . . . The echoing thunder of crashing portfolios and shuttering institutions rolled on and on. It got so bad that the two U.S. presidential candidates momentarily halted their campaigns to talk over a mutual plan for how to cope with the crisis. By December, unemployment in the city of High Point had reached 8.8 percent, the highest in a quarter century and almost double the rate from just a year earlier. By January, it was 10.3 and still climbing. And of course, the same thing was happening nationwide.

As the crisis deepened, so did my concern for the fate of our university. People everywhere were going to feel the severe effects of this crisis. They were losing their savings and 401(k) plans, watching as their home values crumbled and retirement plans evaporated. Families would be needing to make some tough choices. Wouldn't it be reasonable to expect that a private liberal arts university tuition might be right near the top of the list of expenses to cut?

The state of our current enrollment numbers was always on my mind because, frankly speaking, it was our continuing increase in enrollment that was fueling so much of our growth and development. Yes, we had borrowed a little money to fund the bulk of our capital improvements, but I was also counting on our growing numbers of students to make the investment a sound one. And I was not the only one. Our banks were looking closely at our enrollment figures too. In order to secure our construction loans, we were leveraging the growth trends in our enrollment data, so our banks were watching these numbers as carefully as we were. There was a lot of pressure to deliver.

What if the numbers stopped increasing?

And what if they started going *down*?

I know I have portrayed myself as a person of habitual confidence, and for the most part, this is quite true. Yet, confidence is not the same as blind trust, and certainly not the same as foolhardiness. It also does not mean there are never times when I worry. Actually, I worry a good deal. I just do it constructively. As I've said, I think of myself as a paranoid optimist, and I am constantly making contingency plans and weighing options and studying scenarios. You cannot be an entrepreneur for any length of time and not discover that plans rarely work out exactly the way you expect them to.

"If you want to make God laugh," as the saying goes, "make a plan."

I knew we had made God laugh many, many times. Normally, I did my best to laugh right along with Him. Still, during my entire time at High Point University, there were three periods when I would wake up in a cold sweat, times when sleep and I could not find each other's company, not even in the deepest hours of the night. Two of these sleepless stretches occurred in 2008—the first one, curiously enough, well before that September.

This first anxious episode had to do with the residential complex that came to be known as The Aldridge Village.

The Benevolent Businessman

As I mentioned earlier, the fall of 2007 convinced me that our student population was growing so quickly that it was outpacing our capacity to house them. We needed to undertake some serious residential construction. I had my eye on a fifteen-acre tract of land just north of the campus that I thought would be perfect for our first foray into building a self-contained, off-campus housing complex.

The gentleman who owned the place, Archie, had started out as a driver for a long-distance trucking company before I was born, and he worked his way up to being president of one of the largest carriers in North America. Archie prided himself on the fact that over the years, as he had built his career and his equity, not once had he ever sold a piece of property he owned. Archie had a personal philosophy that was just five words, two sentences long: "I buy. I never sell."

I needed him to sell.

I went to have a talk with Archie at his home in High Point. His wife, Emma Louise, brought us coffee, and we chatted a bit. He knew, of course, why I was there—that I was interested in buying this particular property— and of course, he told me I had no chance.

"I buy," he told me.

"I know, I know," I responded. "You never sell. But Archie, let me explain. If I don't have that property, then I won't be able to build a residential facility for our upperclassmen, and if I can't accommodate these students, it's going to impede the growth of our city's university. I'm not just here on a whim; I don't just want this property. Archie, we *need* to have this property."

He still was not going to budge. Fortunately for me, I had an in.

Emma Louise.

"Archie," she said, "you need to help Nido out."

She turned to me and smiled her sweet smile. Archie and Emma Louise were both Quakers, and among the nicest people you'd ever meet. Archie could be a stubborn businessman, too. But perhaps in Emma Louise, he had met his match.

"I still remember when he first came to town," she continued, talking to Archie about me in the third person, even though I was sitting right there. "He was such a cute boy, and all the girls at church liked him."

She went on like that for a while, reminiscing about the old days in High Point, me doing my best not to blush, or at least not too obviously.

Nearly forty years earlier, as a boy of twenty, I had arrived in town fresh from Mount Olive and enrolled at High Point College to further my education. I had met Archie and Emma Louise, and evidently, I had made a favorable impression on Archie's wife. God is good.

Emma Louise concluded her monologue.

"It's Nido, Archie. You need to help him."

Archie shook his head.

"Well, I don't know," he said. "I'll have to think about it."

In the end, Archie agreed to give me the fifteen acres as long as we donated $900,000 to the school at his church. Deal. The property is now worth $15 million, land alone.

That autumn, as the plans were drawn up and we prepared for construction, I suddenly grew worried. Archie was in industrial transportation. He'd had petroleum tankers and had hauled bunker fuel, textile chemicals, and other sorts of potentially problematic freight. The land we'd gotten, I was pretty sure, had been at some point used as a trucking terminal.

"Oh no," I asked myself, "what if there's residual contamination there?"

We ran a Phase I environmental site assessment, then a Phase II environmental site assessment, and then a Phase III environmental site assessment. It was a little nerve-wracking: These things take time (to say nothing of money!), and we didn't have forever. We came out with a clean bill of health, thank goodness, but by the time the studies were completed, we were already into 2008. We would have more than 500 upperclassmen expecting to move in that August—and all we had at this point was a bare patch of land!

Okay. Onward. We had barely eight months to build this thing. It was going to cost some $34 million. "Nerve-wracking" was putting it too mildly.

Construction hummed along throughout the winter and spring. The buildings went up. Samet Construction brilliantly delivered the project on time—in eight months, working around the clock. We knew this place was going to be an amazing facility. In addition to the 560 students in residential suites, it would feature a volleyball court, its own fitness rooms complete with cardio machines and weight equipment, a pool, a restaurant-style dining room, and a free shuttle to campus. We didn't just want to house our upperclassmen. We wanted to house them safely and with useful resources.

This was not only an expression of our students-first philosophy. There was fiscal logic to this strategy, too. I have already emphasized the significance of freshman enrollment, but this was not the sole financial indicator we had to watch. Retention was also hugely important. Every student who chose to leave HPU after just a year or two added to the pressure on new admissions to make up that tuition loss. Or to put it the other way: the higher our retention, the less stress on our Office of Undergraduate Admissions.

Beyond consideration of numbers and dollars, strong retention was also essential to fulfilling our entire purpose. If our mission was to prepare these young people to make a solid and meaningful contribution to their world and we had four years to do it, if they left halfway through that process, then where did that leave us in the fulfillment of our mission?

The Aldridge Village was not only central to our goal of housing our growing student body, but also to helping strengthen retention. It had to be an attractive place to live.

Then, it hit me.

"What if the students just don't want to live there?" I asked myself. "What if they all say, 'You know, I'd really rather live right on campus.'"

I had been going on the assumption that the idea of living off-campus, in this brand-new complex with its various amenities, would be something upperclassmen would find appealing. But what if they didn't? It wasn't as if we could *force* them to choose off-campus residence. We could be sitting there with a $34 million white elephant as we tried to figure out how to squeeze an extra 560 students into campus housing. This could be a disaster!

One night, as I lay awake, my mind raced. It occurred to me that the architects had designed all the rooms for single beds. I almost smacked myself in the forehead with the palm of my hand. (I didn't, but only because I didn't want to wake my wife.) Most of these students had no doubt grown up with double beds! They wouldn't want to move to some place with beds narrower than what they were used to.

The next day, we immediately canceled the order for all the single beds and put in a new one for double beds. The decision meant that the actual living space in all the rooms had suddenly grown smaller and more crowded.

Yes, this was a summer of sleepless nights praying feverishly for God's grace. And yet it all worked out.

The Village was completed in the middle of August 2008, just as students began returning from summer vacation. It was 100 percent occupied. I breathed a huge sigh of relief. Today, students love it so much that they stay there year after year. Plus, the campus has grown so much that The Village is no longer off-campus.

And then a month later, the economy imploded—and I was once again waking up in a cold sweat.

Time to Pray

The week Wall Street crashed, we had just sunk the pilings and laid the foundation for our largest construction project to date—a 277,000-square-foot university center consisting of five floors of multiuse programming, with a 250-seat movie theater, four restaurants, a library and study space, a massive central courtyard, and more than 500 residential beds filling its wings.

As much as we needed The Village residential complex, it alone would not handle the swelling student population, not even at its 100 percent occupancy. If our growth trends continued, we would badly need this new building, too. And we would need it soon. We needed it not only for its residential capacity, but we also needed the additional dining facilities it would offer. We were starting to burst at the seams, and this new project would help us handle the growing stress on our campus facilities.

In fact, just getting to the point where we had a place to build had been quite a saga in itself. The site of this building was directly behind the Slane Student Center, on the other side of the pond-filled park that we planned to build between the two, in a one-two-three punch of architectural magnificence.

But that site was not entirely available, at least not when we first started the planning process. There were still quite a few private dwellings located there. One by one, we were able to purchase those homes and help the owners to relocate, until we reached the point where we had secured the entire parcel we needed . . . except for one single-family home, sitting on the corner of North Avenue and West College Drive. I had met with the man who owned this house many times and tried to persuade him to sell. He refused. Without this property, we wouldn't be able to move forward.

So, I met with him again, a dozen more times. Still no dice. What could I do? I kept meeting with him. He had been living there for fifty years. He was now in his midseventies, and he said he just didn't see the purpose in moving now. I pointed out that his neighbors were all gone, and his was the only house left. He would be surrounded by students.

We had met more than thirty times when he finally said, "Okay." (In my mind, I high-fived myself.) "But I want $600,000 for it," he added. (Perhaps the high-five had been premature.)

"Are you kidding me?" I asked.

The house was valued at barely a third of that amount—and we're talking about a one-family home on a postage stamp of land. I have to give him credit, though: He held firm. In the end, there was no way out of it. I had to pay him $600,000. Although I did negotiate with him that upon his death, his estate would give the university a $300,000 donation.

In any event, it had been a long and challenging planning process, but now we were full steam ahead. By the fall of 2008, the area had been bulldozed and contoured, the foundation prepared, the steel pilings sunk deep into the earth. We had on order a massive inventory of steel, brick, and other materials. We had already invested some $22 million in the project when Lehman Brothers went belly-up and the banking industry started coming unglued.

The worry I'd felt a few months earlier, when we were building Aldridge Village, now seemed like a calm spring day. I was practically nostalgic for that worry. This . . . this was something else. With Aldridge Village, we'd had a $34 million facility in the balance. But now? Now it felt like the future of the university itself hung in the balance.

Our entire strategy had been predicated on the continuing growth of the student body, and up to this point, that strategy had been entirely vindicated. We had begun that fall semester with 870 freshmen, far and away our largest freshman class ever, and a total of more than 1,900 residential students. We still had a long road ahead of us, and we knew that. Our long-term goal was to have a total undergraduate student body of about 5,000. We believed 5,000 students would be just about right, with perhaps a thousand graduate students. We were well on our way.

At least, we had been. But now?

On Friday, October 10, with the news of that week's precipitous stock market crash ringing in my ears, I closed up my office, walked over to the construction site, and stood. I stood there for a few minutes, looking at the steel-and-concrete foundation stretching out for what looked like a mile. It was after 7:00 p.m., dusk had already fallen, and the day's waning light cast the scene in cold grays and purples.

I was scared. I admit it. Then, I started to pray.

A Pivotal Conversation

You may have heard it said that a leader can never show fear. I don't entirely agree.

Yes, as a leader, it is your job to lead. It was my job to lead our staff and faculty and show everyone there that I had full confidence in our future and in our pathway for getting there. As a leader, I know I have to send signals of strength, even when I'm feeling weak, because if the leader is worried, then the whole fabric starts to unravel.

There is a wonderful passage in the book of Exodus that exemplifies this essential quality of leadership. Shortly after bringing the Israelites across the Red Sea, Moses leads his people into a battle where their side is badly outnumbered. The odds are not looking good. Joshua does his best to lead the ground troops, but it is up to Moses to keep the entire operation in motion somehow. The people are scared. The fight looks impossible. Moses is an old man. What can he possibly do?

Standing atop a nearby mountain, he holds his hands in the air. That's it. And that is enough.

The sight of him up there, hands outstretched, keeps the people going. Every time he lowers his hands, the tide of battle starts turning back the other way—so he *has* to keep them airborne. Eventually his arms grow simply too tired to stay up, so he has two aides stand at his sides and literally prop his arms up in the air. The arms never go down, and that unvarying show of support wins the battle.

That is what a leader needs to do.

Still, leaders are human. Here is something else about leadership that my years in business had taught me: When you are frightened, you have to let it show—to *someone*. To a carefully selected, deeply regarded few. Knowing who those few are and being able to fully confide in them—that, too, is leadership. Sometimes, in moments of crisis, you need to reach out to someone you trust, someone you can talk to.

That night, I called Dick Vert, who was the HPU treasurer, chair of our finance committee, and a trusted friend.

"Dick," I said, "we just laid the groundwork on a $50 million building." (It would actually end up costing us $73 million, but $50 million was our current projection.) "You know what's going on out there in the world. The sky is falling. What do you think we should do?"

He asked what I saw as our options.

"Well, we could stop right here, freeze the process in its tracks."

This path would have some pretty serious implications. The brick and steel were already ordered, and it was tons and tons of the stuff. This was a five-story, 277,000-square-foot building, the most massive thing we'd ever built. You can't just call suppliers for something as vast and complex as that and say, "Oh, never mind."

"Or," I continued, "we can go ahead and build the thing."

With borrowed money, I didn't need to add. Dick knew that as well as I did.

"But what if we build it," I added, "and the students don't come? People are losing their 401(k)s, their home equity, their savings. People are losing their net worth. It's a bloodbath out there."

There was a moment's pause on the line. Then, Dick replied:

"Nido, you're building a great school. Look at what you've done. In just three years, you've more than doubled the freshman enrollment."

Which was true: Freshman enrollment had gone from 412 in the fall of 2005, to 870 in our current class.

"Look at what you've done," he repeated, "and think about these students and parents, and how much they love what you're doing. You know what? I think these people are *always* going to send their kids to college. I think they'll find a way. I think college is not a luxury for these people. They're going to send their kids to college no matter what."

"Yeah," I said, "but they could always send them to state schools."

He laughed.

"Yes, they could," he said. "But they won't. Nido, they want the God, family, country values and life skills HPU has become famous for. I think I would keep going."

I didn't sleep a wink that night. The next morning, I got up, dressed for work, and looked at myself in the mirror.

"Okay, then," I said. "We'll just continue on with faithful courage."

A few days later, I met with the full board of trustees and laid out the situation as I saw it. I reviewed the reasons we had launched this project and the investment we'd made so far. I explained the same options I'd described to Dick, though with a bit more detail. Then, I did my best to quantify the risks.

And here was the hard part: It was *all* risk. Going forward meant spending tens of millions more, spending borrowed money to erect a structure that we wouldn't need and certainly wouldn't be able to afford if enrollment should collapse the way the stock market had just done and the global economy was in the process of doing.

But if the students kept coming, then we couldn't afford *not* to build it. We couldn't afford to have our own growth outpace our capacity to that degree because it would create a chaos of crowding that would choke our progress. And what would it look like to have this gigantic expanse of poured concrete sitting smack in the middle of our campus? Would it become a testament to unfulfilled ambitions and unkept promises? A monument to the art of the *impossible*?

We could call an immediate halt, stop construction in its tracks, circle the wagons, and wait out the storm. But what if that threw a wrench in the gears of growth? What if, rather than the safer course, that turned out to be an irreversible act of self-sabotage?

No matter how you turned this thing or from which angle you looked, it was fraught with hazard. We were in perilous territory. Whatever decision we made, it would take both great faith and great courage. *Faithful courage.*

One by one, the trustees spoke, and every one of them supported the idea of moving forward. They echoed sentiments and assessments similar to what Dick had said, and as a board, they voted unanimously to keep going and build that University Center. They had faith in my leadership, and they trusted my presidency. I am eternally grateful.

I brought our executive team together and had everyone go through a contingency budget exercise. If you had to cut 5 percent, what would you do? Where would you cut it, exactly? What about 10 percent? 15 percent? If you had to cut X number of staff from your department, who would you cut? I asked them to identify those people, specifically.

"We can't afford to come back later and make these decisions when we're under the gun," I said. "We have to put ourselves under the gun now."

Each person went through their department, giving the names and positions of the people they'd cut if they were forced to. It was a painful exercise, but these were painful times.

I went to our finance people and asked them to rework our budgets for the following year, starting with a worst-case scenario. Again, paranoid optimism at work.

"What if new enrollment plummets, everyone quits coming to college, and we have to cut our budget to the bone?" I asked them. "Let's start with that, and then budget backward from there."

They came up with five different levels of budget we could fall back on if we needed to, depending on what actual impact the recession would have. (In business, this is typically called *sensitivity modeling*.) It was an immensely complicated planning process, as fine-tuned as a space shuttle launch—but it was necessary.

Once we had a plan in place, at least I could sleep at night.

"I Need to Find New Architects"

As the fall of 2008 ground on and the economic crisis worsened, construction on our new University Center proceeded.

I tapped one of our retired vice presidents, Dr. Roy Epperson, who had served earlier as a chemistry professor. I hired him to serve as a special project coordinator. I met with him every single morning at 7:00 for about ten minutes to discuss whatever phase of construction was going on that day. We threw ourselves into this in a way above and beyond anything we had done before. Every day, I watched the structure taking shape, and every day I reassessed what we were doing to see if it truly expressed the value of *extraordinary*. I still do this today with every project we build. I check the progress daily. On site. Leadership demands that you inspect what you expect.

Now, back to the University Center.

One day, I noticed that the stairs leading down to the lower level were placed fairly close to the front entrance and immediately saw a problem. I'd seen all the details of the plan before, on paper, but this hadn't occurred to me (or anyone else, clearly) until I was standing there looking at it. I found the foreman in charge that day and brought him to the front to show him what I was talking about.

"We can't do it this way," I said. "This doesn't work. We want a big lobby. We want this whole entrance area to be a vast, open space. We want this to be a vaulted entrance hall with soaring glass and sunlight. A space that speaks to endless possibilities, that inspires hope and high aspirations in our students as they walk through the front doors."

The foreman consulted the architects, and he came back to me with their answer.

"They say, structurally, it's impossible," he told me. "They can't do it."

"Then I need to find new architects," I replied.

Within a week, our architects came back with a solution after all. Vaulted entrance with soaring glass and sunlight it would be.

This kept happening. Time and again, I would see some feature in progress and say, "No, wait. Stop. That's not right; we need to move that wall. We need to open up that space. We need to put that function somewhere else."

In the food service area, the architects wanted to place walls that blocked off the space.

"We can't have that," I said. "We want this all open."

They told me that was a problem. They felt the security monitoring the place would prefer the blocked-off space because that would make it easier to check everyone who entered and exited.

"I do care about what they prefer," I responded. "I care about what they think and feel. But I have to tell you, I care a good deal more about how the students feel."

It was that business of primary and secondary again. We were not in the business of building something for the security staff, or the hospitality staff, or the architects. We were constructing a building to take care of our students. With every decision, every choice, every set of options, our primary focus had to be how did we make it an inspiring environment for the people who would eat here, study here, live here?

My discussions with the architects didn't end there. They had drawn up a health clinic on the top floor. I didn't like that either.

"Wait a minute, we can't put a clinic up there," I said. "That could go anywhere. This is beachfront property!"

This spot, on the top floor of this magnificent building, was going to be a unique location, and I knew we needed to do something in this space that would be extraordinary—something we could showcase, something that would make an unforgettable impression. So, I nixed the clinic and mentioned another idea, and we built a larger and better clinic elsewhere on campus.

"Why don't we create a world-class fine-dining restaurant?" I asked.

"Oh, I get it," one of the architects said. "For parents, visitors, potential donors, VIPs like that?"

"No," I said. "For the students, staff, and faculty. And by the way, they *are* VIPs." (Although we don't call them that; we started out doing so but then changed it to VIFs: Very Important *Friends*. I didn't tell the architect that, though. One paradigm shift at a time.)

"We'll put a premium restaurant here and use it as a learning lab, to teach students global protocol and dining etiquette."

I'm not sure whether they thought I was a genius or crazy, but we built the restaurant.

This, of course, became 1924 PRIME, HPU's immersive learning lab that helps students develop business and social etiquette skills and understand global cuisine. The menu features a different international country every month. Just another example of why we're a premier life skills university.

I have no doubt that our architects and contractors thought I was a bit pushy during the whole process. But I wasn't concerned about what was easy or what was the shortest line between two points. We were determined to create an extraordinary experience for our students.

Prior to coming to HPU, I had never been involved in constructing buildings, and I am certainly no architect. But I trust my gut on how a space will make people feel. If architects say, "The wall has to go here," we don't necessarily take their word for it. I know that what they're saying makes sense in architectural terms, but that isn't our principal concern. We care about how the space will make students feel. We wanted to create a space that inspired students appropriately to learn and grow. Not to pamper them, but to prepare them to thrive in an ever-changing, highly competitive global marketplace.

Onward with Faithful Courage

For months, the bad economic news kept rolling in like waves of endless toxic tides. The months of January and February 2009 comprised the worst two-month opening of any year in the history of the Standard & Poor's 500. By March, the Dow Jones had plunged to less than half its former high point in October 2007.

Week after week, we kept our eyes trained on those contingency budget numbers and on every performance indicator—total enrollment, early decision, number of new inquiries, number of campus visitors, cash flow, interest on capital borrowing, budget projections, and actual expenditures. It felt like we couldn't afford to blink. If the numbers didn't hold, we were poised to hit the button and start scaling back.

From October 2008 through the late spring of 2009, we held our breath. By June, we knew.

The storm was still raging out there. Unemployment nationwide would not hit its peak until the start of 2010, and people would be digging out from the financial wreckage for years. But we'd been through the eye of the storm, and our ship was intact.

We never had to go to any of our fallback plans. We never cut a single budget or displaced a single employee. We didn't freeze any salaries; in fact, we gave raises. We were not spendthrifts; we were prudently cautious. Yet, we were able to keep moving forward because the numbers were there. Our parents kept believing in us. Our students kept coming. Not only did enrollment and tuition hold, but the numbers kept going *up*.

The *News & Record*, the daily newspaper in nearby Greensboro, penned an editorial about what they observed happening in High Point in the face of the Great Recession. They wrote: "The economic downturn has wounded higher education, leading to layoffs and halting construction at public and private colleges alike. But someone forgot to tell Nido Qubein."

The editorial pointed out that we had hired thirty-five new faculty and staff members since the first of the year, with stated plans to hire sixty more by August.

Once we got through that first admissions cycle without any ill effects, I realized that we were going to have a few years when everybody else was going to be scared to do anything and this ironically would create an environment that could actually work to our advantage. Much like investors buying into the market when it hits the bottom, it was a situation where a perceived weakness could be used as a strength. Because nobody was building, this meant we could procure materials for less and build at significantly lower cost than we'd originally projected. So yes, in the course of our campus construction, we—that is, I—had added a great deal of extra cost, but this was mitigated in part by the muting effect of the recession in progress.

On campuses around America, construction slammed to a halt. At High Point University, meanwhile, we *accelerated*. It was our version of Warren Buffett's famous investment dictum, "Be greedy when others are fearful; be fearful when others are greedy."

In April 2009, we dedicated the Plato S. Wilson building, whose 60,000 square feet housed a stock trading room with live financial databases such as Standard & Poor's and provided finance and business students with the same technology they would find on the actual stock trading floor in New York. With its Center for Entrepreneurship and Innovation, the academic building would prepare students for careers in marketing, sales, entrepreneurship, operations management, supply chain management, human resource management, and more.

On September 15, 2009, on the one-year anniversary of Lehman Brothers' bankruptcy filing, we opened our brand-new School of Communication. Also 60,000 square feet, this building featured state-of-the-art media and communications technology, including high-definition television studios, audio recording studios, editing suites, computer labs, and a screening room. A gaming studio was later built where students could create and test interactive games. We also added a neuromarketing analysis lab, a podcasting studio, a TV news station, and more. Its new undergraduate majors included electronic media, games and interactive communication, journalism, media and popular culture studies, and organizational communication.

And on October 13, a year almost to the day since that sleepless night when I'd called Dick Vert to ask him what he thought we should do, we held the dedication of the new University Center. Today, it is named for Ron Wanek, the founder of Ashley Furniture Industries and the grandfather of four HPU graduates.

"We Chose Not to Participate"

In the fall of 2010, at our annual community leader luncheon in mid-September, two years after Lehman Brothers went belly-up and I had begun losing sleep over our fiscal future, we announced a plan for additional new growth by 2020 that totaled more than $2 billion. Bold indeed!

In the five years from 2005 to 2010, High Point University had increased in size from 91 to 230 acres and built $300 million in new construction, including fifteen new buildings and two stadiums. We had built a brand-new building for our School of Business, and we had established the School of Communication.

Our freshman class, which had grown from 412 to 870 by the fall of 2008 when the economy started to crash, stood at 1,210. Freshman inquiries, at 14,000 in 2005, had risen to more than 42,000. With retention up from 70 percent to 85 percent, all these numbers spoke to a robust continued growth in our student body.

"Skeptics wonder how long we can keep this up," I told our assembled group of friends and community leaders. "But here is what they do not understand: We are not just flying on blind luck and chutzpah."

There was a ripple of laughter at that one. Everyone present remembered a headline that had appeared in the local paper way back in February 2005, a month after I arrived: "Qubein's Chutzpah Pays Off."

"No," I said, "we are following strong business fundamentals. We are not simply building new construction. We are building appreciated *value*. And to the skeptics and the naysayers?"

I waved one hand toward a window in a dismissive gesture, as if to say, *So what?*

"We heard there was a recession. We chose not to participate."

As for the low discount rate HPU had, it was increased as we sought to increase diversity on campus and help more students who needed financial aid. Today, of the $80 million in aid, much of it is need based. And our unfunded discount rate is at over 30 percent. Interestingly, our inquiries surpass 200,000 annually, and freshman applications alone are more than 17,000.

A Pandemic Response

In March 2020, I was scared—again. As I mentioned earlier, leaders need not be afraid to show fear. Leaders are humans, and when you are frightened, you have to confide in someone you trust. That, too, is leadership. So, when we had to tell our students to stay home after spring break to take their classes online because of a global pandemic, I confided with my vice presidents that I feared many students might not return in the fall. In the middle of the pandemic, we refunded students more than $17 million in room-and-board fees, and I had begun hearing horror stories from other colleges and universities about their worries about staying financially solvent. So, we knew we had to act; I had to focus. I cleared my decks of everything and began digging into what we needed to do—and what we had to do. I've heard it said that courage is really fear saying its prayers. Oh, I prayed. I prayed a lot. I got on my knees and prayed to God Almighty to give us the wisdom to help HPU get through this. Then, my team and I began working harder than any other time in my life.

And that's saying something.

When I was twenty-three, I rented a room in an old man's house and sustained myself on peanuts and TV dinners as I started my first business from scratch. I also taught a three-hour class at a local community college and created my first publication, *Adventures with Youth*, a newsletter to assist youth leaders to create successful programs for young people. I pored through telephone books trying to find customers and typed labels on a typewriter using two fingers. After two years, I had thousands of customers in thirty-two countries. I *believe* in the art of the possible. And I'm grateful for my faith.

I've told people that is the hardest I've ever worked. But this work—finding a way to help High Point University survive the pandemic—was much harder. I was dealing with the deadly respiratory illness known as COVID-19 that threatened the livelihood of our employees and students and the future of our school. I brainstormed daily with our vice presidents and deans, talked frequently to university presidents and others I knew in higher education, and asked for guidance from our experts at Novant Health, a medical network partner headquartered in nearby Winston-Salem.

I also asked God for grace.

I hated what had happened to our students, that they had to stay home in the middle of their semester and miss their classes, their friends, their graduation, their everything. I wanted to come up with something that showed our students we cared about them and their future. Then, I had one of those moments that come out of the blue while I'm shaving or showering and letting my mind roam.

"Why don't we offer every student a fifth-year master's degree in Communication and Business Leadership? Tuition free! As a gift for their suffering and as a gesture of our caring?"

I broached the idea with Dr. Virginia McDermott, dean of our School of Communication, and Dr. Jim Wehrley, then the dean of the School of Business. They quickly helped craft the program and get its accreditation approved. We sent a letter to our seniors, and 240 students quickly enrolled. We started to gain momentum, and I could feel it.

That spring, we created the HPU Cares Fund, and in its first month, the initiative received more than 682 gifts and nearly $1 million from families and individuals impacted and transformed by HPU in some way. Contributions ranged from $25 to more than $50,000. Like I do often with our staff and faculty, I filmed a series of videos to keep in touch and keep them calm. Me too.

"These are times when we have to forget about all the things we must do and think about the things we must be," I said in the video to our employees that spring. "We need to think, 'Who must I become in a time like this?'

"We need to reach out with both hands to support our brothers and sisters in this world, and we as a university, as an academic institution, must continue our service to our students. We must keep our school open."

That fall, the students responded. They believed in us. As private university enrollment dropped by an average of 14.2 percent nationwide, we at High Point University had a 5.6 percent increase in our enrollment. We welcomed 5,617 students—our largest enrollment in the university's history.

We had a full house. That included 1,000 graduate students, the largest graduate enrollment in the university's history. Meanwhile, our team rose to a level of excellence. We knew some students would test positive for COVID-19. To think otherwise would be naïve. But we had ample resources, continuous education, and faithful courage to manage these cases with love and compassion.

We commissioned a Health and Safety Task Force, chaired by our provost, Dr. Dan Erb. They crafted a multipronged approach to mitigate the risk and to create a protocol that would provide a medical safety net for the sick and the well.

That approach included a new student health center, a new full-time medical doctor, a new quarantine area for sick students, and a slew of new precautions on campus—from mandating masks to requiring daily health checks through a monitoring app. And the many signs. So many signs. The #KEEPHPUHEALTHY reminders were everywhere.

We asked students to wear masks on campus and follow all other protocols on campus. Then came the contact tracing, spearheaded by Gail Tuttle, then the senior vice president for HPU's Office of Student Life, and guided by health education from Johns Hopkins University. To complement these efforts, we recruited what we called HPU Health Heroes. This on-campus group reminded students they saw unmasked and standing too close to others to keep physically distanced and to put on a mask to be safe.

By the time students moved back to campus, there were 56 faculty members, 71 staff members, and 186 students who were Health Heroes. Grand total: 313. That number only grew.

We also created a command center staffed around the clock. If a quarantined or isolated student emailed and needed anything—from seeing a doctor to needing an iPhone cable—they received a response within three minutes. Meanwhile, a fleet of campus volunteers carried to the students in quarantine their meals, mail, and school supplies.

Cases rose as high as 170 on a campus that hosted 7,600 students, faculty, and staff. But at a time when a global pandemic had closed colleges and universities nationwide and sent students home to take classes online, we remained on campus. By the end of the fall semester, we had survived. We had made it. We had help.

HPU families, alumni, and other supporters contributed more than $30 million to help us weather our country's biggest public health crisis in a century. Meanwhile, we spent $17 million out of an annual university budget of $300 million on pandemic-related measures.

And of course, I made a point to walk around campus every day. I did that before the pandemic, slipping into The Café to talk to students and our employees. But during the pandemic, I slipped on my purple HPU mask and talked with students, staff, and faculty about how they were doing. I wanted to make sure they felt safe and secure.

In my Happy New Year video message to students, families, and alumni, I could barely contain my excitement. I told them: "Thank you, dear friends, for standing beside us through thick and thin, pandemic and all. Your university is going places and making a difference, and you've helped it make a difference in America and in the world."

By the spring of 2021, no more than thirty or so students, faculty, and staff had been diagnosed with COVID-19. As vaccines nationwide became available, those numbers dropped to one or two COVID-positive cases out of 8,000 faculty, staff, and students. A miracle. I breathed a sigh of relief. We had learned much about ourselves and the relationship of our university to thousands of people. We also learned we needed to believe we can do what's necessary to pull us forward and move in a direction that says, "All things are possible for those who have faith."

As fears of the pandemic reemerged in the fall, we employed the same protocols of maintaining space at eight nearby hotels to house quarantined students, to deliver food, provide nurse supervision, and ensure their virtual attendance in all their classes. Through it all, our faculty and staff demonstrated the ultimate levels of commitment, and our parents were trusting and patient.

What I saw happening around me reminded me of a quote I sent our faculty and staff a few weeks before Christmas 2020. It's from Mother Angelica, the entrepreneurial Catholic nun from Alabama who used $200 to create the world's largest religious media network at a monastery in Birmingham, Alabama. She said: "Faith is what gets you started. Hope is what keeps you going. Love is what brings you to the end."

I do believe that with all my heart. Always will.

CHAPTER 10

Aim Beyond Success to Significance

I t was a perfect North Carolina Wednesday, 80 degrees and not a cloud in the sky.

Hundreds had gathered here on campus, including the mayor of High Point and the governor of North Carolina, to mark the official groundbreaking of our health sciences and pharmacy building complex, HPU's most ambitious project to date.

"Ten years ago, High Point University had a dream," I told the assembled crowd. "And now, we're living that dream, day after day. This, what we're witnessing today, is what happens when you believe in the fundamental principles that built this country.

"This, what you're seeing here, is the American Dream made manifest."

It was September 9, 2015, exactly one decade since city leaders strolled into the nearby fine arts building and saw blown-up posters of our expansion plans while trumpeters blew a royal fanfare.

Quite a full-circle moment.

Many of the city leaders present that Wednesday had been here ten years earlier, and they appreciated the historic resonance without me having to point it out. What the assembled crowd did *not* see was the enormous sigh of relief I gave (in my mind, not outwardly!) as I spoke. Because getting here had been a journey that at times felt like a 50K race across an active minefield—in a hailstorm. As one area newspaper put it, "The project was not completely pain-free."

That's the understatement of the decade.

Yes, we survived the economic crisis of 2008 and 2009 intact, even coming out of it stronger. And yes, by 2013, when that annual *U.S. News & World Report* survey ranked us No. 1 in our class, our strategies had proven themselves and our numbers offered undeniable evidence that our plan was clearly working. We had outlasted the critics, and we had not just survived but thrived. We had triumphed; we had arrived. If this were a movie, that 2015 achievement might have been the final crowning moment just before the closing credits.

But living, breathing reality doesn't work that way. Just because we'd hit our numbers and proven our critics wrong did not mean all our challenges were behind us. In fact, they kept on coming, harder than ever, and the pathway to that sunny September day in 2015 had taken us through perhaps our biggest and most difficult battle yet.

Our New Focus

It started five years earlier in September 2010. I announced our intention to build a new building (then at an estimated cost of $50 million) to house two new schools, a School of Health Sciences and School of Pharmacy. Really, it started two years earlier than that because this announcement itself marked the culmination of two years of quiet preparation.

Establishing a new academic school is an enormous undertaking: You have to create curricula, attract new faculty, build the physical structure that houses it, bring in the necessary technology, enroll students, and secure accreditation. It's no wonder that it normally takes years and years to fund a new academic school. In this case, part of our preparation involved lining up agreements for our future students for clinical residency placements at medical organizations across the region. We hired a dean for our still-nonexistent School of Health Sciences and a director for our not-yet-launched physical therapy program. Both came from Duke University. We began laying the foundation for a major new funding and staffing drive. The programs these schools would offer would also mean hiring anywhere from 50 to 100 new staff and faculty.

This was a new area of focus for us. For the first five years I was at HPU, we had focused on building and strengthening our core undergraduate program, and we had not put a high priority on building our graduate studies. Now, we were ready. We had about 325 graduate students, and our original goal was to grow that to 1,000. Once these new programs were up and running, they would educate 1,500 new students or more a year—and some would be earning doctoral degrees, a first for High Point University. Today, we enroll 1,000 students in a dozen graduate programs.

As part of our preparation, we applied for authorization from the Southern Association of Colleges and Schools Commission on Colleges to be able to offer doctoral degrees. By the fall semester of 2010, we had our plan in place. We had the money. All the logistical preparation was well underway. So, we made the announcement.

The question now was, where did we put it?

We began looking at Oak Hollow Mall, a relatively modest mall sited about a mile and a half north of us. The economic downturn had not been kind to Oak Hollow Mall. Stores shuttered and remained closed, including a Circuit City and a Goody's department store. What remained was a Dillard's and a Sears. Neither store generated a lot of traffic.

We hired engineers, experts who knew malls inside and out, to give us a feasibility study. They reported back and told us what we had in mind was entirely doable there. The plan was greenlit. In February 2011, we bought the mall for $9 million and announced our intentions to locate a new graduate school campus there.

This, though, did not exactly work out as planned.

Throughout 2011 and 2012, we worked on our plans for the mall. In the summer of 2012, we hired a dean from the highly ranked pharmacy school at the University of Kansas. In November 2012, we unveiled our new Biomechanics and Human Physiology Lab in the former Circuit City building. The lab became one of the most sophisticated of its kind in the country. It featured a DEXA scanner for measuring bone density; an anti-gravity treadmill; a 24-camera, 360-degree motion analysis system; and an environmental simulation chamber that could be set to any climate and altitude parameters. It was truly breathtaking.

Yet despite all the progress, we had a problem.

Here was what the team of engineers could not have predicted—the human factor. Try as we might, we could not persuade the people at Dillard's to sell us their property (which they still own). The same was happening with the people at Sears (who also owned their property). I just couldn't see having a graduate school campus with a Sears and a Dillard's plopped in its middle. And I could not go on negotiating and keeping our construction plans on hold forever. We'd already put so much time and energy, money, and resources into the project. We had to build some-where, and we had to find that somewhere soon.

A strategy devoid of back-up plans is no strategy at all. I'd known from the start that the mall location was not a certainty, and I had several other options tucked away in the back of my mind, though I hadn't discussed any of them yet with anyone. Now, it was discussion time.

In March 2013, we announced plans to build the health sciences build-ing right on our existing campus. We could no longer wait on the Oak Hollow Mall. I assured city leaders and members of the press that we would not be shopping for any new land for the building. "Our land-buying days are behind us," I said. "We're comfortable with the size we are." (At this point we were at about 4,000 resident undergraduate students, which was 80 percent of the way to our goal of 5,000.) Rather than locate at the mall, we would build the 220,000-square-foot building on the northwestern edge of the campus on an existing parcel of land right next door to one of our athletic centers.

That didn't quite work out, either.

We soon realized that this site just wouldn't suit this purpose, for a variety of logistical reasons. In fact, the only location that would work was a spot on the opposite side of the campus, right at the southern edge, just south of the Plato Wilson building.

Except that this presented a whole new problem.

Montlieu Avenue, which at this point defined the southern border of our property, cut right through there, between the parking lot immediately behind the Wilson School and the southern parcel of land where we were now considering placing the new building. Not good. Having our campus sliced in half by a main thoroughfare, with our new Health Sciences and Pharmacy Schools hanging off the southern end like a severed limb? That was no more acceptable than having the place right next door to a department store. The only way this could possibly work for us would be if we could persuade the city and the state to close this section of Montlieu Avenue altogether, at which point we would prepare it for sinking the footings and pouring the foundation for our new building.

Except that Montlieu Avenue was not like the little streets we had absorbed during our earlier expansion. This was a state road, a major thoroughfare that connected the city from one end to the other. Closing a main thoroughfare meant we would need to negotiate with the citizens of High Point.

This was going to be difficult.

Our relationship with the civic and business leaders of High Point had been strong from the start. From the mayor to prominent nonprofit leaders to local CEOs, key community leaders were all enthusiastically on board with our plans. But the population itself? The citizenry, the neighbors, our friends, and townspeople at large? That had been a more delicate proposition.

As one city councilwoman was quoted in the local paper as saying, "I think [things with HPU] got off to a little bit of a rocky start."

For example, with our baseball stadium scoreboard.

The Challenge of a Billboard

Back in May 2006, with the inspiring words from Queen Noor's commencement speech still echoing in the ears of students and parents streaming away from campus for summer vacation, we began building our new baseball stadium. There had been a baseball field there already, but it was fairly primitive, the sort of field where you had to move the numbers on the scoreboard with a big stick. We wanted a professional quality field, complete with a big scoreboard driven by the latest technology.

We opened the stadium a year later, in the spring of 2007, and it looked like a million bucks. Which is no coincidence, because that's about what it cost then—plus another half million for its state-of-the art electronic, computer-operated scoreboard. And that thing looked *fantastic*.

It looked fantastic until you drove around behind that big board and looked at it from the back. All the mechanics of its operation were plainly visible and, frankly, it wasn't very attractive. We thought, why don't we cover up those ugly mechanics with a nice big picture? We drew up a beautiful poster showing three of our smiling students wearing HPU T-shirts and sweatshirts, in front of an American flag and an HPU flag, bordered by the slogan "Choose to Be Extraordinary" below and "High Point University" above. Patriotic, inspirational, attractive. We learned that even though this was on our own land, we needed to get an additional permit from the city to put up a large poster because it was visible to our neighbors. We applied for the correct permit.

And then all hell broke loose.

There was one neighbor who could see the new board from his house, and he refused to let us put the picture up there. The city council sided with him. So did some other residents. Others piled on. For the next six months, it became a highly publicized stand-off, with newspaper editorials and readers weighing in through the letters to the editor columns. People talked about it and argued about it all over town. For some disgruntled citizens, it became a *cause célèbre*, the focal point of a civic drama.

Soon, I found myself pouring dozens of hours into the dialogue.

Why, you might be wondering. How important was this, really? Why would a university president fritter away so much time into winning the right to put up a billboard on the back of a baseball scoreboard? For me, it became a matter of principle. I knew that if we backed down on this one, it would be that much harder to prevail on any other important issue in the future. And if our neighbors opposed us successfully on this, they might oppose us on many future projects. There were far too many important challenges ahead of us. We couldn't afford to let this set a precedent of weakness or misunderstanding. We needed a reasonable solution.

What's more, I genuinely believed that this was the right decision, not only for us but for the city, too. For our neighbors. For *everyone*. We weren't talking about putting up an eyesore. We were talking about taking an existing eyesore and making it look positive and attractive.

I met with the neighbor who had the objection, talking with him as persuasively and graciously as I knew how. He was still dead set against it. I met with him a few more times. He remained steadfast in his opposition.

Okay, that wasn't going to work.

Next, I invited one city council member to come take a drive in my car. I drove her by the place, pulled to the side of the road, and stopped the car. We turned and looked up at the board together.

"Look at that thing," I said.

We could plainly see all the board's machinery; it was like staring under the hood of your car or looking at the back of a television set with the cover removed. It was, in a word, ugly.

Then, I pulled out a matted reproduction of the picture we wanted to put up there.

"This is what we propose," I said. "We want to honor the American flag and show how these young people are the pillars of tomorrow."

I didn't have to say the next point, because it was obvious: *How could this picture possibly be worse than that ugly display of circuitry and mechanics?*

I invited another council member to take the same drive. And another. And all the rest, too.

Finally, in February 2009, nearly two years after we first unveiled the stadium and its scoreboard, the council took another vote on the question.

Our baseball-sign poster slipped through like the narrowest of Supreme Court victories: 5 to 4.

Over the years that followed, as we continued to build and grow, we found ourselves in this position again and again—negotiating with neighbors and townsfolk, going before the city council, and waiting like expectant fathers outside the delivery room to hear the outcome of their vote. Again and again, we squeaked by on decisions that went in our favor by a margin of a single vote. It was always our intention to respect our neighbors and to honor their concerns. Growth demands change, and change creates discomfort.

But in all those years, we'd never yet tried to close a main thoroughfare.

God's Grace

By mid-2013, we had completely ruled out the former options and decided to press ahead in our efforts to locate our new health sciences building (now at an estimated cost of $100 million) on the land south of the School of Business. That decision meant we needed to secure permission to do something big.

Close Montlieu Avenue.

Our first step was to go to the state level. We went to the governor's office and the N.C. Department of Transportation in Raleigh, North Carolina, and explained our situation. They told us if it was fine with the city of High Point, it was fine with them.

Okay. Big breath. Time to meet with the city.

We met with the city council in small groups and showed them what we wanted to do, why it was important to the city, how many students it would attract to the school, and what important levels of economic impact it would have on the city.

Then, we explained the alternative, the most radical alternative yet—leave High Point altogether and go to the neighboring city of Greensboro or Winston-Salem and build our schools of pharmacy and health sciences there.

At the time, there were only three pharmacy schools in all of North Carolina, and none of them were located in the Piedmont Triad, a seventeen-county region in central North Carolina of 1.7 million people. Having our region's only pharmacy school would be an exceptional draw that would benefit its host city in all sorts of way. Which of the three Triad cities would they rather see all that benefit accruing to—Greensboro? Winston-Salem? Or High Point?

This was a persuasive argument, especially when we heard that the other cities wanted it. We could see that at least some of the city council members were leaning our way. However, they told us that this would need to go before a public meeting prior to their vote, to give High Point residents a chance to object and the council members a chance to consider those objections.

And object they did.

We started getting slammed with phone calls, people posting online, and angry letters to the editor in the local papers. It was the baseball scoreboard all over again, only at a whole new level. This time, it wasn't just a question of aesthetics that people were worried about. Residents were concerned that shutting down this thoroughfare would change traffic patterns in ways that would hurt the city and be incredibly inconvenient to them personally. And what if police or fire trucks had to get through, and now they suddenly had to reroute? How would city services be able to respond to emergencies? All legitimate concerns and fair questions.

Of course, we had already talked with the fire department, police department, and ambulance services. They all carefully studied the whole situation, and we knew this would not be a logistical problem for them. Still, we also knew that people absolutely would be inconvenienced because they no longer could get from North University Parkway over to Main Street by zipping out on Montlieu. If we got our way, that section of road would be closed, and they would be forced to take another route. Conceivably, it could take you a mile or more out of your way.

The controversy raged for weeks. We understood the pain it would cause and the options it would test. We respected the spirit of the concerns and worked hard to balance our neighbors' needs and the growth of the university.

On a Monday evening in January 2014, the public meeting finally happened. The only reason people had for attending was to oppose the plan, and we knew that whoever showed up would be against it. More than 350 people came.

For the first thirty minutes or so, I talked about how and why I came to America, what High Point meant to me, and the role we wanted our university to play in our city.

I laid out exactly what we planned to do as fully and as objectively as I could. I then laid out what was at stake for the city of High Point.

"Now, we don't have to do this," I said. "In fact, it would in some ways be more advantageous for us to locate this pharmacy school in Greensboro because then we would attract support from a whole new community. Or in Winston-Salem, because then we would attach to the prestige of Wake Forest University. We have even looked into ways we might loosely affiliate the new school with Wake Forest.

"But that's not what we really want. What we really want is to locate it right here in High Point—because we believe in High Point," I continued. "We are High Point residents ourselves, and at the risk of making a less favorable business decision, I would rather keep it here out of loyalty to my community. To do this, though, we need your support.

"I am not naïve. I do not expect all of you to agree with what I'm saying. And we *know* that this will inconvenience some of you. We *know* that you would rather we not do this. But we're asking you to go along with this plan because it will help us grow our university, and in the long run this will only benefit the city of High Point, economically and socially."

City Manager Strib Boynton stood up and thoughtfully told the crowd that they had studied the proposed change carefully. It currently took ambulances about seven minutes to get from the vicinity of High Point Regional Hospital to the city's Five Points area. They had conducted test runs using the alternate routes that Montlieu's closure would necessitate and found that those rerouted runs came out to about—dramatic pause here—seven minutes. Their conclusion: Response time for police, fire, and EMS crews would not be affected by the closure. What's more, he said, there were fire stations on both sides of the proposed closure, and since firefighters are typically the first on the scene at emergency calls, that amounted to an additional layer of assurance that the public's safety would not be compromised in any way.

It was not an easy event. Emotions ran high. A few key staff and I stayed after the meeting to talk with individuals for as long as they wanted to, which proved to be a fairly extended time. In the next morning's edition of the local paper, thrive as they do on controversy, they printed quotes from those who were most vocally against it.

The city council met. One member happened to be out that day, so there was not going to be any 5-to-4 split for us this time. What would happen if the vote came to a tie?

As it turned out, we needn't have worried. The council voted 8 to 0 to close Montlieu Avenue.

Thank you, Lord.

In July 2014, after the six months it took to work out details of the transfer, that segment of the road was finally closed to the public and officially became property of High Point University. We brought in the jackhammers and soon the road disappeared, and what remained was a bare patch of land. And one year later, on a hot and cloudless September day, we were celebrating the building's newly poured foundation—and I was breathing a silent sigh of relief.

There we all were—Gov. Pat McCrory, High Point Mayor Bill Bencini, and me, as well as hundreds of supporters.

"This is what happens when you believe in the fundamentals and principles that built this country," I told the crowd in front of me. "This day is another page in our history book because when you make the right choices and have God's grace as your guide in all you do, good things happen."

Today, neighbors are satisfied that we collectively made a good decision to grow the university. Furthermore, they now benefit from a Pro Bono Physical Therapy Clinic as well as our pharmacy students and our physician assistants volunteering across our city.

All good things. With God's grace.

Why I Said "Yes"

Let me revisit briefly the purpose of this whole adventure, and why I embarked on this mission in the first place. Today, friends still ask, "What made you do it?"

In 2004, I had a successful career going at full stride. The academic world was not even remotely on my radar as a career choice. Why did I give up everything I was doing to undertake this unlikely journey?

The answer comes down to a single word: impact.

There's no question that it's all been quite rewarding with the challenges we've had to face and the mountains we've had to climb. I cannot deny it, I love the thrill of the chase and the exhilaration of confronting what seem like impossible odds. There are few endeavors I cherish as much as the pursuit of "impossible" aims to a successful conclusion.

Yet, it is about more than just success.

If success were what drives me, then I would likely have stuck to the career path I was on in 2004, and when the unexpected offer of the president's chair came, I would have replied, "Thank you so much, but I must decline." Or, if I had said yes purely for the challenge of taking a few years out to effect a brisk turnaround in this entirely unfamiliar setting—which was, let's face it, what I *thought* I was doing at the time—then I would have stepped down by 2007, or 2010, or surely by 2013, once the ball was rolling and our success was assured.

Yet, it isn't about success alone. It is about *success and significance*.

Which brings me back to the biomechanics lab at Oak Hollow Mall.

A Better Quality of Life

As we shut down the facility and began moving all our programs of instruction over to the new health sciences complex on campus, we repurposed the fully equipped building left behind toward a new mission: a community rehabilitation clinic that would offer pro bono physical therapy and rehabilitation treatment to community residents.

HPU's Pro Bono Clinic sets our Doctor of Physical Therapy (DPT) program apart from others nationwide.

Patients can come in without having insurance or seeing a doctor, and since opening in December 2017, the clinic has seen thousands of patients. Many of the patients who come illustrate the growing diversity of North Carolina.

They speak eighteen different languages and come from thirty-five different countries. At the clinic, HPU graduate students earning a doctorate in physical therapy take care of them. Under the guidance of local licensed physical therapists and a clinician at the clinic, small teams of DPT graduate students see patients. They spend one day a week at the clinic for three semesters before they start full-time clinic rotations nationwide.

Meanwhile, our undergraduate students assist those patients in every way possible from checking their blood pressure to giving them food grown in our community garden behind the clinic. Reserved for the clinic's patients, the clinic's food pantry helps them eat healthier. A poor diet, which leads to poor health, leads to more stress-related illnesses.

But that's not all. Elementary, middle school, and high school student groups get the chance to tour the clinic and be exposed to STEM (science, technology, engineering, math) topics and careers in health care.

I think of the clinic—and what we've done five minutes from campus at the Oak Hollow Mall—as incredibly ironic. We dealt with the dustup over the baseball scoreboard, the closing of Montlieu Avenue, and every other skirmish and struggle we've gone through with some members of the community. In the final analysis, we have always aimed our own development toward the goal of serving the people of High Point.

I hear that from the patients we serve and the students who volunteer at the Pro Bono Clinic.

A part-time cashier from High Point in her fifties was suffering from a pinching pain in her lower back. She has no insurance. So, she came to the clinic.

"I'm glad to have this," she tells our doctor. "I'm tired of the pain."

A resident from Salisbury, North Carolina, a small city an hour south of campus, came to the clinic after he suffered a significant stroke in 2017 on the night of his twenty-eighth birthday. He had to use a wheelchair to get around. Today, he's beginning to walk.

"Look at me," he says to the physical therapy students helping him. "I'm able to walk and drive better because of everyone here. These students are like brothers and sisters to me."

The clinic opened his eyes to how he could discover a better quality of life.

Sowing Seeds, Greatness Taking Root

Since 2005, HPU has grown measurably and responsibly. Our freshman class alone is now larger than the entire traditional undergraduate student body was when I first assumed office. We have invested almost $3 billion in the past eighteen years. In the midst of the recession and a global pandemic, this extraordinary university continued to fulfill its vast potential. We founded ten new schools. We've hired talented academics and quadrupled the size of our faculty, our campus, and our number of students. As of 2023, we have constructed 108 new and renovated buildings and expanded our campus from 91 acres to more than 550 acres. But High Point University is more than just bricks and mortar, and our national rankings among our peers tells us that. Since 2013, we've been ranked No. 1 by *U.S. News & World Report* among the Regional Colleges in the South, and Princeton Review has named us as one of the country's top 386 institutions.

We didn't tackle this vast change because we were impatient. We tackled this vast change because we didn't believe that incremental changes would lead to substantive results. We also didn't believe that transactional behaviors would lead to the kind of significant growth that would carry this university upward now and into the future.

That kind of change has attracted attention. Week after week, we have the representatives from more than 400 universities come visit us and ask us questions. Lots of questions.

How did you do it all?

How did you raise the necessary funds?

How did you grow your brand so quickly?

How did you plan and complete so many projects so fast and so well?

How did you get the support of your board of trustees?

There are no easy answers. The miracle is in the mix: a clear vision, a solid strategy, practical systems, and a stubbornness to execute consistently.

The magic of what we have accomplished lies in the phrase I mentioned earlier. It's "intentional congruence." That means everyone in the HPU family—stellar faculty, committed staff, engaged students, supportive parents, visionary trustees, generous alumni, and helpful city residents and officials—all fully understood where we were headed and why we were going there. They then wholeheartedly supported our mission with their ideas, involvement, and stewardship.

I'll always remember a particular Wednesday in May 2021. I was sitting in the front row of Callicutt Auditorium, in Congdon Hall, with a big smile across my face as I listened to our dental medicine dean talk about the excitement of founding the only private university school of dental medicine in North Carolina. Our investment will involve creating 300 jobs in our home in the Piedmont Triad. When the dentistry enrollment reaches its full capacity, we will have nearly 270 students attending a school located on campus in what we call our Innovation Corridor, a $450 million section of campus.

Not a penny will be borrowed to build our School of Dental Medicine. Nor will we borrow any funds to construct academic buildings for law, nursing, optometry, or the School of Entrepreneurship.

Or for our new residential and Student Life facilities.

Or our new library.

Since announcing the initiatives, three families blessed HPU with $140 million in philanthropic gifts and paid their commitments within eighteen months.

I do believe when God breathed life into our nostrils, He intended for all of us to do something worthwhile. We at HPU know we have to do our part in preparing tomorrow's leaders and creating a better future. We believe in planting seeds of greatness in the minds, hearts, and souls of our students. As I write these words, we are playing a leading role in revitalizing downtown High Point. Our relationship with the city of High Point has steadily improved, strengthened, and deepened over the years. It was always our intention, from Day One, for this to be not simply High Point University but High *Point's* University. Transformation creates opportunity. Not just for the university, but for the city itself.

And there's no better example of that than what now exists just five minutes from campus—a growing and energetic downtown.

CHAPTER 11

"Let's Play Some Baseball"

I wake up very early every morning and brew a strong cup of Turkish coffee. Then, I sit down for my Me Time. I read somewhere that a writer calls this time in our day our "white space." It's that time you set aside to add clarity to your life. For me, it's time way before daybreak when I read, research, and fill notepad pages with ideas of what needs to be done next at High Point University. And of course, I pray. There are some days I've gotten down on my knees and prayed for guidance because what I was about to do felt so much bigger than I could ever be. I did just that on a Wednesday morning in May 2017 because I was slated to speak at the annual meeting of the High Point Convention and Visitors Bureau at the High Point Country Club. I needed to find the right words because I knew I had to persuade my fellow citizens that we needed to go in a new direction in our beloved city. And with whatever I said, it boiled down to four of the most important words you can ever say, "I need your help."

> *Dear God,*
> *Please do not let my emotions take over this morning. Please do*
> *not let my preferences obscure and dominate the realities of our*
> *community. Let my words move the hearts, minds, and souls of*

the people I see. May they influence our citizens and energize our
city. This is their home. This is my home too.

A few hours later, I walked onstage flanked by several American flags. Ever since I came to America as a teenager, I have believed in what the flag represents, and that morning, I wanted to talk about the ingenuity, personal initiative, and private enterprise that have made our country great. I knew what I was about to say would surprise almost everyone in that audience, especially local attorneys Doyle Early and Aaron Clinard, chairmen of Forward High Point; and Tim Mabe, president and CEO of the High Point Convention and Visitors Bureau. They had come to me earlier asking me to endorse the idea of building a downtown baseball stadium, their "catalyst project," which would bring a professional baseball team to High Point.

But what they really needed me to do was more than just endorse. They boldly asked me to finance and negotiate the purchase of the baseball team, which was needed as an anchor tenant, and they asked me to secure the naming rights for the stadium. These were the two necessary components to ensure financing of the project through bonds.

In the President's Seminar on Life Skills, which I teach every fall to all HPU freshmen, I tell students that commitment involves feeling as well as thinking, and when I see their quizzical looks, I tell them to think of this math equation: Thoughts + Feelings = Action. And at the CVB meeting that day, action was needed. I've always believed that a thriving university like HPU needs a thriving downtown to create jobs, enhance economic impact, keep some graduates in our city, and create inspiration for our entire region.

Building a Better Future

When I arrived in High Point in 1968, downtown was alive. I was a student at then High Point College, studying human relations and working at the High Point YMCA, creating for its Camp Cherrio a newsletter known as the *Bugle*. I was a budding entrepreneur, full of ideas and fresh from earning an associate degree from Mount Olive College. I enjoyed going downtown, and I found High Point's Main Street full of activity. Retail shops lined city blocks, and furniture companies all around downtown gave High Point its manufacturing muscle that earned the city its nickname—Home Furnishings Capital of the World.

Then came the North American Free Trade Agreement. It took effect in January 1994 and eliminated the barriers of trade and investment between the United States, Canada, and Mexico, and reduced the cost of commerce. Known as NAFTA, the agreement spurred investment and growth. Furniture company CEOs realized that to compete, they had to save on labor costs by manufacturing their products beyond our country's borders. So many were forced to source their products outside High Point. It was outsource or die.

I always saw High Point as my home city, and Mariana and I have created a life here. Given the scope of my international work, we could have moved to any city in the country, but we chose to stay in High Point. Mariana and I both graduated from High Point College, we are both immigrants, and we grew to love this city. We were raising our four children in High Point and worshiping at Wesley Memorial United Methodist Church and getting involved in local organizations.

I was privileged to serve as the director or chairman of many nonprofits in High Point. In fact, at one point, I even chaired both the High Point Chamber of Commerce and the High Point Economic Development Corporation, and since 1994, I had been a member of the board of trustees at High Point University. There was no question in my mind that the city and the university could work together to build a better future for all.

Taking Bold Steps

As I stood onstage at the High Point Country Club, I felt my emotions well up inside me. I don't remember exactly what I said, but I do know how I wanted the audience to feel. I wanted them to feel my love for the city of High Point, and how this community—our home, my home—could be transformed in a wonderful way if we all worked together, with faithful courage, toward a common goal. And it could all start with Forward High Point's goal of building a baseball stadium.

But I wasn't thinking about just baseball and a baseball stadium. I was thinking about apartments and a hotel, a park and a playground, a children's museum, and an events center.

Before that speech, I had already talked to my friends, the developers Roy Carroll and Chris Dunbar, to inquire about their interest in investing in downtown High Point. I knew our mayor and our city council were ready to take some bold steps. They were ready to help. Roy agreed to build a hotel in downtown High Point, and Chris wanted to build at least 200 apartments around the ballpark. Also, after talking with both Tim Mabe and Doyle Early, I knew I had to sell this idea because both Tim and Doyle told me more than 50 percent of our citizens didn't support building a baseball stadium—yet. Tim and Doyle heard it constantly, "Why do you need a baseball team when neighboring Greensboro *and* Winston-Salem both have one?" I knew I had to convince those in the audience not to get hung up on baseball. This was bigger than baseball. It was about High Point's future. So, like I had during my time at High Point University, I felt this urgency, this responsibility to act.

That morning, I told the crowd of 500 leaders that I pledged to put together an ownership group for the professional baseball team and sell the naming rights for the proposed $35 million multipurpose stadium downtown. I also pledged to raise $50 million in private funds to help build a hotel and apartments and $38 million to build a children's museum, an events center, and a park. I told the audience we would raise all that in private donations and investments in four months.

I had become bullish about our city's future because I saw people of impact and influence willing to step up and step out to make High Point a better place to live, work, worship, and play. I saw that energy with Forward High Point and the city council and staff. They all cared deeply about High Point, and in 2016, they quietly went about buying twenty-five properties in downtown so the city could build a multipurpose stadium for baseball, soccer, lacrosse, and big events on eleven acres off Elm Street. I was honored to join their effort and help create what we all believed needed to happen—to encourage more development downtown.

I brought up the earlier construction of the Slane Student Center. But I failed to talk about its origins. It dated back to 2005, when I drove Marsha and Jack Slane around campus and parked in front of the student center that bore their name.

"Look at that," I told them. "That's not a student center. It's got a cafeteria, sure. But there's nothing for students in there. If we're going to have a university where students *want* to come, we *have* to build a place for them to gather. And it starts right there with the Slane Student Center. Here's what has to happen. We have to enlarge it."

"But Nido, you have a street here," Marsha said.

"We can move the street," I responded.

She looked incredulous. So did Jack. But I told them what I tell our students: Don't mistake the difficult for the impossible. We ended up moving the street, and with the help of Marsha and Jack, we built, in 2006, a 45,000-square-foot addition to the Slane Student Center. A decade later, the college rating organization Best College Values would name Slane the No. 1 student center in the nation. And it all began with that conversation in my car with Marsha and Jack.

I had a vision, and I wanted them to see it. They did.

The Blessing of Adversity

My creative mind was borne out of necessity. I had to pay my bills, by golly.

Earlier I mentioned how I was a twenty-three-year-old entrepreneur in 1971, a High Point College graduate trying to figure out how to effectively use the graduate degree in business I had earned from UNC-Greensboro. I barely had two nickels to rub together. For dinner, I sometimes ate a fifteen-cent bag of peanuts or bought three Swanson TV dinners on sale for $1 to get me through the week. I worked as a youth director at a local church and earned $5 an hour teaching a three-hour class at a local community college.

But I also wanted to start my own business, my first business, and like the Law of Identification, which I teach now, what became personal became important. I looked everywhere for some sort of guidance to help me with my new job as a church youth director. I found nothing, and I knew I was far from alone. There were so many other youth directors just like me searching for advice and tools they could use. That's when I got my idea for my first business. I created my first publication, *Adventures with Youth*, a newsletter to assist other youth leaders like myself in creating successful programs for young people.

But I didn't go into detail about how I found my customers. I had the help of a man named Bill Hylton.

I knew I needed the names of customers, and I knew I could find them in the yellow pages of telephone books. The only place I knew that had stacks and stacks of telephone books was NorthState, a company headquartered in High Point that began in 1895 as the High Point Telephone Exchange. That's where I met Mr. Hylton. I told him about the business I wanted to start, and I asked to borrow the company's telephone books. Initially, he told me no. I then promised him I would pick up NorthState's telephone books at 5:05 every weekday afternoon and bring them back at 7:55 the next morning. Day after day, week after week, I did that. It worked. I'd work deep into the night, typing out names and addresses on a typewriter using two fingers, and I'd bring the telephone books back to Mr. Hylton first thing in the morning.

"Son," Mr. Hylton said, "you are a salesman."

"Mr. Hylton, sir," I responded, "I'll take that as a compliment."

You know the rest of the story: In two years, I had thousands of customers across the U.S. and overseas.

I employed that kind of discipline and focus throughout my life. When I was a student at then High Point College, I began speaking at local churches about growing up in the Holy Land as a Christian. I had someone transcribe and type up my story about my childhood, and I stapled it together and turned it into a booklet I sold for $1 at every speech I gave. I then sold the booklet for $2. At one speech, I had a minister come up to me and tell me they couldn't afford to pay me, but they would give me a "love offering." Remember, English was my second language, and I thought they were going to hug me and kiss me. Really.

But I found out a "love offering" was a way for the group to express their appreciation by putting money in a basket and giving it to me as a gift.

For me, adversity was a huge blessing. It led to abundance, and it all reminds me of a fish, a koi fish.

Put a koi fish in a fishbowl, give it food and water, and it'll grow no more than two inches. But put it in a pond, where the water is deeper and colder, and it'll grow at least to a foot in size. That happens because you have taken a koi fish from the comfort of a fishbowl to a spot where it takes more effort to survive. It has to grow bigger, stronger, and more resilient to deal with the difficulties it will face.

I am like that koi fish.

When I was in my early twenties, living on peanuts and TV dinners, I had to be more creative and more innovative. I wanted to be successful, and I wanted to tackle ideas bigger than myself. I had a hunger for that, and I found inspiration in one of my favorite books, *The Strangest Secret* by Earl Nightingale. In his short book, taken from his famous motivational recording in 1956, he writes about what that secret is: believe and succeed. The key to success and to failure is becoming what we think about.

"We must control our thinking. The same rule that can lead people to lives of success, purpose, wealth, happiness and all the things they ever dreamed of for themselves and their family, is the very same law that can lead them into the gutter. It's all in how it is used for success or for failure. This is the Strangest Secret in the world."

With the baseball stadium and other catalyst projects, there was no secret. I knew I had to be diligent about bringing people to the table, and I had to convince them that investing in downtown High Point was investing in their own future. I worked hard. I talked with people and used my words once again like an artist employs colors. I wanted them to see what

I saw on the canvas in their mind. Five months later, on a late Wednesday afternoon in September 2017, I announced what I had discovered with the help of my friends.

My Rolodex had paid off. Once again.

A Hopeful Vision

On September 6, 2017, a Friday, at least 700 people arrived on campus and filled Hayworth Fine Arts Center. They arrived probably not knowing what to expect. I really didn't know what to expect either. For the first time, though, I did write out some notes I was going to deliver from a lectern. It was something I've hardly ever done. But I wanted everyone in the audience to understand how important this announcement was. Beyond that, I didn't know what I was going to say. Oh, during my hour-long walk that morning I had thought about some other points I needed to hit on, and I had flashy graphics and numbers ready in my PowerPoint presentation. But did I know what I would say? Not really. But like I had the morning of my announcement at the High Point Country Club, I prayed. That, I know, always helps.

> *Dear God,*
>
> *These people are just like me. They want the same thing I want. So, please give me confidence and strength of clarity to explain the importance of it all. And this is so important for our city, everything we hold dear.*
>
> *What I'll say today is not for the faint of heart. I know that. What I'll say is for believers. So, let my words spring from your guidance and help convince them to believe. Let them see what I see, feel what I feel, so we all can shout from the mountaintops, "Yes, we can!"*
>
> *Grant me the wisdom to help them understand and let them see clearly that our present circumstances don't determine where we can go. They merely determine where we can start.*
>
> *And this is a great place to start.*

A few hours later, I stepped onstage at the Pauline Theatre inside the Hayworth Fine Arts Center and walked to the lectern. I wanted my delivery to be more serious because I wanted the people in the audience to understand what we were about to undertake—the city's most important endeavor in a generation. That afternoon, I invited two friends to dash any doubts, two people to endorse our vision and eliminate chatter about competition or the question about the need for a third team in the Triad.

Up came Billy Prim, CEO and chairman of Primo Water Corp. He had helped raise the money to build a stadium and bring the Winston-Salem Dash to the Twin City. Also to the podium came Jim Melvin, former mayor of Greensboro and president of the Bryan Foundation. He had helped raise the money to build a stadium for Greensboro's minor league team, now known as the Grasshoppers. Both Prim and Melvin told the audience that building a stadium and bringing a baseball team to High Point would be the smartest thing we could ever do.

"As they say in golf, 'Nido, you're the man,'" Melvin told the audience. "Without your vision, we'd end up going nowhere." Jim has always been an encourager, and even at eighty-eight years old, he is moving full throttle forward to make our region better in every way.

I sure did not want to end up "going nowhere," and we didn't! Not by a long shot. Eleven investors came forward to help. Together, we didn't raise $38 million. We raised $63 million, and that included a lead gift from High Point University, approved by our board of trustees. I've always believed every institution of higher learning can help instill higher living by being a good steward in their community where it sets down roots. Roots are important. Every May, on a stage in front of Roberts Hall, I tell our graduates that their parents give them roots; we give them wings. This time, with the multipurpose stadium and the other planned projects, the university could do the same thing for the city. But as I mentioned many times before, it wasn't just about baseball. With the construction of the stadium, I brought in supporters that unveiled the following:

- The Carroll Companies, Roy Carroll's real estate development company in Greensboro, would build a hotel in the downtown stadium area.

- David Couch and Chris Dunbar's Blue Ridge Companies would build 200 apartments in the downtown stadium area.

- BB&T (now known as Truist Financial Corporation) would underwrite naming rights for the stadium for fifteen years.

- Frank Boulton, chairman and founder of the Atlantic League of Professional Baseball, agreed to relocate a franchise to High Point from Bridgeport, Connecticut. I negotiated the purchase of the team from him and put together a nonprofit board to run the operations of the stadium and the team.

By the end of a nearly two-hour presentation, I could feel the excitement in the Pauline Theatre. Not only had we raised $63 million, but we also had brought in $50 million in private investment. I relied on my circle of influence, the people I know and trust. The greater your circle of influence, I've come to find, the smaller is your circle of concern. With a greater circle of influence, you learn to be vertical in your thinking. You're more adept at solving problems, finding solutions, and making decisions. You then can build capacity and bring around you a team to reach one mountaintop and then look for another to scale.

That happened with raising money for downtown.

We said we needed to raise $38 million, and we raised $63 million. We said we needed to secure naming rights, and we did it. We said we were going to get a baseball team, and we did it. We said we were going to attract private developers, and we did it. High Point needed a shot in the arm, and we did it. And then some.

As a city, we were becoming creative. Moreover, though, we were becoming innovative. I've always seen creativity as the agent of change, but innovation as the agent of excellence. I've seen it in my decades in the business world. Innovation establishes a defining line between managers and leaders. Managers deal with the present reality and try to make it work under new circumstances. But leaders improve the present reality to meet the future's requirements. And we in High Point were doing just that. We weren't afraid of our future. We saw it as an adventure, and I could see we were going to enjoy the ride because of what we all felt.

Hope.

Afterward, as I talked to my friends in the audience, I thought about what we had become—one city with common interests. We wanted to attract young people to live in High Point, and we wanted to re-create a bigger sense of collective pride. We were coming together to make a better life for everyone in the Home Furnishings Capital of the World. And connecting the city even *more* with High Point University.

"The Time Is Now . . . "

When I left Mount Olive and enrolled in High Point College more than a half century ago, I knew hardly anything about furniture, let alone how to build it. But I soon learned that in High Point, furniture is like the water we drink. It is vital.

After World War II, almost 60 percent of all furniture made in the United States was produced within a 150-mile radius of High Point. People flocked to High Point for jobs and opportunities. Furniture buyers and designers did, too. They still do. They come for the High Point Market every April and October. Today, more than 150,000 people of all professional stripes come for the High Point Market every year. It has become North Carolina's biggest economic event. It generates billions every year as well as all kinds of internships and job opportunities for so many, including our students at High Point University.

Yet, for years, those cavernous showrooms have remained empty for months at a time. That has always worried community leaders, particularly recently. In early 2021, two leading furniture organizations—High Point Showroom Association and High Point x Design—merged to bring together their combined membership of sixty brand showrooms. Their

initial mission: work toward establishing High Point as a year-round destination for designers to shop outside of the biannual market.

The compelling reason for the merger is a move to what so many of
us saw in High Point. The furniture industry needed a boost. I remember
reading in July 2019 the *New York Times* story about the rebirth of High
Point's downtown and HPU's role in that work. The story appeared under
the headline "Furniture Was a Savior. Then It Was a Handicap." The *New
York Times* wrote the following:

> *The showrooms provide tax revenue and support the furniture
> market. But for most of the year, they are dark, and downtown
> is quiet. You don't see people ducking in and out of shops on foot
> as you do in vibrant urban centers with a mix of retail offerings.*

During a twenty-year period that ended in 2012, research showed that
40,000 furniture workers lost their jobs in North Carolina because of plant
closings, layoffs, and overseas competition.

Those layoffs and plant closings have hit High Point hard. As co-chair
of the Piedmont Triad Partnership, I work closely with the most influential
leaders in our region to attract new companies and new job opportunities
for our citizens. Meanwhile, we in High Point began looking for ways to
reinvent our city. We wanted to transform it, make it a gleaming city on
a hill.

As I told the audience that afternoon in September 2017, we had all
the pieces of the jigsaw puzzle. We simply had to put them together—with
their help.

"Ladies and gentlemen," I told them, "let me be very clear: The time is
now; the person is you."

My Life Lesson from Algebra Class

I liked algebra, and I had a tough teacher in high school.

We had a test one time, and I must've handed in two pages of equations.

I was proud of myself, and I felt confident I had scored 100 on the test. I didn't. When I got the test back, I saw the teacher had given me a 0. When I saw that, I marched straight up to his desk.

"Do you have no heart?" I asked him, showing him two pages of equations. "Did you look at these two pages? I understand the principles of algebra! Just look. I solved it!"

The teacher just looked at me.

"The answer was wrong, Nido," he said. "The process may have been right, but the answer was wrong. Think of it this way: If you got into a car to deliver a package from me to Mr. Smith, and you delivered it to the wrong Mr. Smith, you failed."

I never forgot that lesson. He taught me the importance of the end result. With the catalyst project, our end result was to make a bigger and stronger university, and with it, a better downtown. We all wanted the same thing—a vibrant downtown that would energize our city. There was no need for dissension. There was a need for unity. In January 2019, five months before the first pitch on Opening Day, I wrote an opinion piece for the *High Point Enterprise* about our transformation and our need to come together.

"Innovation is sometimes messy," I wrote. "It doesn't always work out the way we planned. Our focus should always be on building bridges of understanding with each other as we work to help our neighbors, our community, and our country. With faithful courage, let's all keep innovating to improve our region and enhance the relationships among us all. The future is bright indeed."

I saw that future materialize on Opening Day at BB&T Point, now known as Truist Point, with a professional team known as the High Point Rockers.

On a late Thursday afternoon in May 2019, I stood on the Fred and Barbara Wilson Plaza and took it all in. What I saw was beautiful. What I saw was hope.

I knew Fred and Barbara would come for the big day, and there they were standing a few feet away. Fred is a big-time supporter of HPU. When I called him a few years back about investing in our new School of Pharmacy, he interrupted me and said, "Nido, how much do you need?"

He did the same thing when I approached him about supporting the catalyst project downtown. He never asked me what I planned to do. He trusted me to be a good steward with his investment. So, when I saw him and Barbara that Thursday, I told them how much I appreciated their help in making a dream in their hometown happen.

"See what happens when we come together?" I said. "When we come together, we can move mountains."

The same thing happened with so many other benevolent stewards. Like Earl and David Congdon and their family, who have already invested in big ways in our downtown. Earl's grandchildren also have wisely invested in bringing a professional soccer team to the stadium, making the facility significantly more attractive in our area.

Showing the World

An hour before the Rockers' first game, I sat on a stage just outside the front gate with a handful of people who had brought baseball and a stadium to High Point. We all had much to say. First up was Jay Wagner, High Point's mayor. He stood before the big banner, "All Of Us," in front of a crowd twenty people deep outside the front gate. He had waited for this day a long time.

"I'm so excited," Wagner told the crowd. "I woke up early, and I couldn't go back to sleep. I've had a vision in my heart of downtown High Point for a very long time, and today, standing here, I'm overwhelmed for my city, our city, and I'm glad all of us are here to celebrate."

I listened to speaker after speaker. They all came up and talked about courageous steps, divine intervention, and the dawn of a new day for High Point. Then, it was my turn. I mentioned stewardship, leadership, and the need to believe in what I called the "art of the possible." And on an afternoon under a cloudless, wide-open sky, I wanted everyone there to absorb this historic moment in the city of High Point.

"Underneath this beautiful blue sky, we can really see this is, indeed, a first," I said. "This is a first for our city and a first for our children. This stadium is a symbol of what all of us can do when we pull together. And when we come together, it shows we have faithful courage. It shows High Point is a greater place because of our commitment, and it shows the world what we can do. Now, let's play some baseball."

Afterward, I couldn't help but stand on the concourse and capture that moment. I looked beyond the right-field fence, and I spotted a hosiery mill built a century ago. The building rises five stories above West English Road, a red-brick testament to High Point's rich industrial past. The mill now foreshadows our city's promising future. The building covers 200,000 square feet. It will feed our economy and offer event space, an entertainment venue, two restaurants, a coffee bar, and the spacious room needed for furniture makers, design professionals, and entrepreneurs to mine their creativity and make their dreams happen.

I remember talking to Earl Congdon and his son, David, about this project. Earl and David ran Old Dominion Freight Line, one of the country's largest publicly traded trucking companies. Both Earl and David are faithful HPU supporters. Their support helped build the Congdon School of Health Sciences, a 220,000-square-foot building on campus. The Congdons recommitted $40 million from their family's foundation toward renovating that historic mill, long closed. That structure is now known as Congdon Yards. The mill has been transformed into a beautiful events center, a business incubator, and a community gathering place. And across the street, a new and modern hotel is also being built. And it's all around a mill that represents High Point history.

The city had fourteen hosiery mills and twenty-six textile plants operating when the Adams-Millis Hosiery on West English Road first started to hum in 1920. Twenty years later, Adams-Millis became the largest hosiery factory in the world and provided millions of socks for soldiers during World War II. Like the Congdons, the Millis family have also been huge supporters of High Point University and many nonprofits in our city.

So today, the old Adams-Millis Plant is now Congdon Yards. Quite the appropriate name.

Then there is Dr. Lenny Peters. He's a High Point physician, medical researcher, entrepreneur, and friend. His real estate company, Peters Development, which is run by his daughter, Elise Peters Carey, has more than a dozen projects underway downtown. His projects include shopping centers, apartments, office space for small businesses, and a restaurant with a rooftop terrace.

As our downtown starts to boom, I sense that same kind of faithful courage across High Point. In the next few years, we'll see in downtown more restaurants, more apartments, a new hotel, and improved landscape. And behind center field at Truist Point, we now see a 50,000-square-foot building known as The Outfields that includes a food hall known as Stock + Grain Assembly.

We do believe in our city and its future. We also believe in its past.

By April 2023, in a former High Point Market showroom on South Hamilton Street, a $10 million structure will unveil exhibits that will detail the people and the products that made High Point the Home Furnishings Capital of the World. The 25,000-square-foot building is the home for the American Home Furnishings Hall of Fame. Construction began in December 2021, and it is supported by my dear friends Ron Wanek and his son, Todd, owners of Ashley Furniture Company. Karen McNeill and her husband, Steve Pond, are the dynamo couple behind this fabulous addition in our city.

It's a beautiful thing to see, the revitalization of High Point's downtown. It reminds me of something broadcast legend Tom Brokaw told our graduates when he gave the commencement address in May 2015.

"Big ideas have always defined America," he said.

That spirit is alive and well in High Point. There's a sense of intentionality as we work together to create an inviting place, a downtown we can share with the people we love. I saw it firsthand on a Thursday afternoon in May 2019, on Opening Day.

As I walked toward the infield for another ceremony, I passed a father and his young son. They were sitting in the left-field bleachers, shoulder to shoulder, talking. The father was grinning big. But what caught my eye is what his son brought to the game. His own glove.

I saw it again when I got to the infield with the team officials, and we all stepped up to the microphone to deliver more comments before the first pitch. Once we finished, I started walking off the field when I saw a blur out of the corner of my eye. I looked left and saw three of my grandchildren dashing toward me. They were all legs and arms, waving. Like the father in the left field stands, I grinned big. I met my grandchildren with a big hug.

You know, the older I get, the more I realize our true legacy in life is reflective of our children and grandchildren.

The Child in All of Us

Every time I walk through our city's new children's museum, I'm so proud of what I see. I walk into this spacious lobby, and I remember what Mariana told me when she saw it all come together.

"We have to have events here not just for children," she said during one of our walking tours of the museum. "We have to have events so our community can see what they have."

So true. I walk into our lobby, and I remember why the idea of a children's museum works. Going with my grandchildren to children's museums in other cities, I remember how every face I saw there beamed with joy. Kids. Parents. Grandparents. Everyone I saw was making a good memory with people they love, and I knew I wanted to see *and* feel that in our city.

As our museum began to take shape at the corner of North Hamilton Street, I discovered that the two-story building with its huge dinosaurs out front had gotten more people excited than the baseball stadium *and* HPU's new conference center, hotel, and arena on campus.

That perplexed me. But I remember what my daughters, Deena and Cristina, told me: "Dad, the community is used to you building beautiful buildings on campus. The museum is different. They don't see this as just another building. It's bigger than that."

I agree. The children's museum touches every fiber of the "familial focus"—love and joy, learning and inspiration. Can't you just imagine how parents and grandparents, aunts and uncles and friends *feel* when they see the youngest among them walk wide-eyed through the two-story structure housing 75,000 square feet of museum activities? Those young ones, from toddlers to young teenagers, find themselves in what one writer has called the "happiest place in High Point." They find a television station, a grocery store, a design studio, a veterinary hospital, a floor piano, and a STEAM lab where they can explore their curiosity with science and technology, engineering, art, and math. They walk upstairs and see a mission control center on Mars and learn about how they can survive and thrive in outer space. Or they can walk outside and find a double-decker carousel where they ride a horse or a dolphin, an alligator or a seahorse. Everywhere I look inside our children's museum, I'm reminded of what I think is important no matter your age: Never let the child inside you die. You can't. Look at what you would lose. It's what makes life worth living. We must remind ourselves to embrace joy.

Yes.

Joy takes center stage at the children's museum every day. It is a $45 million investment, including an endowment, to help buoy the future of High Point and improve the quality of life for families everywhere. I remember when I talked to my sons, Ramsey and Michael, and my daughters about investing generously in this museum. They were all in. They are involved in almost everything we do, and I see us as a team. I believe in partnerships. I tell our students that it's important to build bridges rather than erect walls with others. And when I say building bridges, I'm not building one from where I am to where you are. No, we must build bridges from where the other person is to where we are. It's all about connection, relational capital, involving others in your life, especially when you're working on something that is bigger than yourself.

I tell my children often, "We're on this journey together."

Building Bridges, Finding Strength

We in High Point have come together for a common purpose—to create jobs, improve our local economy, and attract and keep young people in our city. Public officials and private leaders march onward with faithful courage. As we do that, we make High Point an even more attractive place to live.

With the help of High Point University and generous friends, we bought the High Point Rockers and brought the team to High Point. We created a nonprofit to own the team. The citizens of High Point own the team. And the stadium. And their future.

With the museum, I simply wanted to set the idea in motion and get out of the way. I'm not even on the board. Barry Kitley is the capable and hardworking chair of the board. Megan Ward is the enthusiastic executive director. Professors at HPU get the students involved in many ways to help them grow as educators, scientists, and engineers. My focus is to work toward helping the museum reach a sizable endowment to make sure it has the funds to obtain new exhibits, make necessary repairs, and remain vibrant. I'm humbled by the generous support we received at the museum from wonderful families named Congdon, Culp, York, Witcher, Millis-Young, Millis-Hiatt, Hayworth, Caine, Couch, Callicutt, and many more. They all stepped up to make our vision a reality.

I'll always remember the challenges we faced closing Montlieu Avenue. Then, in August 2021, city officials surprised me by naming the stretch of Montlieu that runs from the center of campus all the way to North Main Street as Qubein Avenue.

I'm humbled by the decisions many have made to transform downtown High Point. I was just one. But I felt I had a responsibility to take the lead, to help make it happen. I believed it could happen. Others believed too. The avenue has benefited from many upgrades, including burying utility lines below the street and adding sidewalks and bike lanes. The university already owns the former Immaculate Heart of Mary church and school across from the university's entrance on North Centennial Street. Since then, we've renovated two houses and turned them into residences for twenty-seven students as well as using that area for more parking. What else we will do with that land is still up in the air. We don't know. Yet, we do know what that land represents—the entrance to a tree-shaded streetscape that creates a gateway from the university to the children's museum. It'll act as a connector from our city's downtown to the university. A bridge, per se.

Always building bridges.

In the Hayworth Fine Arts Center on campus, right there inside the entrance, is one of my favorite Bible verses. It's from Luke 12:48: "To whom much was given, of him much will be required." These words are Jesus's instructions to His disciples regarding their responsibilities when He returns to His Father in heaven. Those words guide me on what I have to do on this earth. And fortunately, they guide so many of my friends who always respond positively when the need arises and they share their talents and money to make good things happen.

Friends like Loraine and John Charman, David Hayworth, Angie and Rick Workman, Jana and Ken Kahn, Ron and Todd Wanek, Christy and David Cottrell, David and Stephanie Couch, Teresa and Don Caine, Fred Wilson, Earl and David Congdon, Bob Stout, Phil Phillips, Mark Webb, Richard Budd, and so many others who regularly endowed HPU with hundreds of millions of dollars to build a beautiful new library and start schools for dental medicine and law. But we are far from done. We have only just begun!

CHAPTER 12

Building a Dream

It was 2014 when we started gathering ideas for a new basketball arena to accommodate the needs of a growing institution. We, including Dan Hauser, our vice president and director of athletics, and other school officials, began visiting universities in Alabama, Ohio, South Carolina, North Carolina, and Kentucky to see what would work—and what wouldn't work—for HPU.

But in my mind, I saw something more than just a basketball arena. I saw something far grander, far more intentional. I saw a conference center, a hotel, and an expansive, high-ceiling atrium with a roof of glass reminiscent of an art gallery. It would be a thing of beauty, an example of practical elegance that would prompt students to believe what we tell them at HPU—Think Big. Dream Big. We needed a perfect place for the new facility, and we found it on the northwest end of campus, on eight acres of land at the corner of University Parkway and Lexington Avenue.

Our architects and a few others I approached didn't think we could build it there. They told me the building I envisioned would not fit on that one piece of land. It was too small, too much like a postage stamp. During my time as president at HPU, we have built 100 new buildings on our campus as we've grown from 91 to more than 550 acres since 2005, and I've learned from experience not to believe in what you see on a blueprint. So, like I did on the property where we built Cottrell Hall and Congdon School of Health Sciences, I walked it.

That's right, I walked it.

I knew every stride I took was about three feet, and I calculated in my head the square footage needed to build what I envisioned. I must've walked that land at least fifty times. Back and forth, back and forth. I walked it at all hours of the day, and I walked it when no one was watching, always counting my number of steps. I then came back to our doubters and said emphatically, "The land is there. We can do it."

In my time on this earth, I've come to see that people will look for the easiest path from point A to point B. They want a straight line. But life is not a straight line. It zigzags like roads in the North Carolina mountains. You have to know how to maneuver life, and to watch for potholes at almost every turn. During my career as a business owner and now as a university president, I've had people tell me, "It can't be done." My response? "I'll find somebody who *can* do it."

When I tell someone that, I often think about the suspension bridges you find in China. There are at least fifty, and some were built without industrial machinery and equipment other than the human equipment of wisdom, diligence, and bravery. So, I knew our team could do this, and we could build on those eight acres the biggest facility yet on campus, an investment of $170 million.

And we didn't borrow a penny.

"Nothing without Divine Guidance"

On a sunny Saturday during Family Weekend in September 2018, more than 2,000 people gathered in the parking lot adjacent to Vert Stadium for the official groundbreaking. No one could get on the site next door because construction had already begun. You could hear the beep-beep-beep of construction vehicles moving dirt on the site beside the parking lot. But that didn't dampen our enthusiasm. We saw from that parking lot the university's future taking shape behind us in more ways than one.

That brings me to my friend Orlando Smith. Everyone calls him "Tubby," a nickname his grandmother gave him because as a youngster he loved bathing in her wash basin.

Tubby grew up in Scotland, Maryland, a farming community beside the Chesapeake Bay where people worked the land and the ocean to make ends meet. Tubby saw that firsthand with his father, Guffrie.

Guffrie farmed, became a leader in the family's church, and worked many jobs to feed his wife, Parthenia, and their seventeen children. Tubby was their sixth, and he learned to play basketball by using a bushel basket nailed to a corn house as a backyard hoop. And he learned to play well.

The University of Maryland initially offered Tubby a basketball scholarship, but they withdrew it after a coaching change. When that happened, Guffrie encouraged Tubby to consider accepting the basketball scholarship offered by a small Methodist school in North Carolina.

Smith followed his dad's advice. In 1969, he came to High Point College to play basketball. Smith played four years, scored 1,539 points, and became the ninth leading scorer in the program's history. After graduation, he started his coaching career at his high school alma mater. By 1979, he moved to the college ranks and joined J.D. Barnett, his former coach at High Point College, at Virginia Commonwealth University in Richmond, Virginia. Tubby found his passion, what really excited him, and his career took off.

Tubby has taken five different schools to the NCAA Men's Basketball Tournament, won a national championship in 1998 with the University of Kentucky, and helped coach the USA Olympic basketball team to a gold medal in 2000.

In 2016, he received the John R. Wooden Legends of Coaching Award. Quite the career.

When the University of Memphis let him go in 2018 after finishing with a 21–13 record, I had an idea. I knew what Tubby had gained from High Point College. He had told me about that many times. He never really talked about games won. He talked about friendships made, maturity gained, and the freshman co-ed named Donna Walls, the college's first Black Homecoming queen. Donna became his wife and the mother of their four children.

"High Point's motto states, 'Nothing without divine guidance,' and that is a good mantra for all of us young and old to live by," Tubby said in 2016 when he was inducted in the inaugural class of the HPU Athletics Hall of Fame. "It is through the instruction received from my parents growing up and here at High Point University that I've been able to reach farther, reach further, and go higher. With proper guidance, support, and inspiration, nothing is impossible."

I believe that too. There are no unrealistic dreams, only unrealistic timelines. And knowing what I know about Tubby, I told myself, "Why not ask him to come back to his alma mater to coach?" He urged me, back in 2006, right after I became president, to build a new basketball arena. Twelve years later, we were set to do just that. So, in March 2018 I met Tubby and Donna at a friend's house beside North Carolina's Badin Lake. At a kitchen table in a picturesque place an hour south of campus, I started our conversation with six words: "We want you to come home."

Tubby did. Six months later, on a sunny Saturday in September 2018 during Family Weekend, Tubby spoke in front of a fleet of TV cameras. Tubby talked about history.

His history.

Our history.

"It's one of the greatest days in the history of High Point University," Tubby told the crowd. "It'll be the largest building, the largest undertaking ever in the history of the school. A grand facility that will be a multi-purpose facility. It's a real privilege and honor in leading this basketball program at this time in its history."

That day, I told the crowd that the future of High Point University was going to be richer and better, more substantive and substantial.

"We're adding facilities that are purposeful, that are on merit, that are not frivolous," I said. "This facility will serve in preparing our students for a life filled with success and framed with significance."

It was, indeed, an historical moment. Something to savor. But now, the work started.

The ABCs of HPU

As the arena, hotel, and conference center took shape, I walked the site almost every day. I'd take notes, survey the progress, and talk to those responsible for the construction. That included the workers on site. And there were many—750 at the highest count. I must've talked with Jason Sweet, HPU's assistant vice president of capital projects, and Barry Kitley, senior vice president of operations, every time I went. I'd talk with them about the smallest of details, like the holes for the hardware on the doors of the hotel, as well as our vision of what the entire complex needed to be.

I had a vision, but it wasn't written on paper. I saw it in my mind. I've had people ask me, "Where did you get the idea for this?" and "Where did you learn that?" Quite honestly, I don't have a definitive answer. I remember asking my oldest son, Ramsey, an international travel journalist, that very question. He had an idea.

"Dad, you're an expert on this because you've been in every major airport, every major conference center, every major cruise ship, and you've seen it all," he told me. "You've been everywhere. You picked up a lot of knowledge."

Ramsey is right.

As a leadership speaker who once traveled the world, I have soaked up like a sponge every place I went. I've given 7,000 presentations across the globe, and I've traveled through the greatest airports, stayed at the best hotels, and spoken at the finest conference centers. I've been exposed to the finest marketing, the finest presentations and finest boardrooms, and I've seen awe-inspiring technology up close, as well as experienced the importance of hospitality and customer service firsthand. And from that experience, I've come to realize that whatever enters your psyche becomes your own personal reference library. And whatever you're doing—whether it's building a huge complex or talking to an auditorium full of corporate leaders—you rely on your own personal frame of reference to help guide you. It's "situational awareness." I've become a student of this wherever I go. I will take photos or mental notes of what I see because I never know how I can use it. And it can be anything as minute as how a door is constructed to how a lamp casts its light a certain way onto a street. Those exercises help to keep me sharp and creative.

To develop creativity, I've always believed one has to rely on their thirst for knowledge. Think of it this way: Knowledge is to creativity what a bed of coals is to a fire. Knowledge provides a reservoir of resources to keep the creative fires burning.

"Believe in Yourself"

In March 2020, the unthinkable happened. A global pandemic slowed down our construction, and we had to deal with everything from supply-chain problems to a shortage of construction labor. When you think about a building that needs at least 2,200 tons of steel, you know you'll need almost everything under the sun to pull it off. Yet, what humbled me was the number of people who stepped up and stepped out to help make this building a reality. Dozens of supporters came forward to create an architectural example of what we're doing at HPU—preparing students for the world as it's going to be and equipping them with the values needed to help them navigate constant global change.

When I think of our supporters, many come to mind. But two stand out in particular: Ken and Jana Kahn. Ken is the president of LRP Media Group, a global media company serving education and business professionals, and his wife, Jana, serves as the chief marketing officer of the LRP Media Group. I met with them at their home in Florida and told them what we wanted to do with the boutique hotel we were building. We wanted to create a new major, hospitality management, and use the hotel as a learning lab for students. Within minutes of starting my conversation, both Jana and Ken agreed to help. They gave the lead gift to build the hotel and, in a couple of years, made a sizeable gift to name the new school of law. Their generosity persuaded our board of trustees to name the hotel after them. The Jana and Ken Kahn Hotel has thirty rooms accommodating sixty guests. Each room has framed watercolors on its walls depicting recognizable campus scenes and a purple "God, Family, Country" pillow on its bed, and some have balconies that overlook Vert Stadium and offer a breathtaking view of campus. Next to the hotel is a Mediterranean-style restaurant known as Alo. It's our second fine-dining restaurant on campus that educates students about business and social etiquette, global culture, and international cuisine. The restaurant illustrates the very definition of its name, a Latin verb that means to develop, foster, and nourish.

That's what we want to do with our arena, our conference center, and our hotel and restaurant. We want to develop, foster, and nourish students for generations to come in a building that exudes this practical elegance and can withstand the test of time. We want prospective students and their parents who visit the campus to come up the escalator and see this panoramic view open up in front of them. They'll take a dozen steps and look down into a bowl-shaped arena designed by the same architects who built a basketball home for the Oklahoma City Thunder. It can hold 5,000 fans who will surround a court named after Tubby and Donna Smith, two of the first supporters of the arena. They'll walk around the concourse and see the history and excellence of HPU unfold around every bend. They'll see the interactive campus map and the exhibit about the leaders who mentor students every semester on campus or who come to campus to speak, coach, inform, and inspire. They'll see the art pieces that depict through an illustration and a few words what students discover at High Point University. Then, they'll see a wall filled with 6,000 photos of students, faculty, staff, families, and fans. That huge mosaic illustrates through images HPU's commitment to students: Choose to be extraordinary.

A commitment, I believe, is like your signature on a contract. It binds you to a course of action, and at HPU, that course of action has brought about a bounty of impressive results. Those results have names. They are our students who have come to know the importance of what every leader masters. It's the ABCs.

Ability.

Belief.

Commitment.

"Believe in yourself," I tell our students. "Know that you have been created for a purpose. And know that you can make a commitment to be extraordinary in your life."

Leadership resides within all of us. We simply have to take advantage of the talents we have. When we do, we will know who we are and become who we want to be.

The arena, conference center, and hotel represent that mindset, a growth mindset that's become a part of our university's academic DNA. It encourages students to be curious, innovative, and unafraid to stretch themselves beyond what they think they can do. The complex has so many opportunities for students to test their talents, follow their passion, and believe in what they do.

Two Students, Two Stories

Emmy Beck-Aden is a Media Fellow, a member of HPU's Honor Scholar Program, and a senior media production and entrepreneurship major from Athens, Ohio. Her interest in media production began when she was eight. That was when she picked up the family's camcorder, the one her dad used when the family went to Disney World. He'd train his lens at Emmy and her three sisters and say, "Look at the camera!" That's how it started.

With the help of YouTube videos, Beck-Aden trained herself in film production as a teenager. She went on to win awards for her short documentaries, including one about the difficulty of finding healthy food in her hometown of Athens. Her work sparked conversations and spurred people to act.

She came to HPU because of its emphasis on life skills, leadership, and her passion for video production. As a senior, she interned with NBC Sports covering the Winter Olympics, and she directed HPU's campus news show, *HPU All Access*. She also has interned with *Side by Side with Nido Qubein*, my weekly television show on PBS North Carolina. In September 2021, she added another line to her resume when she and a team of her talented friends steered the first broadcast in our new arena during its grand-opening weekend. Emmy, her friend Thomas Hart, and other media production students helped broadcast on big screens the concert by the rock band Train. After the concert, she turned to her friends and exclaimed, "This is what I want to do after I graduate!"

Practical education at its finest.

"It just shows you how purposeful, intentional, and caring High Point University is," she said. "The faculty and staff always go out of their way to provide students opportunities beyond the classroom. It's what you can put on a resume and what can give you an edge wherever you go.

"No matter where I go, I know I have the experience to be successful. I also know I have a university that will continue to support me."

Before the Train concert, the famous Lee Greenwood sang "God Bless the U.S.A." I love that song. So does Matt Redbord. He's a senior finance major from Ocean, New Jersey, and a member of HPU's Air Force ROTC. He got to talk to Lee and introduce him onstage that Saturday night in the arena.

"It was such a surreal honor," Redbord said. "Mr. Greenwood and I worked on the details together of what I was going to say, and the whole time, I was sort of starstruck. Such a superb opportunity. It shows how High Point University feels about ROTC, the military in general, and how much trust they put in us, their students, someone like me."

I'm glad Matt got that opportunity. He wants to be a fighter pilot, and like Emmy, he knows HPU will support him every step of the way. We are a God, family, country institution, and we don't make excuses for that. It is who we are. I tell our students, if you don't stand for something, you'll fall for anything, and we at HPU stand tall for what our flag represents. Every time Lee sings "God Bless the U.S.A.," I think back to when I filled out those thirty-eight forms, both front and back, to become an American citizen. That was more than a half century ago. Still, it feels like yesterday to me. I'm an immigrant by birth, an American by choice. When I hear Lee sing the chorus from his well-known song, "God Bless the U.S.A," I feel a tug of emotion that floods me with gratitude. It did that Saturday night.

"A Unique Place"

Wherever I speak, I always make sure there is an American flag onstage. And in our new arena, there is an American flag no one can miss. We designed the structure of a magnificent flag at the top of the escalator. It is a rippling flag with three words underneath it that have become the philosophical foundation of HPU: God, Family, Country.

Those words are forged from the 3,000 pounds of steel originally used to construct the World Trade Center in New York City. That steel came from D.H. Griffin Company during its restoration work following the infamous date we all know well: 9/11.

I talked about those three words when I addressed the crowd during the grand opening celebration Friday night inside the conference center.

"This is a unique place, and it's unique because it's a God, family, country school," I said. "It's a unique place because its president is an immigrant who understands wholeheartedly that even with all the blemishes this country has in its past, each of us living on this land ought to express appreciation every day for the oxygen that we breathe, for the opportunities that we have, for the freedom that we enjoy, and for the friendships we so appreciate.

"No student who enters these hallowed hallways to learn shall exit these hallowed hallways without learning that when God breathed into his or her nostrils, God intended for them to be extraordinary.

"That means to appreciate the land in which you live and the family who loves you. And the God who created you.

"We are an inclusive campus, and we welcome one and all from all backgrounds and all religions and all countries of our world. Yet, we're a campus that's very clear on the values in which we stand. Those values are stable, they're foundational, they're principled, and we shall not give them up."

Indeed, HPU is a unique place because of its distinguished faculty and distinctive focus of excellence and significance in life. I do believe that with every fiber of my being.

Our Moon Shot

Sometimes, when I'm walking around campus and talking to staff, faculty, and visiting families, I get so energized about what High Point University has become—and continues to become—I will point to the sky and say, "This school is going to the moon!"

I do get my share of quizzical looks. When that happens, I remind them about how we at High Point University have created "appreciated value." The life skills students learn at HPU have helped them understand how to adapt and overcome obstacles in a let's-figure-it-out world.

As I say at every commencement, their families give them roots; we give them wings. Families recognize that, particularly three families from Florida. Those three families helped us make history on a Wednesday morning in March 2022.

When I stepped up to the podium inside Callicutt Auditorium in the Congdon School of Health Sciences, I could barely contain my excitement. I looked out over the audience and saw so many familiar faces. Donors and supporters. Local leaders and alumni. Faculty, staff, and friends. And in the very back, I saw a swath of white coats worn by graduate students studying to be physician assistants. Those students represent for me HPU's foray into the medical sciences and how we want to help an aging population, a need that is going to grow. And that morning, I announced how we would continue that educational trajectory. We *were* going to the moon, and I unveiled how our big news, our huge news, would further raise the profile of HPU and transform the lives of hundreds of students.

"Look, I know you came here wondering, 'What is he going to announce this time?'" I said. "Actually, we're announcing nothing. I just wanted to see if you would show up."

Laughter rippled through the auditorium.

"No, we have some important things to talk about."

With clicker in hand, I motioned toward the wide screen behind me, and one big number appeared—$100,000,000. All from three families. All raised in thirty days. As soon as the numbers appeared, I heard someone exclaim from a few rows back.

"Wow."

Three families gave us a combined $100 million in thirty days—a record at HPU. These families own and operate businesses in health care, insurance, and publishing, and they believe in us. We at HPU are grateful for any support we receive, but this news was big. I had never heard of another university in the Piedmont Triad of North Carolina ever making this kind of announcement, especially with just three families. They chose to invest in the future of the university and the future of students to come. I am forever grateful to them. I told our audience as much. But I wanted them to understand why such a contribution happened. It wasn't by accident.

"Ask yourself why anybody would commit that kind of money to what some of us used to think of as 'little ol' High Point College'?" I said. "And then ask yourself a second question: 'Why do we ever doubt ourselves? Why?'

"We have to have faithful courage. We have to believe in the art of the possible. It's possible when you have an idea and are willing to work for it, and you're willing to dedicate yourself and commit yourself to excellence. Our community on this campus does that every day. When that happens, you know all things are possible. No exception to that rule.

"There are no unrealistic dreams; there are only unrealistic timelines.

That's what we have found out at High Point University. And that's why we come to work every single day—all of us—with a sense of dedication, a sense of belief that our tomorrows will be better than our yesterdays, and that the future generations who enter the hallowed hallways of learning will exit the hallowed hallways to serve and change the world in meaningful ways.

"Others talk about it. We're doing it on this campus. Every day."

But that was just the beginning of our big news that Wednesday morning. Through a number of slides, I showed our audience how our campus would grow and create a space for students who want to become attorneys and optometrists, entrepreneurs and nurses. We would create four new schools—a School of Law, a School of Optometry, a School of Nursing, and a School of Entrepreneurship. That would bring our number of schools on our campus to fourteen. In 2005, we had just three.

We didn't stop there. That morning, I announced that our board of trustees had unanimously approved a $400 million academic expansion to be completed by May 2025. That will include building a $95 million, five-story structure at the corner of Farris Avenue and Panther Drive. Known as Panther Commons, that building will house 300 additional graduate and undergraduate students as well as a new restaurant on the top floor and retail businesses on the bottom floor.

Other investments from that $400 million would include:

- The construction of 32 new student houses and cottages; HPU will now own 212 houses and cottages, including 20 tiny homes!

- The construction of a 1,200-space parking deck

- Campus improvements to Parkway Commons and the land HPU bought from a funeral home near the corner of University Parkway and Lexington Avenue

- The acquisition of at least twenty dental practices across North Carolina to hire dentists as mentors and provide clinical rotation placements for our HPU dental students

So, you can see why I was excited that Wednesday morning. We wouldn't borrow a cent or take on an ounce of debt. Every contractor and subcontractor we would hire would come from the Piedmont Triad.

"Forgive my enthusiasm," I said, "but I believe in this institution. I believe in the mission and vision and values of this institution, and I believe God has blessed this place in ways only the truly faithful can imagine.

"I believe in part we're blessed because we do dare to say we are a God, family, country school. And we do dare to salute the American flag. And we do dare to talk about the values of civility and kindness and inclusivity and equality and caring for our fellow men and women in society.

"If you're a person of faith, you know that the Bible says you've got to do for the least of these, your brothers and sisters. We're all equal one to the other. We all have a responsibility to stand tall, create opportunities, help others when we can, and invest liberally and generously in evolving, developing, transforming, and growing the future leaders of this country that we love and appreciate. That's our students. They can come here and do amazing things."

Remember in 2005, on my first Monday as president and at my first official meeting with the university's vice presidents, I gave them all a single piece of a puzzle. I wanted them to put together a puzzle that showed a beautiful photograph of Roberts Hall. I told them then how together we could create a wonderful picture of our future. On that Wednesday morning in March 2022, I said the same thing. We all are putting together a puzzle of a beautiful future, and each of us is a crucial piece.

"We can't have twenty jigsaw puzzles," I told our audience. "We have to have one. Each of us has to put our piece into that puzzle so the picture is complete. Then, with intentional congruence, we move onward in magical ways."

On a Friday in March 2022, two days after our big announcement, the editorial board of the *News & Record* wrote about our plans. They mentioned how we've had our share of skeptics through the years. These skeptics all thought we were, as they wrote, "living in a bubble" with all our growth since 2005. I'd heard it too. But there was no bubble, only faithful courage. The *News & Record* ended their editorial this way: "Early on, when Qubein first began to dazzle us with fundraising coups and land acquisitions and new buildings, seemingly by the sheer force of will, it was easy to be a doubter. Not anymore."

A few months later, we made another big announcement. Our School of Law became the Ken Kahn School of Law, after the longtime HPU supporter who graduated from Harvard Law and started his own legal and professional book publishing company. The founding dean of the Ken Kahn School of Law is Mark Martin, the former chief justice of the N.C. Supreme Court.

We do believe our job here at High Point University is to nurture and prepare future generations that will make our country and the world a better place. We model for our students the capacity to make things happen. Life is always filled with risk. But life is not about risk avoidance, it's about risk management. And faith. At High Point University, High Point's university, we do have faith in the good we can do for students, our community, our country, and the world. Our goals are ambitious. Yet, we believe in the art of the possible. And the possible has come to be.

The "Wow" at HPU

As I enter my twentieth year as president and as we celebrate our centennial, I see so much excitement happening across campus.

Take our fifteen Success Coaches headquartered on the second floor of Cottrell Hall. Really, though, they operate across campus—from a table at Starbucks in Slane to a bench along the Kester International Promenade. They act as academic advisors and counselors, mentors and coaches, and they help freshmen and sophomores navigate one of the biggest transitions of their young lives—college.

As I walk around campus every day, I see potential everywhere I look, and often, I have conversations with the students I see. Those are some of my most enjoyable conversations. I hear about their families or their classes or their hobbies or their goals, and it reminds me of the importance of what we do every day—educating the next generation of leaders.

I also have frequent meals with our faculty groups, and it helps me connect and listen to their suggestions and field their questions. We share breakfast, lunch, or dinner, and every time, I'm reminded of the bright minds we have on campus. They are heroes, models, and mentors to our students. And when faculty members share stories about their research with their students or how they have connected with them beyond the classroom, I see how we at High Point University are fulfilling our mission statement consisting of these seventeen words:

> *At High Point University, every student receives an extraordinary education, in an inspiring environment, with caring people.*

Good examples of those words can be found everywhere on campus. Just walk into the Culp Planetarium or Caine Conservatory. You'll see for yourself.

The Caine Conservatory opened in early 2020 with the help of a lead gift from HPU supporters Don and Teresa Caine. They owned Camco Manufacturing, a company the Caines started in 1966, a year after Don graduated from High Point College.

Situated in the $450 million section of campus known as the Innovation Corridor, the conservatory is a 15,000-square-foot building that contains a restaurant, a classroom, and two production-style research greenhouses with a collection of plants for hands-on education. Inside the conservatory, collaborations unfold from every university discipline. Those pedagogical combinations, professors tell me, make the Caine Conservatory a model to follow for education in the twenty-first century.

Then there is the Culp Planetarium inside the Wanek School of Natural Sciences. It is 6,000 square feet of visual and audio production magic created by a lead gift from HPU supporters Rob and Susan Culp. Rob served as the treasurer on the HPU Board of Trustees and was the executive chairman of Culp Inc., a mattress and upholstery fabric company in High

Point. He passed away in 2018. His wife, Susan, is a member of the HPU Board of Visitors. The planetarium opened in the fall of 2019 and made science as relevant to anyone as the oxygen we breathe.

The planetarium has 125 seats and five surround-sound speakers under its fifty-foot dome and gives students from communications and education to physics and music the chance to collaborate and produce their own documentary. They'll write the script, write the music, and produce the audio and the visuals. They end up creating pieces that can be used at planetariums across the country.

Down past the Millis Athletic Center is our new outdoor ice rink. We installed it during the pandemic to give students a chance for exercise and fellowship. We had more than 3,000 students and visitors take advantage of the chance to put on skates. They had a ball, so the ice rink is now a permanent part of our campus.

But as I mentioned before, we are far from done.

A Wonderful Circle

Everywhere I go and everywhere I look, I am reminded that our work at HPU has brought my life full circle. Let me explain.

While I was enrolled in graduate school at UNC-Greensboro, I started working as a youth director at a church in High Point. From that job—and my first business, the newsletter *Adventures with Youth*—I gained the confidence as well as the encouragement of others to write my first book, *What Works & What Doesn't in Youth Ministry*. I hadn't read that book in years. I picked it back up recently, skimmed through it, and discovered on page 7 this sentence: "The joys and rewards of working with young people may be few and far between, but when they come, they make enduring all the pains worth it."

That's how I felt then. That's how I feel today. Young people may occasionally cause you some pain or trouble, but when the joy comes, it comes in waves. Young people can give you an endless supply of that, and it makes working with them so worthwhile. Today, I see my life completing a wonderful circle. I started working with young people. In the middle, I worked with corporate leaders around the world. And now, I'm ending my career working with young people once again. That is so rewarding for me.

Every day, we think about how we can make HPU more useful, more interesting, and more purposeful for students and those who lead them. We have become High Point's university, and we have become the foundational strength for our city, my hometown. The future for us and our city is bright.

What does Earl Nightingale say in his book, *The Strangest Secret?* What is *the* secret?

Believe and succeed. And when you believe, you discover what's important in life.

It reminds me of a short film from Albania titled *Sorry*, which won an Oscar in 2020. I discovered it the following summer and sent it to our faculty and staff as a source of inspiration. Every day, I look for inspirational material to share. And this short film was definitely that. It shows a teacher hitting a student on the hand with a ruler after he arrives late for school day after day. Then, the teacher happens to be riding his bike one morning and sees why the boy is late. He's taking care of his brother, pushing his brother's wheelchair to his brother's own school. When the boy comes in late for school once again, the teacher lays the ruler in his hand, kneels down, kisses the boy's hand, and hugs him.

Not a word is spoken. At the end of the film are three lines in Albanian. Translated to English, the lines read: *Do not prejudice anyone; treat people gently because you do not know their troubles.*

Something to remember. Something we all should remember.

"Our Modern-Day Bill Friday"

I think about the people who have graced us with their talents. There have been so many. Here are a few.

The Rev. Dr. Michael Brown helped create a program that introduced HPU to the rest of the country. Michael, a retired minister, is a member of our board of trustees, and recently in 2021, he delivered a Christmas sermon to a packed crowd inside Hayworth Fine Arts Center. That service was produced and broadcast by ABC Network nationally on Christmas Eve 2021.

Then, there is Lindsay Bierman. He was the CEO of PBS North Carolina. He had approached me about doing an interview show like what I had done before on his network. This time, the show would be a thirty-minute weekly program aired in primetime right after the acclaimed *PBS NewsHour*. Lindsay reminded me that someone else had done a show just like that when PBS North Carolina was known as UNC-TV.

That someone was Bill Friday, the beloved educator from small-town North Carolina who rose to become the head of the UNC system for three decades.

"Bill Friday had a big show on this network, and we're trying to revive that show," he told me. "And Nido, I've watched you a long time, and we at PBS North Carolina all felt you could be our modern-day Bill Friday."

I was humbled by the opportunity and very much appreciated Lindsay's exaggeration. I could see how I could bring in guests I know and talk about subjects that have always fascinated me: leadership, inspiration, and my guests' life experiences. Lindsay came up with a name for the show, *Side by Side with Nido Qubein*, and suggested we would tape it onstage on the campus of High Point University. Today, David Crabtree leads the network with creativity and vigor.

I remember one of my first guests was Dr. Harold Martin, the chancellor at North Carolina A&T, the largest historically Black university in the country located in nearby Greensboro. I asked him about the heroes, models, and mentors he'd had in his life. He told me about his high school basketball coach. Then, Harold turned the tables on me. He asked who my biggest mentor was. I knew right away. My mother. She may have had a fourth-grade education, but she had a graduate degree in common sense.

When my father died when I was six, she had to raise five children by herself. I was the youngest, and I saw the power in her messages and the strength of her resolve in how she provided for us. Necessity always seems to be the mother of invention. She never said, "We can't afford that!" She always found a way to encourage her children and focus us on the possibilities that lay ahead.

I told Harold about that. But later, as I reflected on that exchange, I couldn't help remembering that one fateful day when I was awakened by the news I'd always dreaded and longed never to hear.

It was the day I found out my mother had died.

My Hero, My Mentor

On January 26, 2005, at 4:00 in the morning, the silence of our bedroom was unexpectedly shattered by the phone ringing.

Life was roaring along at a fairly hectic pace in these early days, hectic even for me. This was my first few weeks in office as president, and while most in the community still thought I was raising $10 million, I was busily engaged shooting for $20 million. At the same time, the machinery for our coming expansion-explosion was already in motion. We had hired architects, interviewed contractors, drawn up plans, and had all gotten ready to work. That week, I had called our first board of trustees meeting to put my budget before them and seek their approval to borrow our first $25 million. At the same time, I was in a flurry of communication with donors and potential donors. I was used to taking calls at all times of day or night.

Still, 4:00 a.m.?

That critical trustees meeting was scheduled to take place at midday that day, but I couldn't see why anyone would be calling me about a board meeting while it was still dark out.

I picked up the phone and answered. It was an overseas call from my brother. He broke the news to me. Our mother had died.

Later that day, I attended our board meeting and made my presentation. The board approved the budget unanimously. We finished our business at about 2:00 p.m. As the trustees started getting up from their seats and preparing to leave, I told them about the early-morning phone call.

"I want to share some personal news with you," I said. "My mother has died. My family and I need to fly to Jordan today. Like right now."

My family was already packed and waiting for me. We raced to the airport and flew, arriving the following day to begin the bittersweet process of saying goodbye.

Three sad days later, we were on a plane back home again. Within a few days, I would be back on campus handing out two tons of Ghirardelli chocolate to the strains of James Taylor singing "How Sweet It Is (to Be Loved by You)."

On that plane ride back to America, I thought about my mother and what she had always told me.

"Choose well, Nido," she said. "You always have choices. Your circumstances never dictate where you end up; they only define where you start. Your choices determine who you become."

Our university is not perfect; I know there is room for advancement. Still, looking back, I know we have made good choices.

I believe our students will make good choices, too. And you know what? My mother would be proud of her youngest son. I still think of her often and what she always said to me.

"It's up to you and God. Together, you make it happen."

And we have. Right here, at High Point University. Together. Always.

Thank God for all His blessings.

Let Your Light Shine

When I walked into our children's museum right after it opened, I couldn't get over what I saw.

With every step I took, I waded into an eclectic cross-section of High Point consisting of hundreds of people. They had brought their children and grandchildren, and everyone I saw was smiling, happy, just a picture of joy.

Everywhere I looked, the children were a blur of energy. They played on the fire truck, crawled under the ginormous furniture, and raced a tiny boat across tiny rapids before heading upstairs to the Mars Academy to figure out how to live in outer space.

Their families were right there, experiencing the joy of the moment too. They even participated. They rode the carousel. I rode the carousel. I went out there with my grandchildren and learned right away that you've *got* to be flexible to ride a big purple panther.

My ride on the museum's two-story carousel reminded me of what I always knew to be true: Never let the child inside you die.

That's something I tell the parents at every open house at High Point University. We need to let the child within us emerge so we can appreciate the beauty of a flower, the delight of eating an ice cream cone, or the fun of riding a two-story carousel beside the children and grandchildren we love.

The museum's a work of stewardship. It's about children. It's about community. It's about the many people who stepped up and stepped out to support the museum in such a magical way.

The children's museum is an extension of our God, family, and country values. It's a place where character is built, where love for country is emphasized, where God's name rises every day, and where families are at the heart of all we are and all that we do.

The same is true at High Point University. Parents see HPU as part of their family, an emotional link to who they are, because we have taken care of their children. And now, their children—our students—have grown into leaders, prepared and ready to take on an ever-changing world. Or as we like to say at HPU, the world as it's going to be.

In this book, I wanted readers to see how that all came to be. Despite the Great Recession, a global pandemic, and a few doubters who questioned the why and how of what we did, High Point University has thrived.

I tell people constantly, "We have a great team." That's how we went from "little ol' High Point College" to an internationally recognized university ranked in our category by *U.S. News & World Report* as the No. 1 Regional College in the South for the past decade.

But I also emphasize that nothing happens without God Almighty. Never underestimate God's grace. Of course, you have to do the work. But God gives us the wisdom and strength to find a way. We found a way at High Point University, and I am humbled and incredibly grateful for the journey.

His grace and His blessings have helped us transform High Point University and assisted in transforming downtown High Point and create a one-of-a-kind museum that's been called the "happiest place in High Point," a place where we all can rediscover the wonder of life through the eyes of a child.

At High Point University, I tell our students success is embedded in the impact, relevance, and appreciated value we bring to others.

I'm constantly asking our team how we can be more creative, more entrepreneurial, and more imaginative in ways that can bring even more joy to more people in High Point and the surrounding region and bring more lasting value in the lives of those who study and work at High Point University.

I do think about what's next for our city and High Point's university. I also think about what's next for me. I've had people ask me about my future as I enter my twentieth year as High Point University's president and celebrate its centennial anniversary in 2024. If anything, I tell them, I'd love to have two things as I commit to continue my servant leadership:

- When I die, I want my kids and grandkids to say, "He lived well. He cared for other people. He honored God."

- And I want us all to inspire others to get more involved in their school, their house of worship, or their community.

As the Bible says in Matthew 5:16: "Let your light shine before others, so that they may see your good works and give glory to your Father who is in heaven."

Life is all about choices. So, be wise. Choose well. Let your light shine.

Acknowledgments

My life is the product of the many heroes, models, and mentors who invested in my growth journey and tolerated my learning curves and ambitious goals.

I'll be eternally indebted to the board of trustees who trusted me to lead our university. Their faithful guidance is immeasurable.

I'm grateful for God's grace. For my family's enduring love and support. For our students and their families. For the faithful alumni who continue to enroll their children and grandchildren at HPU. For our stellar faculty who exude entrepreneurial agility and a genuine love for discovering applications of knowledge in life. For the dedicated staff who serve every day with enthusiasm. And for our city's leaders who advocate our work, and for the extraordinarily generous philanthropists who believe in our future.

Transformation is never easy. And so I share my gratitude for fellow college leaders from across the country who patiently withheld any judgment of our strategies and tactics while we went about, in our own way, creating solid academic schools, learned student scholars, and wonderful graduate outcomes. Our transformational journey at HPU looks quite different from the traditional playbook of higher education. But I've always appreciated the private encouragement shared by so many of my contemporaries.

Special thanks go to John David Mann and the many others who read the manuscript and contributed to make it better.

About the Author

Nido Qubein is an internationally known business speaker and consultant who returned to his undergraduate alma mater in 2005 to serve as president. By all accounts, he led High Point University from a "sleepy small school" to a dynamic and highly successful institution of higher learning.

Student enrollment and the number of faculty quadrupled. National rankings topped the *U.S. News & World Report*'s "Best Colleges in the South." The campus grew from 91 to 550 acres and the number of buildings expanded from 22 to 128. With an investment of almost $3 billion, the university evolved from three academic schools to fourteen. Graduation rates, learning outcomes, and career placements moved up measurably.

The author enjoys an international reputation as a dynamic speaker, much-in-demand business advisor, and a respected member of corporate boards. He has authored many books on communication and personal development and has been featured widely in national publications. He has received many prestigious awards and distinctions, including The Ellis Island Medal of Honor, induction in the Horatio Alger Association of Distinguished Americans, DAR Americanism Medallion, and the National Speakers Hall of Fame. And he has even been honored in the Senate chambers in Washington, D.C., for his commitment to higher education, leadership, and philanthropic endeavors.

You may reach Nido Qubein via email at nqubein@highpoint.edu.

You are invited to download free the HPU+ app and sign up for daily motivation.

Watch for author and book updates at highpoint.edu and nidoqubein.com.